COASTAL CUISINE

Texas Style

A Collection of Recipes
served up by the
**Junior Service League
of Brazosport**

Additional copies may be obtained at the cost of
$16.95 plus $3.00 postage and handling, each book.
Texas residents add $1.31 sales tax, each book.
Send to:

Junior Service League of Brazosport
P.O. Box 163
Lake Jackson, TX 77566

Profits from this cookbook are used to fund community service projects
sponsored by the Junior Service League of Brazosport

Library of Congress
Catalog Card Number
93-079087
ISBN: 0-9637804-0-9

Copyright © 1993
Junior Service League of Brazosport
Lake Jackson, Texas

First Printing - 5,000 quantity
November 1993

Second Printing - 5,000 quantity
June 1994

Printed in the USA by

WIMMER
The Wimmer Companies, Inc.
Memphis • Dallas

A Crossroads of Cultures,
A Variety of Cuisines

The cluster of cities known as Brazosport along the upper Texas coast lies at a crossroads of cultures, with ties both to the Deep South and to the Old West. Our cuisine reflects that cultural diversity, with popular local specialties ranging from spicy Tex-Mex to ranch-country barbecue to authentic French Cajun to fresh-from-the-ocean seafood. In addition, residents come to our community from across the globe, bringing with them treasured recipes from the lands they left.

COASTAL CUISINE, Texas Style celebrates that diversity with a collection of favorite recipes that range from elegant offerings suitable for formal gourmet dining to down-home dishes just right for a back-yard barbecue.

Even as we celebrate our heritage, however, the recipes in COASTAL CUISINE reflect modern-day needs for good nutrition, convenient preparation and safe food-handling practices. Low-fat, nutrient-rich recipes have undergone review by a registered dietician to gain their designation as "❤ Heart Healthy." Recipes that can be on the table in less than 20 minutes carry the tag, "✓ Quick to Fix". The cookbook also provides tips for safe handling of food and, in keeping with the U.S. Department of Agriculture's current recommendation to avoid eating raw eggs, uses only recipes in which eggs are cooked before consumption.

These treasured recipes come from members of the Junior Service League of Brazosport, who understand the desire to both prepare healthy, hearty fare for their family, and to present distinctive dishes for special occasions. We think you'll turn here first for either need.

The vibrant young women who are members of the Junior Service League of Brazosport are dedicated to volunteerism and to helping make their community a better place in which to live. Proceeds from the cookbook are used to fund our community service projects.

COOKBOOK COMMITTEE
General Chairperson: Barbara Franklin

Recipe Collection and Selection
Chairperson: Christy McConnell
Cindy Cathcart, Janis Keller, Leah Martin

Publishing and Layout
Chairperson: Cynthia Lancaster
Terrie Lumsden, Wendy Mathews, Cindy Williams

Design and Graphics
Chairperson: Delight Fails
Helen Baker, Sandra Frazier, Bonnie Novosad

Quality and Development
Chairperson: Marty Dunn
Doris Aldrich, Jackie Brewer, Linda St. Lawrence

Marketing and Publicity
Chairperson: Nancy Standlee
Denice Foose, Peggy Schrott, Marilyn Woody

Production Assistance
Marcie Allen, Jody Epps, Diane Hill, Karen Johnson,
Helen Jones, Karen Moran, Donna Paul

Registered Dietician for Nutritional Review
Katy Engen

ACKNOWLEDGEMENTS
Thank you to all Junior Service League of Brazosport members
and their families who so graciously shared favorite recipes
for publication in this cookbook.

We wish to thank two special ladies who gave of their time
and talents to help capture the spirit of our community in this project.
Schelli Martin, for her illustration of Texas, and
Susan Chester, for her graphic interpretation,
which became the cover for our cookbook.
Susan also designed the back cover and divider pages.

TABLE OF CONTENTS

Junior Service League of Brazosport

*God grant that we do noble things
and always respond to the best that is in us.
Open our eyes to the needs of others,
and help us to be faithful to our task.*

Since its origin in 1970, the Junior Service League of Brazosport has given thousands of hours in volunteer service to community projects.

The young women who make up the membership of this service organization truly do "open their eyes to the needs of others."

Service projects take many forms, and vary from year to year, but are always selected with one main goal in mind: to fill needs that are otherwise not being met.

The projects range in scope from sponsoring free "Discovery Days" for school children at the Brazosport Museum of Natural Science to providing cardiopulmonary resuscitation training to community residents. Members serve as hostesses in the Brazosport Memorial Hospital emergency room, visit intermediate schools to provide timely information about major health concerns, and sponsor an annual Christmas used-toy sale for residents who could not otherwise afford gifts for their children.

In addition to volunteer time, the Junior Service League of Brazosport also gives thousands of dollars to the community each year, in areas ranging from scholarships for outstanding local high school graduates to budgeted donations for area organizations.

Junior Service League counts on fund-raising projects to finance its many service projects. Proceeds from the sale of the COASTAL CUISINE cookbook will help underwrite our community services, projects and donations.

Appetizers
and Beverages

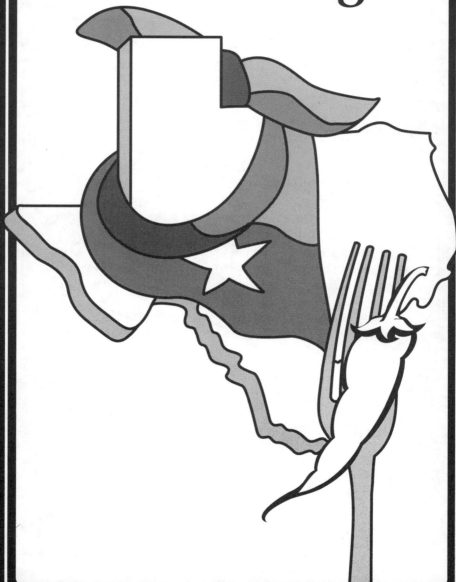

EMERGENCY ROOM HOSTESS
1988 - 89, 1990 - to present

Families facing the strain of bringing a loved one to the emergency room at Brazosport Memorial Hospital don't have to go it alone. Volunteers on duty from Junior Service League are ready to provide coffee, telephone calls or a shoulder to lean on. JSL volunteers are trained to assist families, facilitate services and give services and give support in any way they can. Members of this service project spend 30 hours in the emergency room each year.

SOUTHWESTERN SALSA

❤ *Heart healthy,* ✓ *Quick to fix*   *Yields about 2 cups*

1 (14.5-ounce) can Mexican-
   style stewed tomatoes
½ cup finely chopped onion
2 tablespoons chopped fresh
   cilantro

2 teaspoons lemon juice
1 small clove garlic, minced
⅛ teaspoon hot pepper sauce

Chop tomatoes in food processor. Add all other ingredients; mix well. Serve with low-fat baked tortilla chips.

Note: *This is an excellent, mild salsa that can be used in many Mexican dishes.*

Wendy Mathews

TEXAS SASS

Yields about 2 cups

2 large ripe tomatoes, chopped
4 green onions, chopped
1 (4¼-ounce) can chopped black
   olives
1 (4-ounce) can chopped green
   chiles
3 tablespoons olive oil

2 tablespoons picante sauce
   (or more to taste)
1½ teaspoons vinegar
1 teaspoon salt
½ teaspoon garlic salt
Pepper to taste

Chop tomatoes and green onions (include bulb and stem.) Mix all ingredients; chill overnight. Serve with tortilla chips.

Lisa Baker

EASY MEXICAN DIP

Serves 6-8

1 (8-ounce) package cream
   cheese, softened

½ cup mild, chunky picante
   sauce (or more to taste)

Mix cream cheese and picante sauce. Dip can be served immediately, but is better if chilled about one hour. Serve with tortilla chips or wheat crackers.

Lynne Vandaveer

TEXAS CAVIAR

Yields 7½ cups

1 pound dry black-eyed peas
2 cups Italian salad dressing
2 cups diced green pepper
1½ cups finely chopped green onion
½ cup finely chopped jalapeño peppers

1 (3-ounce) jar diced pimiento, drained
1 tablespoon finely minced garlic
Salt to taste
Hot pepper sauce to taste

Soak black-eyed peas in enough water to cover for 6 hours or overnight. Drain well. Transfer peas to saucepan, add enough water to cover. Bring to boil over high heat. Reduce heat, allow to boil until tender, about 45 minutes. Do not overcook. Drain well, transfer to large bowl. Blend in Italian dressing, and let cool. Add remaining ingredients; mix well. Refrigerate. Serve with tortilla chips.

Hint: This dish can also be served on a lettuce leaf as a salad. Serve with grilled chicken for a cool summer meal.

Lisa Baker

PINTO BEAN DIP

Yields 2 quarts

4 (15-ounce) cans pinto beans (plain or with jalapeños), well drained
1 clove minced garlic
½ small spice bottle of freeze-dried chives

3-4 jalapeño peppers
1 teaspoon jalapeño juice
1 cup (2 sticks) real butter
1 (8-ounce) package Velveeta cheese

Puree well-drained beans in blender, one can at a time. With the last can, add garlic, chives, jalapeños and jalapeño juice. In a pot, warm butter and Velveeta cheese until melted, then add pureed beans. Simmer until ingredients are well mixed. Serve with chips.

Note: This recipe can easily be halved. Dip is best if made ahead of time.

Bonnie Novosad

WOWIE GUACAMOLE

Yields 2 cups

2 ripe avocados
½ medium onion, finely chopped
1 small tomato, finely chopped
1 (4-ounce) can chopped green
  chiles

1 tablespoon lemon or lime juice
1 teaspoon salt
½ teaspoon pepper
½ teaspoon garlic powder
Few sprigs cilantro, chopped

Mash avocado pulp in bowl; add all remaining ingredients, beat until creamy. Cover well, refrigerate until served. Serve on lettuce leaves for salad, as an accompaniment to Mexican food, or with tortilla or corn chips for dip.

Cynthia Lancaster

MEXICAN LAYER DIP

✓ *Quick to fix*   *Serves 12*

1 (6-ounce) can bean dip
3 ripe avocados
1 (8-ounce) jar picante sauce,
  mild or hot to taste
1 envelope taco seasoning mix
1 cup (8-ounces) sour cream

½ cup diced onion
2 tomatoes, chopped
2 cups (8-ounces) shredded
  Cheddar cheese OR Colby-
  Jack cheese blend

On a large platter, layer the ingredients: Spread bean dip on platter. Peel and mash avocados, mix with picante sauce; spread on top of bean dip. Mix taco seasoning with sour cream; spread on top of avocado. Sprinkle on diced onion and chopped tomatoes. Top with shredded cheese. Serve with tortilla chips.

Linda Jordan

~ *Selecting avocados: If you need them tonight, choose slightly soft avocados that yield to gentle pressure on the skin. For use in a few days, choose firm avocados and leave at room temperature to ripen.*

HOT ARTICHOKE DIP

Serves 6-8

1 (16-ounce) can artichoke hearts, drained, chopped
1 (7-ounce) can diced green chiles, drained
1 (8-ounce) package cream cheese

¾ cup sour cream
½ cup mayonnaise
1 cup (4-ounces) grated Monterey Jack cheese
½ cup grated Parmesan cheese

Chop artichoke hearts; combine in bowl with all other ingredients. Pour into shallow baking dish; bake at 350° for 30 minutes. Increase heat to 400°, stir dip, and bake another 15-20 minutes. Watch closely to prevent burning. Serve hot with crackers, melba rounds, bread sticks or vegetable sticks.

Nancy Germano

SPINACH-ARTICHOKE DIP

✓ *Quick to fix*   *Serves 6*

1 (6-ounce) jar marinated artichokes, drained
5 ounces frozen spinach, thawed and drained
2 green onions, chopped
¼ cup grated Parmesan cheese
1 (3-ounce) package cream cheese

½ cup mayonnaise
½ cup sour cream
Dash of cayenne pepper OR hot sauce
Salt and pepper to taste
1 cup picante sauce (optional)
1 cup sour cream (optional)

Drain artichokes; cut in very small pieces or chop in food processor. Mix artichokes, spinach, green onions, Parmesan cheese, cream cheese, mayonnaise, sour cream, cayenne pepper, salt and pepper to taste in saucepan; heat on medium until cheese melts. Serve hot or cold with tortilla chips. If desired, serve with bowls of picante sauce and sour cream for a triple-dip treat.

Tonya Heard

~ Room temperature: Serve cheeses at room temperature to enjoy their true flavor. Remove full-flavored cheeses from the refrigerator an hour before serving. Milder cheeses can come out a half-hour ahead.

DILL LIGHT ARTICHOKE DIP

Serves 8

1 (14-ounce) can artichoke
   hearts or bottoms, drained
1 cup fresh ground Parmesan
   cheese
½ cup light mayonnaise

1 (8-ounce) package light cream
   cheese, room temperature
½ teaspoon dry dill
¼ teaspoon minced garlic

Preheat oven to 400°. Place ½ the artichoke hearts in food processor, and chop. Add remaining artichokes, chop coarsely. Add Parmesan cheese, mayonnaise, cream cheese, dill and garlic. Process until smooth. Pour into 10-inch pie plate; bake at 400° until hot and bubbly, about 15 minutes. Serve immediately with bread sticks or crackers.

Note: *Dip can also be served at room temperature, uncooked.*

Katy Engen

CENTERPIECE SPINACH DIP

♥ *Heart healthy,* ✓ *Quick to fix*   *Yields 3 cups*

6 green onions
1 cup low-fat cottage cheese
1 cup plain non-fat yogurt
1 (10-ounce) package frozen
   chopped spinach, thawed and
   well drained

2 tablespoons fresh lime juice
1 teaspoon salt
Pinch of pepper
1 large purple cabbage
Assorted fresh vegetable dippers

Cut green onions into 1-inch sections. Using knife blade in food processor, chop green onions. Add cottage cheese and yogurt, process 1 minute or until smooth. Add spinach, lime juice, salt and pepper. Pulse 2-3 times, or until well mixed. Chill until serving time.

To make cabbage centerpiece container, cut off base of cabbage to set securely. Peel back largest leaves, but keep leaves attached to cabbage. Cut off top ⅓ of cabbage, and hollow out center. Fill center with dip; serve with assorted fresh vegetable dippers.

Susan Laver

~ **Instant fruit dip:** *Create a healthy fresh dip for fruit by combining equal amounts of applesauce and yogurt.*

CREAMY FRUIT DIP

✓ *Quick to fix*   *Yields 1 cup*

1 (8-ounce) package cream
   cheese, regular or light
2 tablespoons milk
2 tablespoons brown sugar

1 tablespoon granulated sugar
1 teaspoon vanilla extract
1 teaspoon cinnamon
¼ teaspoon nutmeg

Allow cream cheese to soften. Combine all ingredients, stir until smooth. Serve as a dip with fresh fruits. Store in refrigerator.

Hint: *This dip is great given as a gift in a nice container with a basket of fruit.*

Tonya Heard

PINEAPPLE FRUIT DIP

✓ *Quick to fix*   *Yields 2½ cups*

1 (8-ounce) package cream
   cheese, softened
1 (3.4-ounce) package vanilla
   instant pudding

1 (15½-ounce) can crushed
   pineapple, undrained
½ cup finely chopped pecans

In a bowl, mix softened cream cheese, dry pudding mix, crushed pineapple (include juice) and pecans. Serve with crackers or fruit. To make a cheese ball, drain crushed pineapple well, form into a ball; chill.

Sharon Schwing

PIÑA COLADA DIP

Yields 2½ cups

1 (3.8-ounce) package coconut
   instant pudding
¾ cup milk

½ cup sour cream
1 (8-ounce) can crushed
   pineapple, undrained

Combine all ingredients in blender or food processor using metal blade. Process 30 seconds (stir after 15 seconds if using blender.) Refrigerate several hours or overnight to blend flavors. Serve with fresh fruit.

Peggy Schrott

MALLOW FRUIT DIP

✓ *Quick to fix*   *Serves 10-12*

1 (8-ounce) package cream
cheese, softened
1 (7-ounce) jar marshmallow
creme
1 tablespoon orange, lemon or
lime juice

1 teaspoon grated citrus peel
(optional)
Dash ground ginger (optional)
Assorted fresh fruit dippers

Allow cream cheese to soften. Use a fork to blend cream cheese and marshmallow creme. Add juice and grated peel; season with ginger if desired. Mix well. Serve chilled or at room temperature with fresh fruit dippers such as strawberries, cantaloupe, pineapple, kiwi, apples or pears. Store in refrigerator.

Linda Meche/ Carol Ann Adam

SWEET PUMPKIN DIP

✓ *Quick to fix*   *Yields 7 cups*

4 cups powdered sugar
2 (8-ounce) packages cream
cheese, softened

1 (30-ounce) can pumpkin filling
2 teaspoons ground cinnamon
1 teaspoon ginger

Combine sugar and cream cheese; beat until well blended. Mix in remaining ingredients. Use a hollowed-out pumpkin for serving, if desired. Serve with gingersnaps. Store dip in refrigerator.

Marty Dunn/ Barbara Lundahl

COCONUT BANANAS

Yields 24 appetizers

4 tablespoons lemon juice
1 (16-ounce) carton sour cream

1½ cups shredded coconut
4 bananas, peeled

Place lemon juice, sour cream and coconut into separate bowls. Cut bananas into 1-inch pieces, dip immediately in lemon juice. Roll banana pieces in sour cream, then in coconut, making sure all sides are coated. Cover with plastic wrap and refrigerate for several hours, or overnight. Serve alone as an appetizer, or as a beautiful addition to a fruit platter.

Delight Fails

RANCH-STYLE CHEESE BALL

✓ *Quick to fix*   *Yields 1 cheese ball*

2 (8-ounce) packages cream
  cheese, softened
1 package dry Ranch-style salad
  dressing mix

1 (2.25-ounce) jar Lowry's
  seasoned pepper

Mix softened cream cheese with dry salad dressing mix. Shape into ball.
Roll ball in seasoned pepper until covered. Serve with wheat crackers.

Kim Gary

DIANNE'S CHEESE BALL

Yields 1 cheese ball

2 (8-ounce) packages cream
  cheese, softened
1 (8½-ounce) can crushed
  pineapple, well drained
2 cups chopped pecans, divided

¼ cup finely chopped bell
  pepper
⅓ cup finely chopped onion
1 tablespoon Lowry's seasoned
  salt

Mix all ingredients, reserving one cup of pecans. Shape mixture into ball;
roll ball in reserved pecans. Place cheese ball in air-tight container and
refrigerate overnight. Serve with crackers.

Karen Parrett

MARTI'S CHEESE BALL

Yields 2 balls or rolls

2 (8-ounce) packages cream
  cheese
2½ cups (10-ounces) sharp
  grated Cheddar cheese
1 tablespoon grated onion
1 tablespoon grated green
  pepper
1 tablespoon chopped pimiento

2 teaspoons Worcestershire
  sauce
1 teaspoon lemon juice
Dash of salt
Dash of red pepper
1 cup (or more) finely chopped
  pecans

Let cream cheese reach room temperature. Grate Cheddar cheese. Mix all
ingredients except pecans, form into ball or roll. Roll in finely chopped
pecans. Wrap in wax paper and refrigerate overnight, or longer for better
flavor. Freezes well.

Marcie Allen

PEPPERED CHEESE ROLL

Yields 2 logs

2 cups (8-ounces) grated sharp
  Cheddar cheese
2 cups (8-ounces) mellow
  Cheddar cheese
1 (8-ounce) package cream
  cheese, softened

2 tablespoons lemon juice
2 tablespoons minced onion
¾ teaspoon garlic salt
Hot pepper sauce — to taste
1 cup finely chopped pecans
Chili powder

Blend grated Cheddar cheeses and softened cream cheese. Stir in lemon juice, minced onion, garlic salt, hot pepper sauce to taste and chopped pecans; blend to mix well. Form two long rolls about 1½-inches in diameter. Roll each log in chili powder, and wrap separately in waxed paper. Chill; then slice to serve with bread or crackers.

Nancy Standlee

JALAPEÑO CHEESE LOG

Yields 4 logs

2 pounds Velveeta cheese
1 pound jalapeño cheese
2 (8-ounce) packages cream
  cheese
1 medium bell pepper, chopped
  fine

1½ cups green onions, chopped
2 jalapeño peppers, chopped
1¼ cups chopped pecans
Chopped pecans for garnish
Jalapeño peppers for garnish

Bring cheeses to room temperature. In a bowl, mix cream cheese, bell pepper, green onion, jalapeño peppers and pecans; set aside. Spray hands with non-stick cooking spray; mix Velveeta and jalapeño cheeses. Press mixture flat on a foil-covered cookie sheet. Pat cream cheese mixture on top of flattened cheeses; roll into 4 logs. Lay on a bed of parsley or lettuce, garnish with additional pecans and jalapeño. Serve with Triscuits or other crackers.

Note: *Best if made a day or two before serving to blend flavors. Logs keep well in refrigerator or freezer. A party favorite!*

Christy McConnell

HOT CHEDDAR DIP

Serves 10-12

1 loaf Sheepherder bread OR
  Hawaiian bread
1 (8-ounce) carton sour cream
1 (8-ounce) package cream
  cheese

4 cups (1 pound) grated sharp
  Cheddar cheese
1 (4-ounce) can chopped green
  chiles
½ cup chopped green onions

Hollow out top of bread loaf. Mix sour cream, cream cheese, grated Cheddar, chiles and onions; spoon into loaf. Wrap in foil; bake at 300° for 1 hour. Serve with chips.

Marty Dunn

CHIPPED BEEF AND DILL DIP

Serves 10-12

1½ cups sour cream
1½ cups mayonnaise
½ pound deli corned beef, finely
  chopped
2 teaspoons dill weed
2 teaspoons dill seed

2 tablespoons dried onion
2 tablespoons parsley flakes
1 teaspoon Beau Monde
  seasoned salt (optional)
Rye or pumpernickel round
  bread

Mix sour cream, mayonnaise, corn beef and seasonings; chill overnight. Carve out bread center and fill with dip. Serve with corn chips or toasted rye bread cubes.

Karen Parrett

HOT BEEF DIP

Yields 2½ cups

¼ cup chopped onion
1 tablespoon margarine
1 (8-ounce) package cream
  cheese
1 cup milk
¼ cup grated Parmesan cheese

1 (2½-ounce) package smoked
  sliced beef, chopped
1 (4-ounce) can mushroom
  stems and pieces, drained
2 tablespoons parsley

Sauté onion in margarine. Add cream cheese and milk; stir over low heat until cream cheese is melted. Stir in Parmesan, chopped beef, mushrooms and parsley; heat thoroughly. Serve with chips or crackers.

Peggy Schrott

MICHAEL'S MICROWAVE CHEESE DIP

Serves 18-20

1 pound ground beef
1 envelope taco seasoning mix
¾ cup water
1 pound Velveeta cheese, cubed

1 (10-ounce) can diced tomatoes
   with chiles
½ can (8-ounces) refried beans
¼ cup picante sauce

Brown ground beef in skillet, drain fat. Stir in taco seasoning and ¾ cup water, simmer on low heat for 10 minutes; set aside. Cut Velveeta cheese into 1-inch cubes; place in 2-quart casserole and cover with waxed paper. Microwave on medium-high heat 2 minutes. Stir, continue to microwave on medium-high until cheese is melted. Stir in diced tomatoes with chiles, refried beans, picante sauce and cooked meat mixture. Microwave 2 more minutes at medium-high heat, or until smooth and heated through. Serve warm with tortilla chips.

Note: *This cheese dip always gets lots of recipe requests!*

Lisa Ondrey

SHRIMP CON QUESO

Serves 8-10

1½ pounds cooked shrimp
½ cup (1 stick) margarine
½ cup chopped celery
½ cup chopped bell pepper
½ cup chopped green onion
1 (10¾-ounce) can condensed
   cream of mushroom soup

1 (10¾-ounce) can condensed
   cream of celery soup
1 (10-ounce) can diced tomatoes
   with green chiles, drained
1 (12-ounce) can evaporated
   milk
2 pounds Velveeta cheese, cubed

Cook and peel shrimp, set aside. Melt margarine in large pan, and add (in order) celery, bell pepper and green onion; sauté until tender. Add both soups, drained tomatoes with chiles, and evaporated milk. Cube Velveeta and add to pan; heat until melted, stirring constantly to prevent scorching. Add cooked shrimp. Serve as a dip with chips, or over rice as a main dish.

Julia Slaydon

~ **Kitchen tip:** *Keep herbs and spices tightly sealed and away from heat and light. Never store herbs above the stove.*

HOT SHRIMP DISH

✓ *Quick to fix*   *Serves 8-10*

1 (7-ounce) can deveined shrimp
1/4 cup (1/2 stick) margarine
1/4 cup chopped green onion
1/8 teaspoon garlic powder (or juice from 1 garlic bud)

1 (8-ounce) package cream cheese, crumbled
1 teaspoon Worcestershire sauce
Few drops of hot pepper sauce
Salt and pepper to taste

Drain shrimp, mash or process briefly in food processor; set aside. Melt margarine in skillet, sauté onion and garlic. Add crumbled cream cheese, stir until melted. Add processed shrimp, Worcestershire sauce, hot pepper sauce, salt and pepper; mix well. Serve warm with chips or crackers.

Wendy Mathews

AVOCADO SHRIMP DIP

Serves 8-10

1 cup boiled shrimp, peeled and deveined
2 cups mashed avocado
1 teaspoon lime juice

1 cup Miracle Whip dressing
2 tablespoons chopped onion
1/8 teaspoon hot pepper sauce
Dash of salt

Cut shrimp in bite-size pieces if large, otherwise leave whole. Mix all ingredients; chill until serving time. Serve with tortilla chips. Don't mix dip too early, or avocados will darken.

Kathy Creel

KING CRAB DIP

Serves 8

1 (6½-ounce) can crab meat
1 (8-ounce) package cream cheese
1/4 cup (1/2 stick) butter plus 1 tablespoon butter, divided

2 teaspoons Worcestershire sauce
2 tablespoons chopped green onion
2 tablespoons slivered almonds

Drain and flake crab meat. Thoroughly mix cream cheese with 1/4 cup butter; add Worcestershire sauce. Stir in crab meat; add green onion, and mix. Spoon into 8"x8" baking dish. Sauté almonds in 1 tablespoon butter, drain. Sprinkle almonds on top of dip mixture. Bake at 350° for 15 minutes. Serve warm with corn chips or crackers.

Barbara Lundahl

PIQUANT CLAM DIP

Serves 16-18

3 (8-ounce) packages cream
  cheese
2 (6½-ounce) cans minced clams
1 bunch green onions, chopped
1 medium bell pepper, chopped

1 teaspoon Worcestershire sauce
½ teaspoon curry powder
½ teaspoon Beau Monde salt
Dash of hot pepper sauce

Place cream cheese in top of double boiler, cook until softened. Drain clams. Mix all ingredients in pan; let flavors blend 5-10 minutes. Serve hot with chips.

Karen Moran

RED-SAUCE CRAB MEAT DIP

✓ *Quick to fix*   *Serves 4-6*

1 (6-ounce) can crab meat,
  drained
½ cup mayonnaise
2 tablespoons chili sauce

½ teaspoon horseradish
Seasoned pepper to taste
Garlic salt or powder to taste

Combine all ingredients, mix well. (Substitute ketchup for chili sauce, if desired.) Serve with chilled vegetable tray of zucchini, carrot, celery, cauliflower, etc.

Polly Galloway

NEUFCHÂTEL SEAFOOD DIP

Serves 10

1 pound cooked shrimp or crab
½ cup chopped celery
¼ cup chopped onion
1 (8-ounce) package cream
  cheese

1 (8-ounce) package Neufchâtel
  (or any garlic cream cheese)
1-1½ cups mayonnaise
½ teaspoon lemon juice
Salt and pepper to taste

Cook shrimp or crab, chop celery and onion; set aside. Blend cream cheese, garlic cheese and mayonnaise. Add seafood, celery, onion and lemon juice. Season to taste. Serve with chips or crackers.

Patti Hoffmann

GRATED SHRIMP DIP

Serves 12-16

½ cup finely chopped celery
½ small onion, grated
Italian dressing
1½ pounds cooked shrimp,
   peeled and deveined
Mayonnaise

1 (8-ounce) package cream
   cheese
½ teaspoon salt
¼ teaspoon black pepper
Dash garlic powder

A day in advance, mix chopped celery and grated onion; add enough Italian dressing to cover. Place in covered container, refrigerate at least 12 hours.

To prepare dip, drain excess dressing from celery-onions. Grate cooked shrimp. Mix shrimp with celery-onions, add enough mayonnaise to form a dip consistency. Beat cream cheese until smooth, add to shrimp mixture. Add salt, pepper and garlic powder, mix well. Spoon into serving dish; refrigerate until ready to serve.

Marilyn Matthews

MARINATED SHRIMP

Serves 25-30

10 pounds shrimp, boiled,
   peeled
4 onions, sliced
1 bunch green onions, sliced
1 cup fresh parsley, chopped
1 bunch fresh cilantro, chopped
4 cups red wine vinegar
⅔ cup olive oil
½ cup fresh lemon juice

1 (2-ounce) jar of capers
1 (12-ounce) jar sliced jalapeños
1 (5-ounce) jar sliced green
   olives
1 tablespoon oregano
1 tablespoon salt
½ tablespoon pepper
1 teaspoon cumin

Boil and peel shrimp. Combine all other ingredients; marinate shrimp 24 hours. Serve by itself, with crackers, or on a salad. Recipe can be cut by ½ or ¼.

Note: *This recipe is delicious, and is great for a party!*

Jo Ann Brown

~ **Don't overcook shrimp:** *Drop shucked shrimp in boiling salted water and simmer 3-5 minutes, then drain.*

SHRIMP-CRAB MOUSSE

Serves 10-12

1 (10¾-ounce) can condensed
  cream of mushroom soup
1 (8-ounce) package cream
  cheese
1 envelope unflavored gelatin

1 cup finely chopped onion
1 cup finely chopped celery
1 cup real mayonnaise
1 (6-ounce) can lump crab meat
1 cup cooked salad shrimp

In saucepan, heat soup, cream cheese and gelatin until warm and blended. Working with ½ mixture at a time, add remaining ingredients; mix until smooth. Grease a favorite seafood mold very well; fill with mousse mixture. Chill overnight. Unmold and garnish as desired. Serve with crackers or vegetable sticks.

Maureen Schefsky

PARTY SALMON

Serves 10-12

1 (16-ounce) can salmon
1 (8-ounce) package cream
  cheese
½ cup chopped pecans
3 tablespoons chopped parsley

2 tablespoons grated onion
1 tablespoon lemon juice
2 teaspoons horseradish
Ripe olive, parsley for garnish

Allow cream cheese to soften. Drain salmon. Mix all ingredients to consistency of smooth paste. Form paste into fish shape on a platter. Add a ripe olive for the eye; shape scales, tail and fins. Chill overnight. Garnish platter with fresh parsley, and serve with Norwegian white crackers.

Delores Smith

PICKLED SHRIMP

Serves 8

2 pounds shrimp, peeled and
  deveined
2 medium onions, cut in rings
1½ cups vegetable oil
1½ cups white vinegar

½ cup sugar
1½ teaspoons salt
1½ teaspoons celery seed
4 tablespoons capers

Boil shrimp for 3-5 minutes until pink and tender. Drain; rinse with cold water. Chill. In plastic, sealable bowl, layer shrimp and onion rings. Mix other ingredients and pour over layers. Seal and refrigerate for six hours, or longer. Shake or invert occasionally. Remove from marinade to serve.

Jane Ray

CONFETTI PARTY MIX

✓ *Quick to fix*   *Yields about 20 cups*

1 (18-ounce) box Honey Graham cereal
1 (16-ounce) box black raisins
1 (16-ounce) box golden raisins
1 (14-ounce) package stick pretzels
1 (1-pound) bag M&Ms plain candy

Mix all ingredients in a large bowl. Serve at card games or other get-togethers.

Delight Fails

CARAMEL CRACKER SNACK

Yields about 9 cups

2 (9-ounce) boxes Ritz Bits crackers
1 cup dry-roasted peanuts
½ cup (1 stick) butter or margarine
1 cup granulated sugar
½ cup light corn syrup
1 teaspoon vanilla extract
1 teaspoon baking soda

Preheat oven to 250°. Combine crackers and peanuts in greased large, shallow baking pan. In a saucepan, bring butter, sugar and corn syrup to a boil; cook for 5 minutes. Remove from heat, add vanilla and soda. Pour caramel mixture over crackers and nuts; stir well. Bake at 250° for 1 hour, stirring every 15 minutes. Pour onto waxed paper; break apart, allow to cool. Store in airtight container.

Penny Daigle

NANA'S CHEESE COINS

Yields 24 appetizers

2 cups (8-ounces) grated Cheddar cheese
1 cup (2 sticks) margarine, melted
2 cups flour
1 cup crispy rice cereal
1 teaspoon cayenne pepper
1 teaspoon salt

Mix all ingredients well; roll into a ball. Chill. Pinch off portions and roll into small balls; flatten on ungreased cookie sheet. Bake at 350° for about 20 minutes.

Peggy McKnight

ZESTY PECANS

Yields about 2 cups

½ cup (1 stick) butter
4 tablespoons A-1 steak sauce

1 pound shelled pecans, halved
Seasoned salt

Melt butter and mix with steak sauce. Add pecans, coat thoroughly. Spread pecans on cookie sheet; bake at 200° for 1½ hours, stirring once or twice. Spread pecans on brown paper and sprinkle with seasoned salt.

Cary Rosenbohm

AVOCADO STUFFED EGGS

Yields 24 appetizers

12 hard-cooked eggs
1 avocado, peeled and mashed
1 teaspoon mayonnaise
½ teaspoon garlic salt

½ teaspoon dry mustard
½ teaspoon pepper
Paprika or cayenne pepper
(optional)

Peel hard-cooked eggs, cut in half. Combine mashed avocado, mayonnaise and seasonings; stuff into cut eggs. Refrigerate before serving.

Linda Meche

SPINACH BALLS

✓ *Quick to fix*　　　　　　　　　　　*Yields 60-70 appetizers*

2 (10-ounce) packages frozen
　chopped spinach
2 cups herb seasoned stuffing
　mix
1 cup grated Parmesan cheese

6 eggs, beaten
¾ cup (1½ sticks) butter,
　softened
Salt and pepper to taste

Cook spinach according to package directions, drain well. Mix remaining ingredients with spinach. Roll into balls the size of a walnut and place on cookie sheet; bake at 350° for 10 minutes. These can be made ahead and frozen.

Alice Rodgers

CHICKEN RUMAKI

Yields 12 appetizers

1 cooked boneless chicken
   breast
4 whole water chestnuts

6 slices bacon
Brown sugar

Teriyaki Sauce:

¼ cup salad oil
¼ cup soy sauce
2 tablespoons ketchup

1 tablespoon vinegar
¼ teaspoon pepper
2 cloves garlic, crushed

Mix all Teriyaki Sauce ingredients thoroughly; set aside. Cut cooked chicken into 12 bite-size pieces. Cut each water chestnut into thirds. Place chicken and chestnuts in bowl, cover with Teriyaki Sauce; refrigerate about 4 hours. Drain. Cut bacon slices in half. Wrap a piece of chicken and a piece of water chestnut in each bacon slice; secure with wooden toothpick. Roll in brown sugar. Broil, 3-4 inches from heat, turning occasionally, 10 minutes or until bacon is crisp.

Note: *Recipe can be doubled, tripled, etc. This is always a big hit at parties!*

Cynthia Lancaster

HOT CHEDDAR MUSHROOMS

Serves 8

1 pound medium mushrooms
6 tablespoons margarine, divided
1 cup chopped onion
1 cup soft bread crumbs
1 cup shredded Cheddar cheese

½ cup chopped walnuts
¼ cup chopped parsley
½ teaspoon salt
¼ teaspoon pepper

Remove stems from mushrooms; chop and reserve. Place mushroom caps in lightly buttered baking pan, brush with 3 tablespoons melted margarine. Sauté onion and mushroom stems in remaining margarine in skillet for 2 minutes. Add bread crumbs, then all remaining ingredients; stir to mix. Spoon mixture into mushroom caps; bake at 350° for 20 minutes. Best if served hot.

Patti Hosack

DEE'S ITALIAN STUFFED MUSHROOMS

❤ *Heart healthy*   *Yields 30 appetizers*

30 medium-size fresh
** mushrooms**
½ cup (2-ounces) shredded part-
** skim mozzarella cheese**

¼ cup minced fresh parsley
¼ cup oil-free Italian dressing

Clean mushrooms with damp paper towel. Remove stems, and finely chop; set caps aside. Combine chopped mushroom, cheese, parsley and Italian dressing in a bowl; stir well. Spoon mixture evenly into reserved caps; place in a shallow baking dish. Bake at 350° for 15-20 minutes, until cheese melts. Each appetizer has about 8 calories.

Dee Eddins

CHILLED MARINATED MUSHROOMS

❤ *Heart healthy*   *Serves 6*

1 pound mushrooms
¼ cup vinegar
1 tablespoon olive oil
1 clove garlic, halved

1 tablespoon chopped parsley
¼ teaspoon oregano
¼ teaspoon salt
⅛ teaspoon pepper

Cook mushrooms in boiling water for 3 minutes; drain. Combine vinegar, olive oil, garlic, parsley, oregano, salt and pepper in a bowl; mix well. Add drained mushrooms. Chill for several hours, stirring occasionally. Remove garlic before serving.

Kathy Carr

BAKED WATER CHESTNUTS

Serves 12

2 (8-ounce) cans whole water
** chestnuts**
Soy sauce

1 cup sugar
1 pound bacon

Cover water chestnuts with soy sauce, marinate for ½ hour. Discard sauce; roll water chestnuts in sugar to coat. Wrap half a slice of bacon around each water chestnut; secure with a toothpick. Place on cookie sheet, bake at 400° for 15 minutes. Drain grease. May be frozen uncooked, and thawed before baking.

Schelli Martin

MUSHROOM LOGS

Yields 48 appetizers

2 (8-ounce) cans refrigerated
 crescent dinner rolls
1 (8-ounce) package cream
 cheese, softened
1 teaspoon seasoned salt

1 (4-ounce) can mushroom
 stems and pieces, drained,
 chopped
1 egg, beaten
1-2 tablespoons poppy seeds

Preheat oven to 375.° Separate crescent dough into 8 rectangles; press perforations to seal. Combine cream cheese, seasoned salt and mushrooms; mix well. Spread mixture in equal portions over each rectangle of dough. Starting at long side, roll up jellyroll fashion; pinch seams to seal. Slice logs into 1-inch pieces; place seam-side down on ungreased baking sheet. Brush each log with beaten egg and sprinkle with poppy seeds. Bake at 375° for 10-12 minutes.

Jeanne Howard/Janice Keller

SAVORY CHICKEN BITES

Yields 40 appetizers

1 (8-ounce) package cream
 cheese, softened
½ teaspoon lemon juice
½ teaspoon dried basil
¼ teaspoon onion salt
⅛ teaspoon dried thyme
1 cup finely chopped, cooked
 chicken

⅓ cup finely chopped celery
1 (2-ounce) jar diced pimiento,
 drained
2 (8-ounce) cans refrigerated
 crescent dinner rolls
1 large egg, lightly beaten
1½ teaspoons sesame seeds

Combine softened cream cheese, lemon juice, basil, salt and thyme; mix until well blended. Stir in chicken, celery and pimiento; set aside. Separate crescent dough into 8 rectangles; press perforations to seal. Spread about ¼ cup chicken mixture over each dough rectangle, leaving ½-inch margin on one long side and no margin on other sides. Roll dough, jellyroll fashion, starting at long side with filling spread to edge. Pinch seams to seal. Brush with egg and sprinkle with sesame seeds. Cut each roll into 5 pieces; place seam-side down on lightly greased baking sheets. Bake at 375° for 12-15 minutes, or until golden brown. To reheat, bake uncovered at 375° for 4-6 minutes.

Janet Steffler

MEXICAN PINWHEELS

Yields 48-60 appetizers

1 (8-ounce) package cream
   cheese, softened
1 cup sour cream
1 cup (4-ounces) grated Cheddar
   cheese
¼ cup minced onion
1 (4-ounce) can chopped green
   chiles, drained

1 (4¼-ounce) can chopped black
   olives, drained
¼ cup chopped green olives
Chopped jalapeño peppers to
   taste (optional)
1 teaspoon garlic salt
12 large flour tortillas

Blend sour cream and cream cheese until smooth. Add Cheddar cheese, onion, chiles, black olives, green olives, chopped jalapeño if desired and garlic salt; mix well. Spread cheese mixture on tortillas, roll up and place seam-side down in glass dish or pizza pan. Chill for several hours, until firm. Slice into ½-inch sections and serve. Pinwheels can be made in advance and frozen before slicing.

Barbara Allen

CHEESE PENNY SNACKS

Yields 48 appetizers

½ cup (1 stick) margarine
2 cups (8-ounces) grated
   Cheddar cheese

1 cup flour
½ teaspoon salt
½ package dry onion soup mix

Bring margarine to room temperature; combine with cheese. Add flour and salt; mix in dry soup. Form into a roll, refrigerate until chilled. Slice in ¼-inch sections; bake on ungreased cookie sheet at 375° for 10-15 minutes.

Sue Allen

CHEESE SQUARES

Yields 24 appetizers

6 eggs
4 cups (1 pound) grated Cheddar
   cheese

2 (4-ounce) cans chopped green
   chiles

Beat eggs, mix in cheese and chiles. Spray 13"x9"x2" dish with non-stick cooking spray. Pour in mixture; bake at 350° for 25 minutes. Let cool slightly before cutting.

Nancy Chamberlain

ARTICHOKE PARTY TOAST

✓ *Quick to fix*   *Serves 15-20*

**2 (14-ounce) cans artichoke
   hearts, drained**
1¾ cups mayonnaise
**1½ cups (6-ounces) sharp grated
   Cheddar cheese**

½ teaspoon onion powder
**¼ teaspoon lemon pepper (or
   more, to taste)**
**1 package party rye slices, lightly
   toasted**

Quarter artichoke hearts. Mix together mayonnaise, cheese, onion powder and lemon pepper. Top toasted rye slices with quartered artichoke hearts; arrange on a broiler pan. Heap a tablespoon of cheese mixture on top of each artichoke. Broil until bubbly. Dish can be mixed ahead and assembled just before serving.

Marilyn Woody

CRAB MEAT CANAPÉS

Serves 20

1 (8-ounce) box Velveeta cheese
½ cup (1 stick) butter
1 (6-ounce) can lump crab meat

**1 package Pepperidge Farm tiny
   rolls, split, OR 1 package
   party rye bread**

Melt cheese and butter in double boiler. Flake and drain crab meat, add to cheese; stir. Spread on split tiny rolls or mini rye slices. Place on broiler pan, broil briefly until warm. The canapés cook very quickly, so need to be watched.

Helen Baker

PUFF PASTRY-SAUSAGE WRAPS

Serves 20

**1 pound ground sausage (deer
   sausage works well)**

**1 (10-ounce) package frozen
   puff pastry sheets**

Divide sausage into 4 equal sections. Form each fourth into a 10" by ¾" strip. Let puff pastry thaw until easy to pinch. Cut each sheet in half to make four sheets about 10" by 3". Place strip of sausage in middle of each sheet, wrap pastry around sausage and pinch edges shut. Slice each roll into ½-inch sections. Lay sections, sausage side up, on a cookie sheet. Bake at 350° for about 30 minutes, until sausage is well cooked and pastry is golden. Drain grease, and serve.

Jane Koontz

ONION-CRAB WEDGES

✓ *Quick to fix*   *Yields 72 appetizers*

9 English muffins, split
Butter
1 (2.8-ounce) can Durkee French
   fried onions
1 (6-ounce) can crab meat,
   drained

1 (4¼-ounce) can chopped black
   olives
2½ cups (10-ounces) grated
   Cheddar cheese
½ cup mayonnaise

Toast and butter muffins; place on greased cookie sheet. Measure out ⁴/₅ of a can of French fried onions, combine with crab meat, olives, cheese and mayonnaise; mix well. Spread mixture on English muffins. Cut each muffin into quarters. Broil 4 inches from heat source until bubbly.

Mary Ann Sosebee

CRAB MEAT WEDGES

Yields 144 appetizers

3 sticks real butter
1 pound fresh white lump crab
   meat OR 3 (6-ounce) cans
   white crab meat
3 (5-ounce) jars Old English
   cheese

1½ tablespoons mayonnaise
   (optional)
2 teaspoons garlic powder
Red pepper, hot pepper sauce,
   Worcestershire sauce to taste
18 English muffins (3 packages)

Soften butter. Stir in crab meat, cheese, mayonnaise if desired and seasonings to taste; mix to spreadable consistency. Cut English muffins in half, spread with crab meat mixture. Cut each muffin into quarters. Bake on ungreased cookie sheet at 350° for 20 minutes. Reduce ingredients by thirds to make smaller quantities. Unbaked wedges can be frozen, then baked without thawing.

Cindy Williams/ Alice Rodgers

BACON CHEDDAR WEDGES: Fry and crumble 1 pound bacon. Mix bacon with 1 cup grated Cheddar cheese and 1 cup mayonnaise. Spread on 12 split English muffins; broil until bubbly. Cut into quarters to serve. (Yields 96 appetizers.)

Sherrie Ezell

STUFFED FRENCH BREAD

Serves 6

½ cup (1 stick) margarine, softened
1 cup mayonnaise (or less, to taste)
3 cups (12-ounces) grated sharp Cheddar cheese

1 bunch green onions, chopped
2 jalapeño peppers, finely diced
1 (4¼-ounce) can chopped black olives, drained
Garlic powder to taste
2 loaves French bread

Mix softened margarine, mayonnaise, cheese, green onions, jalapeños, olives and garlic powder. Hollow out bread loaves to form bowls, being careful not to cut through bottom crust and leaving the end crusts uncut. Fill each loaf with ½ the filling. Bake at 350° until filling is bubbly. Allow to stand until cheese firms somewhat before serving. Serve as a light meal or cut in small sections for appetizers.

Hint: *Use 6 individual-size loaves to make serving easier.*

Jane Ray

SAUSAGE BREAD

Yields 15 slices per loaf

3 loaves frozen yeast bread
2 pounds pork sausage, hot or mild to taste
1 medium onion, chopped
1-2 bell peppers, chopped

1 pound (4 cups) grated Cheddar cheese
1 pound (4 cups) grated Monterey Jack cheese

Thaw bread. Sauté sausage, onion and bell pepper until tender. Roll out each bread loaf to an 8"x15" rectangle. Divide cheese and sausage into three equal parts. Fill each bread rectangle with cheese, then sausage; fold over and pinch to close. Fold ends, and pinch to close. (At this point, you can wrap bread in foil and freeze, if desired. When ready to bake, allow approximately an hour for bread to thaw.) Spray cookie sheet with non-stick cooking spray, and bake seam-side down at 350° for 30 minutes, or until done. Slice and serve hot.

Note: *Reduce sausage, Cheddar cheese and Monterey Jack cheese amounts by ½-pound each, if desired. Sliced sandwich ham can be substituted for sausage.*

Marty Dunn/ Delight Fails

KATHY'S GREEK BREAD

Yields 48 appetizers

1 loaf French bread
½ cup margarine, softened
2 cups (8-ounces) grated
   mozzarella cheese

½ cup chopped green onions
½ cup mayonnaise
1 (4¼-ounce) can chopped black
   olives, drained

Split French bread in half. Combine softened butter with cheese, green onions, mayonnaise and olives; mix to a spreadable consistency. Spread mixture on both halves of French bread. Refrigerate for 24 hours or overnight to blend flavors, if desired. Bake at 350° for 15 minutes. Cut each loaf in half to serve 4 as a meal, or cut loaves into 48 pieces for appetizers. Greek Bread can be prepared in advance and quick-frozen before baking. Wrap loaves in aluminum foil to freeze.

❤ *Heart healthy hint: This recipe tastes just as delicious using fat-free mayonnaise, fat-free cheese and diet margarine.*

Cindy Williams/ Barbara Monical

DIANE'S PEPPERONI BREAD

Serves 10

1 loaf Bridgeford frozen bread
   dough
2 cups (8-ounces) shredded
   mozzarella cheese
1 egg
1 tablespoon parsley flakes

¼ teaspoon garlic salt
¼ cup Parmesan cheese
1 package thinly sliced
   pepperoni
¼ pound thinly sliced deli ham
¼ pound sliced hard salami

Let dough thaw and rise. In a bowl, mix mozzarella, egg, parsley, garlic salt and Parmesan. Spread dough into a large rectangle. On top of dough, layer the pepperoni, ham and salami. Spread the cheese mixture on top. Roll up the dough short-side to short-side, pinching the ends together firmly as you go. Place on cookie sheet seam-side down. Bake at 350° for 40 minutes. Slice, serve warm. Serves 10 as an appetizer, or 6 as a main course.

Note: *The loaf can be prepared the night before and refrigerated until baking.*

Wendy Mathews

EASY FRUIT SLUSH

♥ *Heart healthy,* ✓ *Quick to fix*   *Serves 2*

1½ cups ice cubes
1 ripe banana, sliced

5 strawberries, hulled
½ cup orange juice

Put all ingredients in blender, mix until smooth and thick. Serve immediately.

Ruth Bondurant

STRAWBERRY-YOGURT SHAKE

♥ *Heart healthy,* ✓ *Quick to fix*   *Serves 2*

⅔ cup skim milk
⅔ cup plain non-fat yogurt
1 medium banana, sliced

1 cup strawberries (fresh or
    frozen)
1 teaspoon honey

Chill two glasses. Combine ingredients in blender; process until smooth and thick. Pour into chilled glasses.

Jane Koontz

ALMOND-BANANA SHAKE

✓ *Quick to fix*   *Serves 1*

¼ cup raw almonds
1 cup cold water

2 bananas, cut in pieces and
    frozen

Place almonds in blender, cover; begin to grind. With blender running, add water slowly. After all water is added, blend 30 seconds longer. Add banana chunks, blend on high until smooth and creamy. Pour into a glass to serve.

Karen Creveling

ORANGE JUICE DELUXE

✓ *Quick to fix*   *Serves 4*

1 (6-ounce) can frozen orange
    juice concentrate
1 cup milk

1 teaspoon vanilla extract
½ cup sugar

Put all ingredients in blender, mix about 30 seconds. Pour into glasses, serve immediately. (Decrease sugar and add a little water, if desired.)

Missy Funk

SPICED APPLE SIPPER

Serves 4

¼ cup firmly packed light brown sugar
1 (3-inch) cinnamon stick
½ teaspoon whole cloves
½ teaspoon whole allspice
1 cup water

1 (6-ounce) can frozen apple juice concentrate, partly thawed
1 (24-ounce) bottle purple grape juice, well chilled
Grape clusters (optional)

In small saucepan, combine brown sugar, cinnamon stick, cloves, allspice and water; heat to boiling. Cover, simmer 20 minutes. Strain into a large pitcher. Stir in apple concentrate until thawed. Stir in grape juice. Pour over ice into tall glasses. Garnish glasses with small clusters of green or purple grapes, if desired.

Nancy Standlee

OLDE VIRGINIA WASSAIL

✓ *Quick to fix*   *Serves 10-12*

1 quart sweet apple cider
2 cups orange juice
1 cup Real Lemon concentrate
2 (16-ounce) cans pineapple juice

1 stick whole cinnamon
1 tablespoon whole cloves
½ cup honey (or to taste)

Combine all ingredients in large pan; bring to a simmer. Strain; serve hot.

Susan Laver

PLANTATION MINT TEA

✓ *Quick to fix*   *Serves 10-12*

6 cups boiling water
5 mint tea bags
¾ cup lemon juice
1½ cups sugar

1 cup pineapple juice
1 pint ginger ale
Fresh sprigs of mint

Boil water; steep tea 5 minutes. Add lemon juice and sugar; stir well. Just before serving, add pineapple juice and ginger ale. Serve over ice; garnish with mint sprigs.

Becky Lowery/ Janet Steffler

LEMON TEA

Yields 7 quarts

6 quarts water
4 quart-size tea bags
2 (12-ounce) cans frozen
  lemonade concentrate

1 cup sugar
Fresh mint (optional)
Lemon slices (optional)

Bring water to boil. Add tea bags, cover; let stand 20 minutes. Remove tea bags. Add undiluted lemonade concentrate and sugar to tea, stirring until dissolved. Add mint leaves, if desired. Serve over ice; garnish with lemon slices if desired.

Eva Kinney

EASY BANANA PUNCH

Serves 25-30

4 cups sugar
6 cups water
1 (6-ounce can) frozen orange
  juice concentrate
1 (46-ounce) can pineapple juice

5 large ripe bananas, mashed
2 (2-quart) bottles ginger ale
Orange slices, mint sprigs, whole
  strawberries for garnish
  (optional)

Bring sugar and water to a boil, cook until sugar dissolves. Cool completely. When cool, add juice concentrates, pineapple juice and bananas; mix well. Freeze in 2 half-gallon containers. About 3 hours before serving, remove from freezer. About 20 minutes before serving, empty 1 container into punch bowl and add 1 bottle of ginger ale. Garnish with orange slices, mint sprigs and strawberries, if desired. Replenish as needed with remaining slush and ginger ale.

Cindy Williams

P.T.A. PUNCH

✓ *Quick to fix*
Serves 12

1 (12-ounce) can Five Alive
  citrus beverage frozen
  concentrate

1 (2-liter) bottle Sprite, chilled
Ice ring or cubes

Mix undiluted Five Alive concentrate and Sprite in punch bowl. Add ice ring or ice cubes.

Linda Jordan

DANDY BRANDY

Yields 1 quart

3 cups sugar
1 (2-ounce) jar instant coffee
2 cups boiling water
1 pint brandy

2 tablespoons bourbon
2 tablespoons vanilla extract or
  1 vanilla bean

Mix together sugar and instant coffee. Add boiling water, stir well. Let mixture cool. Add brandy, bourbon and vanilla. Age one month in a dark bottle. Serve with iced milk or over ice cream, if desired.

Becky Lowery

JEAN'S PARTY PUNCH

Serves 25

1 (12-ounce) can frozen orange
  juice concentrate
3 juice cans water
1 (6-ounce) bottle frozen lemon
  juice

1 (46-ounce) can pineapple juice
½ cup sugar
1 (1-liter) bottle ginger ale

Combine orange juice concentrate, water, thawed lemon juice, pineapple juice and sugar; mix well. Pour a portion of punch into a ring mold; freeze. Chill remaining punch overnight. Just before serving, mix punch and ginger ale in a punch bowl. Add frozen ring. Ladle into punch cups.

Mary Ann Sosebee

PUNCH FOR A BUNCH

Serves 30

2 (3-ounce) packages strawberry
  gelatin
1 quart (4 cups) boiling water
1 (46-ounce) can pineapple juice

1 (6-ounce) can frozen
  lemonade concentrate
2 cups sugar

Dissolve gelatin in boiling water; simmer 3 minutes. Add pineapple juice, lemonade and sugar; stir. Cool in refrigerator. Add enough ice and water to make 2 gallons.

Hint: *For a special Halloween Brew, use orange gelatin and serve over dry ice.*

Sharon Schwing

FIVE-JUICE PARTY PUNCH

Yields 5 quarts

3 cups apple juice
2 cups unsweetened pineapple
 juice
3 cups cranberry juice
1¼ cups lemon juice

1 (6-ounce) can frozen orange
 juice concentrate
2 cups sugar
2 (2-liter) bottles ginger ale

Mix all ingredients; serve chilled with a festive ice ring.

Marcie Allen

ALL-OCCASION FROZEN PUNCH

Serves 12-15

1 (3-ounce) package lime-
 flavored gelatin
2½ cups sugar
1 cup boiling water
7 cups cold water
1 (12-ounce) bottle lemon juice

1 (46-ounce) can unsweetened
 pineapple juice
1 teaspoon almond extract
3 drops green food coloring
 (optional)
1 quart chilled ginger ale OR
 1 bottle chilled champagne

In a large saucepan, dissolve gelatin and sugar in boiling water. Add 7 cups cold water, lemon juice, pineapple juice, almond extract and food coloring. Pour into large freezer-safe container; freeze. About 2 hours before serving, remove from freezer to make slush. At serving time, pour into punch bowl; add ginger ale. If desired, omit ginger ale; substitute 1 bottle of chilled champagne. Any color gelatin and food coloring may be used to suit the occasion.

Jody Epps

SHERBET SHOWER PUNCH

✓ *Quick to fix*   *Serves 20-25*

1 (46-ounce) can pineapple juice
1 (12-ounce) can frozen
 lemonade concentrate
2 lemonade cans of water

1 (half-gallon) carton pineapple
 sherbet
1 (2-liter) bottle Sprite
1 (2-liter) bottle ginger ale

Mix pineapple juice, lemonade concentrate and water. Add sherbet, mix well. Just before serving, add Sprite and ginger ale.

Janis Warny

CRANBERRY PUNCH

✓ *Quick to fix* *Serves 25*

1 (3-ounce) package cherry
  gelatin
1 cup boiling water
1 (6-ounce) can frozen
  lemonade concentrate

1 quart cranberry juice, chilled
3 cups cold water
1 (12-ounce) bottle ginger ale
Ice ring or cubes

Dissolve gelatin in 1 cup boiling water. Stir in lemonade concentrate. Add cranberry juice and cold water. Pour into punch bowl; add ginger ale and ice.

Note: *This is a very tasty punch that even children love!*

Cheri McBurnett

TEXAS SUNSHINE PUNCH

✓ *Quick to fix* *Serves 15-20*

1 quart light rum
1 quart pineapple juice
1 quart orange juice

1 quart lemon-lime soda
1 pint peach flavored schnapps

Mix all ingredients; serve over ice. Increase to any quantity using equal parts rum, pineapple juice, orange juice and soda with ½ part peach schnapps.

Wendy Mathews

BOURBON-RUM MILK PUNCH

✓ *Quick to fix* *Serves 6-8*

½ cup bourbon
½ cup light rum
1 cup milk

2 cups vanilla ice cream,
  softened
Dash nutmeg

Mix bourbon, rum and milk; combine with softened ice cream. Spoon into individual serving cups; top with nutmeg.

Hint: *Serve as a holiday party alternative to egg-nog.*

Cheryl Whitten

HOT BUTTERED RUM

Yields 25 cups

1 pound butter, softened
1 (16-ounce) package light
  brown sugar
1 (16-ounce) package powdered
  sugar
2 teaspoons ground cinnamon

2 teaspoons ground nutmeg
1 quart vanilla ice cream,
  softened
Light rum
Whipped cream, cinnamon
  sticks

Combine butter, sugars, cinnamon and nutmeg; beat until light and fluffy. Add softened ice cream, stir until well blended. Spoon mixture into a 2-quart container; freeze. To serve, thaw slightly. Place 3 tablespoons mixture and 1 jigger of rum in a large mug; fill with boiling water, stir well. (Unused mixture can be refrozen.) Top with whipped cream, and serve with cinnamon sticks.

Hint: *Keep this mixture in the freezer during the holiday season to have ready when guests stop by. Mixture keeps up to 3 weeks in freezer.*

Marilyn Woody

HOME-MADE BEER

Yields 8 gallons

1 can Blue Ribbon beer-making
  malt
10 pounds sugar

8 gallons warm water (not hot)
1 package dry active yeast

Put malt, sugar, warm water and yeast into a non-metal crock. Leave for 72 hours; strain through cloth and bottle; serve.

Lisa Baker

*~ **Beverages:** How much serves how many:*

***Orange juice:** 1 gallon = 32 (4-ounce) servings*

***Lemonade:** 2 gallons = 32 (8-ounce) servings*

***Iced tea:** 2 gallons = 32 (8-ounce) servings*

***Coffee:** 1 pound = 56 (6-ounce) servings*

***Beer:** 8-gallon keg = 85 (12-ounce) servings*

***Wine:** 1.5 liter bottle = 10 (5-ounce) servings*

Salads and Vegetables

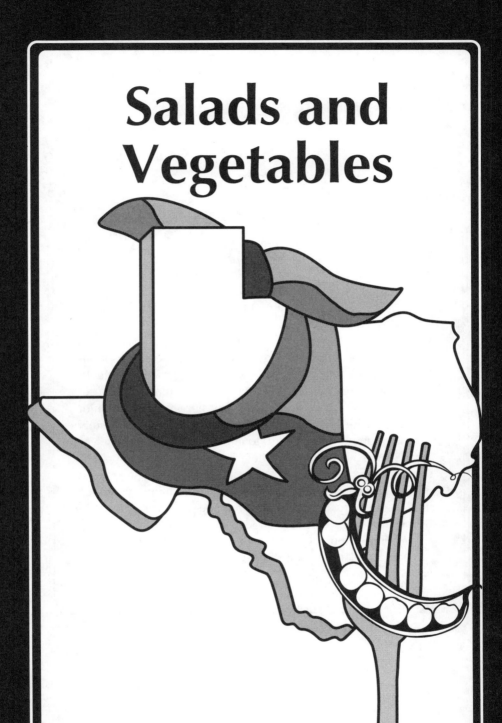

BARGAIN BOX
1973 - to present

Junior Service League operates Bargain Box, a resale shop located at 213-A Parking Way in downtown Lake Jackson, as both a service project and a way to finance community projects. The Bargain Box carries delicately used clothing and household goods, which are sold to the public at nominal cost. Junior Service League also works with churches and community organizations to donate items to families who find themselves in need after a house fire or other tragedy. Bargain Box is a self-supporting project managed and staffed by JSL volunteers with all profits channeled directly into JSL's community service fund. Every Junior Service League member works at the Bargain Box during the year. The shop depends on tax-deductible contributions from the community, as well as JSL members, to provide a variety of household items and good quality used clothing.

SWEET BASIL DRESSING

✓ *Quick to fix*   *Serves 4*

1 cup dried fresh basil
¼ cup apple cider vinegar
¼ teaspoon salt

1 cup safflower oil
¼ cup honey

Put all ingredients in blender, blend until creamy (approximately 30 seconds.) Serve over Romaine lettuce and sliced red pepper.

Ruth Bondurant

TEXAS FRENCH DRESSING

✓ *Quick to fix*   *Yields 1 quart*

1 (10¾-ounce) can condensed
    tomato soup
1 cup salad oil
¾ cup apple cider vinegar
¾ cup sugar

2 tablespoons grated onion
1 tablespoon prepared mustard
1 teaspoon Worcestershire sauce
1 teaspoon garlic salt
1 teaspoon pepper

Combine all ingredients in a quart jar, shake vigorously.

Janis Warny

BINNIE'S OWN FRENCH DRESSING

✓ *Quick to fix*   *Serves 6*

1 cup salad oil
⅓ cup vinegar
1 tablespoon sugar
½ teaspoon onion powder
½ teaspoon dry mustard

½ teaspoon paprika
½ teaspoon salt
¼ teaspoon garlic powder
Dash of pepper

Mix all ingredients in shaker or blender; chill. Serve over spinach, bacon and egg salad.

Binnie Bauml

MANDARIN ROMAINE SALAD

✓ *Quick to fix*   *Serves 6-8*

½ **head Romaine lettuce**
½ **bunch green onions, sliced thin**

½ **cup blanched almonds, toasted**
1 **(11-ounce) can mandarin oranges, drained**

Dressing:

1 **cup safflower oil**
½ **cup tarragon vinegar**
3 **teaspoons white sugar**

1 **teaspoon tarragon spice**
1 **teaspoon Dijon mustard**
1 **teaspoon salt**

Wash lettuce, tear into bite-size pieces. Add sliced green onions, toasted almonds and mandarin oranges. Combine all dressing ingredients; mix well. Pour dressing over salad just before serving.

Marcie Allen

WARMED SPINACH SALAD

Serves 4

1 **small bunch fresh spinach**
4 **slices bacon, crisp-fried**
2 **tablespoons tarragon vinegar**

2 **tablespoons white vinegar**
Salt and pepper to taste

Wash spinach leaves in cold water, dry well, and place in mixing bowl. Fry bacon until crisp; crumble over spinach leaves. To bacon drippings, add vinegars; warm the mixture. When ready to serve, season spinach with salt and pepper to taste, and pour warmed vinegar over spinach. Toss and serve.

Polly Galloway

~ *Salad smorgasbord: Let guests create their own luncheon salads, buffet-style. Fill a large salad bowl with crisp-chilled torn salad greens. Surround with small bowls containing a variety of ingredients: thin strips of meat; cheese; hard-boiled egg wedges; sliced fresh vegetables, mushrooms and onions; tomato wedges; kidney or garbanzo beans; sprouts; sunflower seeds; croutons; raisins; olives, or cubed fruits such as avocado, apple or peaches. Provide a choice of popular dressings.*

BERMUDA SPINACH SALAD

✓ Quick to fix   *Serves 6*

1½ pounds fresh spinach,
   washed
1 cup salad oil
⅓ cup cider vinegar
¼ cup sugar
1 tablespoon grated onion

1 teaspoon salt
1 teaspoon dry mustard
1 Bermuda onion
Mushrooms (optional)
1 (11-ounce) can mandarin
   oranges, drained

Tear cleaned spinach into bite-size pieces, set aside. Combine salad oil, cider vinegar, sugar, grated onion, salt and dry mustard in an electric blender; mix at medium speed. Cut Bermuda onion into rings and slice mushrooms. Drain juice from oranges. Toss spinach with dressing, garnish with onion, mushrooms and oranges.

Terrie Lumsden

BACON-MUSHROOM SPINACH SALAD

✓ Quick to fix   *Serves 8*

1 pound fresh spinach
½ pound fresh mushrooms
6-8 green onions chopped
8 slices crisp-cooked bacon
1 cup salad oil
⅔ cup sugar
½ teaspoon dry mustard

½ teaspoon onion juice
½ teaspoon salt
⅓ cup cider vinegar
1 (11-ounce) can mandarin
   oranges, drained
Salt and pepper to taste

Remove stems from spinach, wash leaves thoroughly and pat dry. Tear into bite-size pieces. Quickly rinse mushrooms in cold water, drain well, and slice thin. Combine spinach, mushrooms, onions and bacon in a large bowl; set aside.

Combine salad oil, sugar, mustard, onion juice and salt in electric blender; blend well. Remove lid of container, slowly add vinegar while blender is running. Toss spinach mixture with dressing until well coated. Garnish with mandarin oranges; season with salt and pepper.

Diane Hill

SUMMER CORN SALAD

❤ *Heart healthy,* ✓ *Quick to fix*   *Serves 6-8*

1 (16-ounce) bag frozen corn,
  thawed
1 cup diced tomatoes
1 cup diced green peppers
¼ cup diced onion
1 cup diced squash

½ teaspoon garlic powder
½ teaspoon onion powder
¼ teaspoon marjoram
¼ cup finely chopped fresh
  cilantro

Combine all ingredients and refrigerate until serving.

Note: *This dish makes a wonderful cold salad or a tasty side dish for Mexican food.*

Alexa Kincannon

CORN RELISH SALAD

Serves 6

1 (12-ounce) can whole kernel
  corn, well drained
¼ cup sweet pickle relish, well
  drained
½ cup sliced black olives
¾ cup sliced celery
¼ jar of roasted diced red
  peppers (optional, for color)

1 teaspoon salt
2 tablespoons champagne
  vinegar or wine vinegar
6 tablespoons olive oil
Lettuce leaves or shredded
  iceberg lettuce (optional)

Combine all ingredients in a serving bowl, chill for several hours. Serve relish by itself on a bed of lettuce leaves, or toss with shredded iceberg lettuce to add crunch and color. Relish will keep up to five days in refrigerator if shredded lettuce is omitted.

Note: *This recipe multiplies well to serve large crowds. If doubling or tripling recipe, cut back on amount of olive oil used.*

Karen Creveling

LOW-FAT POTATO SALAD

♥ *Heart healthy* *Serves 8*

2 pounds potatoes (about 6 medium)
¼ cup finely chopped onion
1 teaspoon salt
⅛ teaspoon pepper

½ cup non-fat Italian salad dressing
½ cup non-fat mayonnaise OR non-fat Miracle Whip
½ cup chopped celery

Wash potatoes. Heat 1 inch water to boiling. Add unpared potatoes. Cover tightly; heat to boiling and cook 30-35 minutes or until tender. Drain, let cool. When potatoes are cool, peel and cube. Combine potato cubes in large bowl with onion. Sprinkle with salt and pepper; coat well with Italian dressing. Cover, refrigerate at least 2 hours.

Just before serving, add mayonnaise; toss until potatoes are well coated. Stir in celery.

Cynthia Lancaster

ITALIAN BEAN SALAD

Serves 8-10

2 (16-ounce) cans green beans, drained
1 (16-ounce) can kidney beans, drained
1½ cups diced celery
1 (8-ounce) can mushrooms, drained

1 (8-ounce) can pitted black olives, drained
1 medium red onion, diced
2 (14-ounce) jars marinated artichokes, drained with oil reserved

Dressing:

Oil reserved from artichokes
¼ cup tarragon vinegar
1½ teaspoons salt (or to taste)
1¼ teaspoons Accent

1 tablespoon sugar
¾ teaspoon hot pepper sauce
¼ cup parsley flakes
2 teaspoons garlic powder

Mix vegetables in a salad bowl, draining canned items well. Reserve oil from artichokes, combine with other dressing ingredients. Blend well, and shake. Pour over vegetables. Salad is best if made 24 hours in advance. It will keep for several days in the refrigerator.

Marilyn Woody

MARCIA'S BROCCOLI SALAD

Serves 6-8

1 bunch broccoli flowerettes
½ pound cooked bacon,
   crumbled
½ small red onion, diced

⅓ cup raisins
⅓ cup sunflower seeds
4 ounces almonds (optional)

Dressing:

1 cup mayonnaise
¼ cup sugar

2 tablespoons raspberry OR red
   wine vinegar

Combine all salad ingredients and chill. Mix together dressing ingredients and pour over salad one hour before serving.

Note: *This salad is perfect for a dinner party or brunch because it can be made ahead of time.*

Ann Ragsdale

CRUNCHY CAULIFLOWER SALAD

Serves 10-12

2 small or 1 large cauliflower,
   chopped
2 tomatoes, diced
½ cup chopped green onion
½ cup diced bell pepper
½ cup chopped green olives
½ cup sliced radishes

1 cup diced American cheese
½ cup Miracle Whip dressing
½ cup sugar
¼ cup horseradish dressing
   (or more, to taste)
1 teaspoon salt
½ teaspoon pepper

Mix all ingredients; chill for several hours before serving.

Barbara Monical/ Marty Dunn

~ **Cutting the fat:** *To reduce fat, use low-fat or non-fat commercial salad dressings. Or, make your own dressings using lemon, lime, herbs and non-fat yogurt.*

MARINATED VEGETABLE SALAD

Serves 6-8

3-4 stalks broccoli
1 pound fresh mushrooms

1½ bunches green onion
1 pint basket cherry tomatoes

Marinade:

½ cup sugar
1 teaspoon salt
1 teaspoon paprika
1 teaspoon celery seed

1 teaspoon onion or garlic
   powder
1 cup vegetable oil
¼ cup white vinegar

Clean all vegetables. Cut broccoli into bite-size pieces. Cut mushrooms in half. Slice onions (include tops). Keep the cherry tomatoes whole.

Mix the marinade ingredients. Pour over vegetables and marinate in refrigerator about 2 hours. Drain if necessary before serving.

Note: *This salad is great for backyard barbecues and picnics!*

Maureen Schefsky

BROCCOLI-CAULIFLOWER SALAD

Serves 10

1 bunch broccoli, chopped
1 head of cauliflower, chopped
1 red onion, chopped
1 cup raisins
1 cup (4-ounces) grated sharp
   Cheddar cheese

½ pound bacon, cooked and
   crumbled (optional)
1 cup unsalted peanuts
   (optional)

Dressing:

1 cup mayonnaise (cholesterol-
free variety, if desired)

¼ cup cider vinegar
¼ cup sugar

Chop broccoli and cauliflower into bite-size pieces. Combine all salad ingredients in a large bowl. To make dressing, spoon mayonnaise into a mixing bowl; use a wire whisk to slowly add cider vinegar and sugar. Pour dressing over salad, and toss. Cover and refrigerate until serving time.

Helen Baker

SUFFERN INN SALAD

Serves 4-6

1 (10-ounce) package frozen
  peas, unthawed
1 cup (4-ounces) Swiss cheese,
  cut in julienne-strips
4-5 green onions, minced
6 tablespoons mayonnaise

2 tablespoons fresh lemon juice
Salt and pepper to taste
2 cups lettuce torn into bite-size
  pieces
8 slices bacon, crisp-fried and
  crumbled

In a covered bowl, combine frozen peas, Swiss cheese, green onions, mayonnaise, lemon juice, salt and pepper to taste; refrigerate for 24 hours. At serving time, add torn lettuce and crumbled bacon to salad mixture (do not drain liquid.) Toss well.

Eva Kinney

LAYERED LETTUCE SALAD

Serves 10

1 head of lettuce
1 (8-ounce) can sliced water
  chestnuts, drained
½ cup chopped celery
¼ cup chopped onion

1 (10-ounce) box frozen peas
2 cups (1 pint) mayonnaise
¾ cup sugar
1 cup (4-ounces) shredded
  Cheddar cheese

Wash lettuce, tear into bite-size pieces. Divide in half, layer one-half the lettuce on the bottom of a large serving dish. Layer additional ingredients in this order: Water chestnuts, celery, onion, frozen peas (do not thaw), and remaining lettuce. Mix together mayonnaise and sugar, spread on top layer of lettuce. Sprinkle with shredded cheese. Refrigerate for 8 hours, or overnight. Recipe can be halved.

Barbara Monical

~ *"Whack" that lettuce:* Using a knife to remove lettuce cores causes discoloration. Instead, hold the lettuce core-end down and whack it on the counter. Use your fingers to lift or twist out the dislodged core.

BLACK BEAN SALAD

❤ *Heart healthy*   *Serves 4*

1 (16-ounce) can black beans,
  rinsed and drained
1 tomato, finely chopped
1-2 serrano chiles, finely
  chopped
½ cup chopped red bell pepper
¼ cup chopped purple onion

2 tablespoons vinegar
1 tablespoon olive oil
¼ teaspoon salt
Fresh cilantro or parsley,
  chopped (to taste)
Chili powder (to taste)
1-2 cloves garlic, finely chopped

Rinse and drain black beans, chop vegetables. Mix black beans, tomato, chiles, bell pepper and onion; coat with vinegar and oil. Add salt, cilantro and chili powder. Add chopped garlic. Mix all ingredients thoroughly and refrigerate until ready to serve.

Note: *This dish is wonderful served with grilled chicken or fajitas. It is also good as a meatless main dish served over hot rice.*

Maureen Schefsky

BLACK-EYED PEA SALAD

                                                                    Serves 4

1 (16-ounce) can fresh-shelled
  black-eyed peas, drained
¼ cup chopped green pepper
½ cup chopped onion
¼ cup chopped sweet pickle
½ cup chopped celery
½ cup chopped tomato

½ cup chopped cucumber
½ teaspoon salt
¼ teaspoon pepper
2 teaspoons sugar
1 (8-ounce) bottle Catalina
  dressing

Combine peas, green pepper, onion, pickle, celery, tomato and cucumber. Add salt, pepper and sugar; mix well. Pour Catalina dressing over vegetables. Allow to chill, and marinate for at least several hours.

Note: *Mix Catalina dressing with a small amount of mayonnaise before pouring, if desired. French or vinegar-and-oil dressing can be substituted.*

Ruth Seiwell

TRAIL MIX RICE SALAD

Serves 6-8

½ cup wild rice
1 cup Texas Basmati rice
2 medium-size red peppers,
  roasted with skin and seeds
  removed (or ⅔ of jar of
  roasted red peppers)

10-12 dried apricots
¾ cup golden raisins
1 cup (6-ounces) dry roasted
  peanuts

Dressing:

¼ cup olive or canola oil (can
  cut with water to reduce fat)
⅛ cup vinegar
½ teaspoon dry mustard

1 to 1½ teaspoons honey
1 rounded teaspoon orange juice
  concentrate (or pulp-free
  apricot or mayhaw preserve)

Cook both rices together according to directions on package. While rice is cooking, cut peppers and apricots into thin strips. In a medium-size bowl, mix apricots, peppers, raisins and peanuts. Stir in warm rice gradually to assure a good ratio between rice and trail mix (there may be extra rice, depending on how wet or dry the rice cooked.) Combine dressing ingredients in a bowl, and whisk until emulsified. Pour dressing over rice mixture. Serve immediately at room temperature, or chilled.

Karen Creveling

CORNBREAD SALAD

Serves 10-12

2 (8½-ounce) packages jalapeño
  cornbread mix
1 cup whole kernel corn,
  drained
1 cup chopped tomatoes
1 cup chopped green peppers
1 cup chopped green onions or
  chives

8 slices crisp-fried bacon,
  chopped
1 cup Cheddar cheese, chopped
  in small pieces
1½ cups mayonnaise
1½ cups sour cream
1 tablespoon chili powder

Bake cornbread according to mix directions; crumble into pieces. Drain corn. Combine with all other ingredients in a large serving bowl; cover and chill at least 1 hour before serving.

Marty Dunn/ Deani Farrar

AVOCADO-TOMATO PASTA SALAD

Serves 4

1 (16-ounce) package spiral
  pasta
3 large or 4 medium tomatoes
3 avocados

2 (4-ounce) cans sliced
  mushrooms, well drained
1 (8-ounce) jar low-fat or non-fat
  Ranch dressing
Salt and pepper to taste

Prepare pasta according to package directions. While pasta is cooking, dice tomatoes and avocados; set aside in a small bowl with drained mushrooms. When pasta is cooked, drain and allow to cool slightly. Place pasta in serving bowl, gently add the tomatoes, avocado and mushrooms. Add Ranch dressing, and toss to coat all ingredients thoroughly. Add salt and pepper to taste. Refrigerate 1-2 hours to allow flavors to mingle.

Hint: If fresh mushrooms are used, sauté them first. Place sliced mushrooms in a non-stick pan and sauté with white wine instead of butter.

Karen Creveling

ITALIAN-STYLE PASTA SALAD

Serves 10

1 (12-ounce) package spaghetti
1 (8-ounce) bottle Italian salad
  dressing
1½ ounces Salad Seasoning spice
  (half of a 3-ounce jar)
1 cucumber, quartered
  lengthwise then sliced

1 large tomato, chopped
1 small red onion, chopped
1 (4¼-ounce) can sliced or
  chopped black olives
Bacon bits, to taste
2 avocados
Croutons

In a 4-quart Dutch oven, cook spaghetti according to package directions, and drain. Return spaghetti to pot. Add Italian dressing, Salad Seasoning, cucumber, tomato, onion, olives and bacon bits. Mix well. Cover pot and refrigerate overnight. Just before serving, chop avocados and add to salad. Mix well. Top with croutons.

Lisa Solis

VERMICELLI SALAD

Serves 8

1 (10-ounce) bag of vermicelli
1 cup Italian salad dressing
½ cup chopped sweet pickle
2 ribs celery, cut fine
1 bunch green onions, cut fine
2 tablespoons parsley

1 tablespoon poppy seed
1 teaspoon celery salt
½ teaspoon caraway seed
¼ teaspoon garlic powder
   or 2 medium garlic buds

Cook and drain vermicelli. Mix all ingredients together; cover and refrigerate for 24 hours. Serve chilled.

❤ *Heart healthy note:* *Using non-fat Italian dressing makes this dish low-fat.*

Becky Lowery

CHICKEN RICE SALAD

Serves 6-8

2 pounds chicken breasts,
   cooked and cubed
1 package chicken-flavor
   Rice-a-Roni mix
1 (6-ounce) jar marinated
   artichokes, chopped
2 tablespoons chopped onion

2 tablespoons chopped bell
   pepper
1 (4-ounce) can mushrooms,
   drained
½ can (2-ounces) sliced black
   olives, drained
⅓ cup mayonnaise
Liquid from artichokes

Prepare salad a day ahead. Cook and cube chicken breasts. Prepare rice mix according to package directions. Drain and chop artichokes, reserving liquid from jar. Mix chicken, rice, chopped artichokes, onion, bell pepper, mushrooms and olives; place in casserole dish. Mix artichoke liquid and mayonnaise, spread on top. Refrigerate overnight. Warm before serving, or serve cold.

Toni Kwan

~ *Refrigerating rice:* *Cover refrigerated rice well so the grains will not dry out or absorb the flavors of other foods.*

CHICKEN SALAD DELUXE

Serves 6

3 cups diced chicken
1 cup diced celery
2 tablespoons chopped parsley
1 teaspoon salt
½ teaspoon pepper

½ cup whipping cream, whipped
1 cup Miracle Whip dressing
2 tablespoons lemon juice
½ cup chopped pecans

Mix ingredients in order: chicken, celery, parsley, salt, pepper, whipped cream, salad dressing, lemon juice, nuts. Chill well before serving.

Cary Rosenbohm

OUR FAMILY'S CHICKEN SALAD

Serves 4

4-6 split chicken breasts
1 cup mayonnaise
½ cup plain yogurt

1 cup chopped celery
3-4 hard-boiled eggs, diced
2 ounces green olives, sliced

Cook chicken breasts for 30 minutes; let cool, and cube. Combine mayonnaise and yogurt in small bowl, set aside. Mix chicken with celery, eggs and olives. Fold yogurt mix into chicken, using only as much as needed for proper consistency. Cover; refrigerate until serving. Recipe can be doubled. Substitute sour cream for yogurt, if desired.

Helen Baker

SPICY CHICKEN SALAD

Serves 4

4 spicy Popeye's fried chicken
  breasts
1 cup mayonnaise or Miracle
  Whip
¼ cup diced celery

2 tablespoons diced sweet pickle
½ teaspoon dry mustard
1 avocado, cut in small pieces
1 tablespoon lemon juice

Remove chicken from bone, chop into small pieces including skin and crust. Combine chicken, mayonnaise, celery, pickle and mustard in bowl. Cover; chill well. Peel and chop avocado; sprinkle with lemon juice. Just before serving, gently stir avocado into chicken mixture.

Cindy Cathcart

EXOTIC CHICKEN SALAD FOR A CROWD

Serves 14-16

8 cups diced cooked chicken
(2 chickens plus 3 breasts)
2 pounds seedless grapes,
halved, OR 2½ cups fresh
cubed pineapple

2 cups chopped celery
1 (8-ounce) can water chestnuts,
drained and sliced
1 (2¾-ounce) package sliced
almonds

Dressing:

3 cups real mayonnaise
1 tablespoon curry

1 tablespoon soy sauce
2 tablespoons lemon juice

A day in advance, combine chicken, water chestnuts, fruit, celery and almonds in a large bowl. Combine all dressing ingredients, add to chicken mixture. Chill overnight. Serve on lettuce leaves.

Note: *This is an attractive recipe to use for luncheons or salad socials.*

Lisa Baker

SHRIMP SALAD

Serves 4-6

½ pound shrimp, boiled, peeled
1 (12-ounce) package tri-colored
pasta curls, cooked
2 teaspoons Miracle Whip
1 teaspoon prepared mustard
Salt and pepper to taste

4 hard-boiled eggs, chopped
4 tablespoons chopped sweet
pickle or relish
2 stalks celery, chopped
Chopped onion to taste
(optional)

Boil and peel shrimp, cut in half if large size. Cook, drain and cool pasta. In bowl, blend Miracle Whip and mustard, add salt and pepper to taste. Stir in cooked pasta. Add chopped eggs, relish, onion if desired, and shrimp. Mix well, refrigerate until serving.

Kristi Abild

~ **Nutrition tip:** *Good sources of Vitamin C include citrus fruits, straw-berries, cantaloupe, Brussels sprouts, broccoli, cauliflower and peppers.*

HOT FRUIT SALAD

Serves 8

2 (20-ounce) cans chunk
 pineapple
2 (16-ounce) cans chunky fruit
 for salad
2 cups juice from canned fruit

2 tablespoons lemon juice
¾ cup sugar
¾ cup flour
1 (5-ounce) jar Old English
 cheese

Drain canned fruits, reserve 2 cups of juice. Combine fruit, reserved juice, lemon juice, sugar and flour in saucepan; cook until thick. Stir in Old English cheese. Spoon into baking dish, bake uncovered at 350° for 45 minutes.

Katy Engen

SHERRIED FRUIT SALAD

Serves 10-12

1 (16-ounce) can pineapple
 chunks, drained
1 (16-ounce) can sliced peaches,
 drained
1 (16-ounce) can sliced pears,
 drained

1 (16-ounce) can apricot halves,
 drained
1 (16-ounce) can Bing or dark
 sweet cherries, drained
1 (8-ounce) jar spiced apple
 rings, drained

Sauce:

½ cup (1 stick) butter or
 margarine
½ cup granulated sugar

2 tablespoons flour
1 cup cream sherry

Spread drained pineapple, peaches and pears on a paper towel; pat dry. Arrange in a 13"x9"x2" glass baking dish. Repeat procedure with apricots and cherries for a second layer. Pat dry apple rings, layer on top.

To make sauce, combine butter, sugar, flour and cream sherry in a small saucepan. Cook over low heat, stirring constantly, until thick. Drizzle sauce over fruit. Cover, and chill overnight. Bring dish to room temperature before baking at 350° for 25-30 minutes. Let cool slightly before serving.

Marilyn Matthews

CURRIED FRUIT SALAD

Serves 6-8

1 (16-ounce) can chunky fruit
  for salad
½ cup red cherries
½ cup black cherries
1 cup black raisins
2 large bananas

½ cup (1 stick) margarine,
  melted
½ cup powdered sugar
2 tablespoons cornstarch
1 teaspoon curry powder

Drain canned fruit, slice bananas and cherries; mix in baking dish. Melt butter, stir into fruit mixture. Combine powdered sugar, cornstarch and curry powder, sprinkle over fruit mixture. Bake at 350° for 15 minutes. Gently stir fruit, and bake for another 15 minutes.

Karen Johnson

SPICED PEACHES

Serves 8

2 (29-ounce) cans peach halves
Syrup from canned peaches
1 cup cider vinegar
1⅓ cups brown sugar
4 cinnamon sticks
2 teaspoons whole cloves

1 (8-ounce) package cream
  cheese
½ teaspoon almond extract
1 (6-ounce) jar maraschino
  cherries

Drain peaches, reserving syrup. Mix syrup, vinegar, brown sugar, cinnamon and cloves in a saucepan. Bring to a boil, lower heat and simmer 10 minutes. Pour hot syrup over peach halves; let cool, then refrigerate at least 4 hours before serving. Soften cream cheese, mix in almond extract. Place a heaping teaspoon of cream cheese in each peach half. Top with a cherry, and serve on a lettuce leaf.

Lana Booher

~ On buying bananas: Unlike most fruits, bananas develop their best taste after they are harvested. Skin color indicates stage of ripeness: Yellow bananas specked with brown have reached full flavor.

24-HOUR FRUIT SALAD

Serves 8

1 (20-ounce) can pineapple
  chunks
1 (16-ounce) can fruit cocktail
1 (16-ounce) can dark, sweet
  pitted cherries
¾ cup pineapple juice from
  canned pineapple

¼ cup sugar
1 tablespoon flour
Juice from 1 lemon
2 beaten eggs
2 cups miniature marshmallows
3-4 bananas, sliced
1 cup whipping cream, whipped

Drain the canned fruit, reserving ¾ cup pineapple juice. Mix together sugar and flour. In a saucepan, combine sugar-flour mix, pineapple juice, lemon juice and eggs; cook until thick. Let cool. Add pineapple chunks, fruit cocktail, cherries and marshmallows to the cooked mixture; refrigerate overnight. Just before serving, add bananas and fold in whipped cream.

Tammi Blevins

FIVE-FRUIT OVERNIGHT SALAD

Serves 8-10

1 cup chunk pineapple
1 (11-ounce) can mandarin
  oranges
2 bananas, sliced

1 (10-ounce) bag whole frozen
  strawberries, thawed, sliced
1 (30-ounce) can peach pie
  filling

Drain pineapples and oranges, reserve juice. Marinate bananas for 1 hour in juices. Discard juice, mix bananas with pineapple, oranges, strawberries and peach pie filling. Cover, and refrigerate overnight.

Jenny Pennington

FREEZER FRUIT SALAD

Serves 10-12

1 (30-ounce) can peach pie
  filling
1 (20-ounce) can undrained
  chunk pineapple

1 pint frozen strawberries,
  thawed
2 bananas, sliced
¾ cup chopped pecans.

Place in freezer until nearly frozen; serve.

Sherrie Ezell

MAMA DEE'S FRUIT SALAD

✓ *Quick to fix*   *Serves 8-10*

1 (16-ounce) carton small-curd
  cottage cheese
1 (8-ounce) carton Cool Whip
1 (3-ounce) package orange
  gelatin

1 (6-ounce) can mandarin
  oranges, drained
1 (20-ounce) can pineapple
  chunks, drained

In a large bowl, combine cottage cheese and Cool Whip. Sprinkle with dry orange gelatin. Fold in well-drained oranges and pineapple. Refrigerate for about 20 minutes.

Barbara Franklin

ORANGE SHERBET MOLDED SALAD

Serves 10

2 (3-ounce) packages orange
  gelatin
2 cups boiling water
Juice of half an orange

1 (11-ounce) can Mandarin
  oranges and juice
1 pint orange sherbet

Dissolve gelatin in boiling water; add orange juice and Mandarin oranges with juice. Add sherbet while mixture is still hot. Mix well to dissolve sherbet. Rinse serving mold in cold water; pour in gelatin. Chill until set.

Note: *This salad goes well with duck, ham, chicken and turkey.*

Bonnie Novosad

CREAMY MINT SALAD

Serves 8

1 (20-ounce) can crushed
  pineapple
1 (9-ounce) box buttermints

1 (3-ounce) package lime gelatin
1 (12-ounce) carton frozen Cool
  Whip, thawed

A day in advance, place pineapple with liquid, buttermints and gelatin in medium saucepan. Cook over medium heat until mints melt; cool completely. Pour mixture into large mixing bowl; carefully fold in thawed Cool Whip. Place in greased 11"x7"x2" pan, cover with foil; freeze overnight. To serve, thaw 10-15 minutes, and cut into squares. Return leftovers to freezer.

Karen Moran

FANCY MELON BALL SALAD

Serves 8

**Various melons and fruits of
    choice**
2 cups sour cream

**2 cups raspberry sherbet, slightly
    softened**

Make melon balls from watermelon, honeydew or cantaloupe. Add
grapes, strawberries, or other fresh fruits. Mix sour cream and sherbet;
pour over fruit immediately before serving.

Jane Ray

CREAMY APPLE-PINEAPPLE SALAD

Serves 10

3 large Delicious apples
**1 (6-ounce) can pineapple bits,
    drained**
**1 (3-ounce) package cream
    cheese**

¾ cup mayonnaise
1 cup whipping cream
**½ package miniature
    marshmallows**

Chop apples into bite-size pieces, drain pineapple bits. Mix cream cheese
and mayonnaise, add unwhipped cream to dilute. Fold in chopped
apples, pineapple and marshmallows. Refrigerate for 24 hours in a
covered dish.

Jackie Brewer

BANANA-CRANBERRY SALAD

Serves 10-12

**1 (16-ounce) can cranberry
    sauce**
2-3 mashed, ripe bananas
**1 (8-ounce) can crushed
    pineapple, drained**

**1 cup miniature marshmallows
    (or less, to taste)**
2 cups whipping cream, whipped
**½ cup chopped pecans
    (optional)**

Combine cranberry sauce and mashed bananas. Add drained pineapple
and marshmallows; fold in whipped cream. Pour into 15"x11" pan, and
freeze. Cut into squares, serve individual squares on a lettuce leaf.

❤ ***Heart healthy hint:*** *Omit pecans and use reduced-calorie Cool
Whip to lower fat content to 3.2 grams per serving.*

Sharon Shaver

PRETZEL SALAD

Serves 10

2½ cups chopped pretzels
1 cup (2 sticks) margarine,
  melted
1 (8-ounce) package cream
  cheese
¾ cup sugar

4 cups whipped topping
1 (6-ounce) box strawberry
  gelatin
2 cups boiling water
2 (10-ounce) packages frozen
  strawberries

Line bottom of 13"x9"x2" pan with chopped (or broken) pretzels; pour melted butter over pretzels. Bake at 400° for 10 minutes; let cool. Mix together cream cheese, sugar and whipped topping; spoon over cooled pretzels. Dissolve gelatin in boiling water; add strawberries. When gelatin is partially congealed, pour over cheese and pretzels. Chill until firm.

Kathy Carr

COMPANY SALAD

Serves 10-12

1 (6-ounce) box gelatin, any
  flavor
3 cups boiling water
1 (15½-ounce) can crushed
  pineapple
1½ cups miniature
  marshmallows
3 bananas, chopped

1 cup pineapple juice from can
½ cup sugar
1½ tablespoons flour
1 egg, slightly beaten
½ pint whipping cream,
  or 1 package Dream Whip
Grated sharp Cheddar cheese

Dissolve gelatin in boiling water, let cool. Drain pineapple, reserving juice. Add pineapple, marshmallows and bananas to gelatin. Chill in 13"x9"x2" glass dish until firm. Heat reserved pineapple juice in a double boiler. Combine sugar, flour and egg; add to pineapple juice, cook until thick. Let cool. Whip the cream, and fold into thickened pineapple juice. Spread whipped cream mixture over gelatin. Top with grated cheese.

Debbie Gentry

~ ***Out of the mold:*** *To unmold gelatin, moisten both the top of the gelatin and a chilled plate. Dip mold, just to the rim, in warm water; lift from the water and shake gently to loosen. Invert moistened plate on mold, then turn the plate and the mold together.*

BLUEBERRY SALAD

Serves 8-10

1 (6-ounce) package black
   raspberry gelatin
2 cups boiling water
1 (16-ounce) can blueberry pie
   filling
1 (8-ounce) can crushed
   pineapple, drained
1 cup sour cream

1 (8-ounce) package cream
   cheese, softened
½ cup sugar
1 teaspoon vanilla extract
   (optional)
½ cup chopped pecans or
   walnuts

Dissolve gelatin in boiling water in 13"x9"x2" glass pan. Add pie filling and drained pineapple; mix well. Chill until firm. Using mixer or food processor, blend sour cream, cream cheese and sugar until smooth. Spread over gelatin layer. Sprinkle nuts on top.

Note: *Substitute 1 (15-ounce) can of blueberries for pie filling, if desired. Use raspberry, black cherry or red cherry gelatin if black raspberry is not available.*

Roberta Hemphill/ Dee Swope/ Julie Zimmerman

PISTACHIO SALAD

Serves 12-15

1 (3.4-ounce) box pistachio
   instant pudding mix
1 (20-ounce) can crushed
   pineapple

1 (12-ounce) carton Cool Whip
½ cup chopped pecans
½ cup miniature marshmallows

Combine pudding mix and pineapple, mix well. Stir in Cool Whip, pecans and marshmallows, chill several hours.

Hint: *Add a festive touch at Christmas by garnishing with maraschino cherries. For Easter dinner or a Spring luncheon, garnish with miniature pastel-colored marshmallows.*

Peggy McKnight

~ **Smell the melon:** *A ripe cantaloupe or honey dew will have a faint, pleasant fruit aroma and will yield slightly to light thumb pressure on the blossom (non-stem) end. For best flavor, "condition" melons by storing them for two to four days at room temperature.*

CHERRY SALAD

Serves 6-8

1 (16-ounce) can pie cherries
1 (8-ounce) can crushed
  pineapple
Juice of 1 lemon
Juice of 1 orange

1 cup sugar
2 (3-ounce) packages cherry
  gelatin
½ cup pecans

Drain juice from cherries and pineapple into saucepan. (Be sure to use pie cherries, not cherry pie filling.) Add lemon juice, orange juice and sugar (add water if necessary to make 2 cups.) Bring to a boil; simmer 5 minutes, stirring frequently. Pour over gelatin, stir until gelatin is dissolved. Stir in cherries, pineapple and nuts. Chill until set.

Patti Hosack

OKLAHOMA JELLO SALAD

Serves 6-8

1 cup applesauce
1 (6-ounce) package raspberry
  or strawberry gelatin

1 (6-ounce) can frozen orange
  juice concentrate
1½ cups water

Heat applesauce in saucepan. Add gelatin, stir until dissolved. Add frozen orange juice, stir until melted. Add water, stir until all ingredients are blended. Pour into gelatin mold or serving dish; chill until firm. This low-fat salad makes a tart accompaniment to ham or chicken.

Becky Gilliland

MEN-LIKE-IT GELATIN SALAD

Serves 8-10

1 (3-ounce) box lime gelatin
1¾ cups boiling water
1 (8-ounce) package cream
  cheese

1 cup crushed pineapple,
  drained
1 cup chopped celery
½ cup chopped nuts

Add boiling water to gelatin, stir to dissolve. Cut cream cheese into small pieces, add to gelatin mixture. Add drained pineapple, stir. Add celery and nuts; stir. Pour into gelatin mold, refrigerate until set.

Missy Funk

FROZEN CRANBERRY SALAD

Serves 8-10

1 (8-ounce) package cream cheese
2 tablespoons mayonnaise
2 tablespoons granulated sugar
1 (16-ounce) can whole cranberry sauce
1 (8-ounce) can crushed pineapple
½ cup chopped pecans
1 cup whipped topping
1 teaspoon vanilla extract
½ cup powdered sugar

Soften cream cheese, mash with mayonnaise and granulated sugar. Add remaining ingredients; freeze six hours in metal pan. Serve on lettuce leaf for a holiday salad, or with whipped topping for a refreshing dessert.

Nancy Chamberlain

CHRISTMAS FROZEN SALAD

Serves 8-10

2 (3-ounce) packages cream cheese, softened
1 cup mayonnaise
½ cup red maraschino cherries, halved
½ cup green maraschino cherries, halved
1 (20-ounce) can crushed pineapple, drained
½ cup chopped pecans
2½ cups miniature marshmallows
1 cup whipping cream, whipped

Combine cream cheese and mayonnaise, mix well. Stir in cherries, pineapple, pecans and marshmallows. Fold in whipped cream. Pour into 8-cup salad ring. Freeze.

Cheryl Whitten

CREAMY CHRISTMAS SALAD

Serves 8

1 (16-ounce) can crushed pineapple, drained
1 (15-ounce) can condensed milk
1 (21-ounce) can cherry pie filling
1 (9-ounce) package whipped topping
1 cup chopped pecans (optional)

Combine drained pineapple, condensed milk and pie filling. Fold in whipped topping. Add pecans; chill until firm.

Kay Wright

GRILLED VEGETABLES

Serves 6

4 medium tomatoes, quartered
4 yellow squash, sliced
1 medium onion, sliced
1 teaspoon minced fresh basil

½ teaspoon salt
⅛ teaspoon pepper
2 teaspoons butter

Place tomatoes, squash and onion on large piece of heavy-duty aluminum foil; sprinkle with basil, salt and pepper; dot with butter. Fold foil edges to wrap vegetables and seal securely; place on grill. Cook over medium coals 20-25 minutes, turning after 10 minutes.

♥ *Heart healthy hint: Use diet margarine for a low-fat, heart healthy dish.*

Lisa Ondrey

BROILED TOMATOES

✓ *Quick to fix*   *Serves 6*

2 large ripe tomatoes or 3 small
   tomatoes, sliced
¼ cup mayonnaise
¼ cup grated Parmesan cheese

¼ cup minced shallot or green
   onion (white part only)
2 tablespoons minced parsley

Slice tomatoes in thirds if large, in half if smaller. Preheat broiler. Combine mayonnaise, Parmesan cheese, shallots and parsley in small bowl, blend well. Gently spread mixture about ¼-inch thick on tomatoes. Broil 4 inches from heat source until lightly browned, about 2-3 minutes. Serve immediately.

Mary Ann Sosebee

~ *Cooking tip: When cooking hot dishes, add herbs near the end or they may impart a bitter taste. Do the opposite in seasoning cold food.*

TOMATO PERSILLES (Parsley Tomato with Pine Nuts)

Serves 6

**6 large ripe tomatoes, halved
and seeded**
**¼ cup plus 2 tablespoons olive
oil**
½ cup pine nuts

¼ cup (½ stick) unsalted butter
3 garlic cloves, minced
1 cup fresh parsley, minced
Salt and pepper to taste

Sprinkle the cut side of the tomatoes with salt, and let tomatoes drain upside down on a rack for 30 minutes. In a skillet, heat ¼ cup of the oil over moderately high heat until it is hot, but not smoking. Sauté the tomato halves for 3 to 4 minutes on each side until softened, but not brown. Transfer the tomatoes to a baking sheet and keep them warm, covered.

In a small skillet, heat remaining 2 tablespoons of oil over moderately high heat until hot but not smoking. Sauté the pine nuts, stirring until golden. Transfer pine nuts to paper towels to drain. Put butter in skillet, and sauté garlic until golden. Add parsley and cook, stirring for 1 minute. Season with salt and pepper to taste. Spoon mixture into the tomatoes, and top with pine nuts.

Terrie Lumsden

GOURMET FILLED TOMATOES

✓ *Quick to fix*   *Serves 6*

3 tomatoes
½ cup herbed stuffing mix
1 clove garlic, minced
3 tablespoons parsley, minced

¼ teaspoon thyme leaves
¼ teaspoon salt
Pepper, freshly ground
⅓ cup olive oil

Preheat oven to 400°. Cut tomatoes in half, and gently squeeze out the juice and seeds. Blend stuffing mix, garlic, parsley, thyme, salt and pepper to taste. Fill each tomato half, and sprinkle with olive oil. Arrange in baking dish; bake for 12 minutes or until tops are golden.

Note: *The filled tomatoes can be made ahead, and baked when needed. They are great for brunch with chicken, fish or pork.*

Ruth Bondurant

BAKED DIJON TOMATO CUPS

✓ *Quick to fix*   *Serves 12*

6 medium tomatoes, halved crosswise
¼ cup Dijon mustard
¼ cup (½ stick) margarine
⅛ teaspoon salt

¼ cup plus 3 tablespoons Italian-style bread crumbs
¼ cup plus 3 tablespoons fresh grated Parmesan cheese
½ teaspoon dried parsley flakes
⅛ teaspoon ground red pepper

Lightly brush tomato halves with mustard. Place tomato halves in a 13"x9"x2" baking dish; sprinkle with salt. Melt margarine, combine with rest of ingredients in a bowl, stir well. Top each half of tomato with one tablespoon of crumb mixture, spreading evenly. Bake at 350° for 10 minutes or until tomatoes are thoroughly heated and cheese melts. Next place tomatoes in broiler; broil 2-3 minutes, until tops are golden.

Note: *These are great for a dinner party!*

Christy Spence

BACON STUFFED TOMATOES

                                           Serves 4

4 large tomatoes
8 slices bacon
1 medium onion, chopped
1 teaspoon dried basil
4 tablespoons minced parsley

1 cup (4-ounces) grated Monterey Jack cheese
Salt and pepper to taste
Bread crumbs
Parsley for garnish

Preheat oven to 350°. Slice top off each tomato and scoop pulp into bowl. Drain tomato shells upside down. Cook and crumble bacon. Save 2 tablespoons bacon drippings, sauté onion and tomato pulp. Remove from heat. Mix tomato pulp, basil, minced parsley, cheese, salt and pepper. Fill tomato shells with mixture. Sprinkle bread crumbs on top and bake uncovered in shallow dish at 350° for 20-30 minutes. Garnish with parsley.

Hint: *A melon ball scoop works well for scooping pulp from tomato.*

Patti Hoffmann

FRIED GREEN TOMATOES

Serves 6

3 large green tomatoes, sliced
  crosswise ¹/₃-inch thick
1 teaspoon salt
1 cup yellow cornmeal

¹/₄ teaspoon cayenne pepper
¹/₄ cup solid vegetable shortening
  or vegetable oil

Arrange tomato slices on paper towels, sprinkle with the salt. Set aside for about 30 minutes to draw out moisture. Dredge slices in cornmeal, and sprinkle with cayenne. Set aside in a single layer.

In a large heavy skillet, melt 2 tablespoons shortening over moderately high heat. When fat is hot, add a single layer of tomatoes and fry, turning once, until golden (about 3 minutes per side). Transfer the tomatoes to paper towels to drain. Wipe out the skillet if necessary, and repeat with remaining shortening and tomatoes. Serve immediately.

Note: *Salting the sliced tomatoes draws out moisture, and helps the cornmeal adhere. This recipe is great for summer gardeners with a bountiful tomato crop.*

Lisa Baker

MUSHROOMS IN SOUR CREAM

Serves 4

¹/₄ cup (¹/₂ stick) butter
1 pound whole, small, fresh
  mushrooms, cleaned
¹/₂ cup minced green onions
1 tablespoon flour

¹/₂ cup beef broth
1 teaspoon dill weed
¹/₈ teaspoon salt
Pepper to taste
1 cup sour cream

In medium size skillet, melt butter. Add mushrooms and green onion. Sauté until tender and lightly browned. Stir in flour, and add beef broth gradually. Stir until sauce thickens. Add dill, salt and pepper to taste. Simmer for 10 minutes. Stir in sour cream, heating until hot, but not boiling.

Karen Moran

WILTED SPINACH WITH TOMATOES

✓ *Quick to fix*   *Serves 4*

1 bunch fresh spinach   **1 teaspoon butter**
2 tomatoes   **1 teaspoon Garam Masala spice**

Carefully wash spinach to remove grit. Pat leaves dry, remove stems. Slice each tomato into 8 wedges, set aside. In a non-stick pan, melt 1 teaspoon butter (or use up to 1 tablespoon, if desired.) When butter has melted, toss spinach in pan and coat with butter. As soon as spinach begins to wilt (watch carefully, as it will wilt quickly), add the tomato wedges. Sprinkle with Garam Masala. Toss several times, just enough to coat mixture and slightly warm the tomatoes. Serve immediately, arranging the tomato wedges on top of spinach.

Note: *Garam Masala is an inexpensive Indian spice mix that combines coriander, cumin, ginger, black pepper, cinnamon, pimiento, carda-mom, bay leaves, cloves and nutmeg. It can be found in the international section of large grocery stores.*

Karen Creveling

SPINACH CASSEROLE

Serves 6

2 (10-ounce) boxes frozen chopped spinach
½ cup (1 stick) butter
½ cup finely chopped onion
2 cups (1 pint) sour cream

1 (14-ounce) can artichoke hearts, drained and diced
½ teaspoon salt
¼ teaspoon pepper
½ cup grated Parmesan cheese

Cook spinach as directed on box; drain. Sauté onion in butter. Combine spinach, onion, sour cream and artichoke, season with salt and pepper. Place in casserole dish, sprinkle Parmesan cheese on top. Bake at 350° for 25 minutes.

Cheryl Whitten

*~ **Nutrition tip:** Good sources of Beta Carotene include deep yellow-orange fruits and vegetables such as cantaloupe, peaches and carrots, and deep green vegetables such as broccoli and spinach.*

VEGETABLE MEDLEY

Serves 6-8

1 medium head cauliflower,
  whole
1 bunch broccoli, trimmed
1 bunch carrots, cut in 2"-3"
  pieces

½ cup mayonnaise
1½ teaspoons prepared mustard
½ teaspoon dry mustard
¾ cup (3-ounces) grated sharp
  Cheddar cheese

Cook cauliflower, broccoli and carrots just until tender crisp. Drain well, and arrange on a large glass serving dish. (Head of cauliflower in center, with broccoli spears and carrots surrounding.) Combine mayonnaise, mustard and dry mustard; mix well. Just before serving, spread mustard-mayonnaise mixture over vegetables. Sprinkle with grated cheese. Microwave until cheese melts, 1 to 2 minutes.

Note: *The vegetables can be prepared ahead of time and microwaved just before serving. This makes a very attractive presentation.*

Marilyn Woody

FRESH VEGETABLE MICROWAVE BAKE

Serves 6

6-7 carrots, cut into strips
½ cup water
¼ teaspoon salt
3 zucchini squash, cut into
  ¼-inch diagonal slices
1 cup patio tomatoes, whole

1 cup herb seasoned croutons
1½ cups cold milk
2 tablespoons cornstarch
¼ cup (½ stick) margarine
1½ teaspoons dried basil
Salt and pepper to taste

Place carrots in microwavable dish with ½ cup of water and ¼ teaspoon salt. Cook, covered, for 6-7 minutes on high. Drain, add squash, tomatoes and croutons. Toss, cover, and cook 6-7 minutes. In a separate bowl or 4-cup measuring cup, combine cornstarch and milk. Stir until dissolved, then add margarine, basil, and salt and pepper to taste. Microwave on medium-high for 8-10 minutes. When mixture thickens, stir and pour over vegetables. Cover and microwave on medium-high for 5-6 minutes.

Delores Smith

GARDEN MEDLEY

Serves 15

2 (12-ounce) cans white shoepeg
   corn, drained
2 (16-ounce) cans French-cut
   green beans, drained
½ cup chopped green pepper
1 cup chopped celery
½ cup chopped onion
1 (8-ounce) carton sour cream

1 (10¾-ounce) can condensed
   cream of celery soup
½ cup (2-ounces) grated sharp
   Cheddar cheese
½ cup (1 stick) butter, melted
1 cup butter cracker crumbs
   (Waverly or Club)
½ cup sliced almonds

Mix vegetables, sour cream, soup and cheese. Spoon into 13"x9"x2"
baking dish. Mix butter, cracker crumbs and almonds; sprinkle on top of
mixture. Bake at 350° for 45 minutes.

Note: *This dish is great for a big gathering, or to split and give half to a
friend. It can be mixed ahead of time, with topping added just before
baking.*

Laura Muskopf

VEG-ALL CASSEROLE

Serves 6-8

1 (32-ounce) can Veg-All mixed
   vegetables, drained
1 cup sliced water chestnuts,
   drained
¾ cup chopped onion

1 cup mayonnaise
2 cups (8-ounces) grated
   Cheddar cheese
½ cup (1 stick) margarine
Ritz crackers, crushed

Mix vegetables, water chestnuts, onions, mayonnaise and cheese. Pour
into buttered 2-quart casserole. Melt margarine, stir in crushed crackers.
Top casserole with cracker mixture. Bake at 375° for 30 minutes, or until
top is browned.

Note: *For a one-dish meal, add 2 cups cooked, cubed chicken before
baking.*

Ann Ragsdale

SAVORY SUCCOTASH

Serves 6

1 (16-ounce) can French-cut
  green beans, drained
1 (16-ounce) can whole kernel
  corn, drained
½ cup mayonnaise
½ cup (2-ounces) shredded
  Cheddar cheese

½ cup chopped green pepper
½ cup chopped celery
2 tablespoons minced onion
1 cup dry herb-flavor stuffing
  mix
3 tablespoons margarine

In a 2-quart casserole dish, mix together green beans, corn, mayonnaise, cheese, green pepper, celery and onion. In a small saucepan, melt margarine and mix with stuffing. Top vegetable mixture with stuffing mix. Bake at 375° for 30 minutes.

Dee Eddins

TWO CORN CASSEROLE

Serves 10-12

½ cup (1 stick) margarine
¾ cup chopped green pepper
⅓ cup chopped onion
1 (17-ounce) can cream-style
  corn
1 (16-ounce) can whole kernel
  corn

3 eggs, well beaten
1 (8½-ounce) package corn
  muffin mix
1 cup (4-ounces) shredded
  Cheddar cheese

Heat oven to 350°. Grease 2-quart casserole. In small skillet, melt margarine and sauté green pepper and onion. In large bowl, combine cream-style corn, whole kernel corn, eggs and muffin mix; blend well. Add onion mixture, mix well. Pour into casserole, sprinkle with cheese. Bake at 350° for 55-65 minutes or until firm and set.

Julie Zimmerman

~ *Filling the gap: Combining vegetables such as broccoli, carrots, cauliflower, squash and beans into a tasty medley bolsters nutrition. Each vegetable helps fill certain nutritional gaps of another.*

FIVE-ALARM CORN CASSEROLE

Serves 10

1 jalapeño pepper, chopped
1 (12-ounce) can shoepeg corn
2 tablespoons milk
¼ cup (½ stick) margarine

1 (3-ounce) package cream cheese
Garlic powder to taste
6-7 slices of Velveeta cheese

Melt butter, cream cheese and milk in a saucepan. When creamy, add corn, chopped jalapeño and garlic powder to taste. Place in casserole dish, top with enough sliced Velveeta to cover, and bake at 350° for 20-30 minutes. This dish can be cooked in the microwave.

Barbara Monical

GRANDMA ECKERT'S CORN CASSEROLE

Serves 6-8

1 (17-ounce) can cream-style corn
1 (16-ounce) can whole kernel corn, drained
1 large onion, chopped
1 medium green pepper, chopped
1 (2-ounce) jar chopped pimientos

⅔ cups milk
1 egg, beaten
1 cup cracker crumbs
1 cup (4-ounces) grated Cheddar cheese
¼ cup (½ stick) butter, melted
Salt, pepper and cayenne pepper to taste

Mix all ingredients, pour into greased casserole dish. Bake at 350° for 1 hour.

Note: *This recipe is very easy, but very good.*

Deani Farrar

~ **Cooking tip:** *Grate cheese before adding to a sauce or casserole. This will prevent toughening and shorten cooking time.*

GREEN BEANS WITH SWISS CHEESE

Serves 6-8

2 (16-ounce) cans French-cut
   green beans, drained
2 cups (8-ounces) grated Swiss
   cheese
2 tablespoons butter, divided
2 tablespoons flour

1 cup sour cream
½ cup grated onion
1 teaspoon salt
¼ teaspoon sugar
1 cup cornflakes or bread
   crumbs

Drain green beans, layer with grated cheese in a 2-quart casserole. Melt 1 tablespoon butter in saucepan, stir in flour to make paste. Add sour cream, stir until thick and creamy. Stir in onion, salt and sugar. Pour sour cream sauce over green beans. Top with cornflakes or bread crumbs sautéed in remaining 1 tablespoon of butter. Bake uncovered at 400° for 20 minutes.

Note: *The dish can be prepared a day ahead.*

Marcie Allen

ASPARAGUS AND PEAS

Serves 8

2 (16-ounce) cans good-quality
   asparagus, drained
2 (16-ounce) cans LeSueur peas,
   drained
2 (10¾-ounce) cans condensed
   cream of mushroom soup
1 (2-ounce) jar chopped
   pimientos

1 (8-ounce) can water chestnuts,
   chopped
1 cup (4-ounces) shredded
   Cheddar cheese
½ cup (1 stick) butter, melted
6 slices white bread, crust
   removed

Cut asparagus stalks in half, and arrange in a 13"x9"x2" casserole dish with cut ends together. Layer with drained peas. Layer mushroom soup on top. Next, layer pimiento, then water chestnuts, then cheese. Dip bread slices (no crust) in melted butter, and layer on top. Bake at 350° until bread is crusty.

Serena Andrews

CONTINENTAL ZUCCHINI

✓ *Quick to fix*   *Serves 6*

1 pound zucchini (about 4 small)
2 tablespoons oil
1 (12-ounce) can whole kernel corn, drained
1 (2-ounce) jar chopped pimiento, drained

2 medium cloves garlic, crushed
1 teaspoon salt
¼ teaspoon pepper
½ cup (2-ounces) shredded mozzarella cheese

Wash and cube zucchini. Heat oil in a large skillet, stir in zucchini, corn, pimientos, garlic, salt and pepper. Mix well, cover, and cook over medium heat, stirring occasionally, for about 10 minutes or until zucchini is tender-crisp. Place mixture in a serving dish and sprinkle with mozzarella cheese. Microwave until cheese has melted.

Note: *This recipe is very easy, and can be done at the last minute. It goes especially well with spaghetti or lasagna.*

Becky Gilliland

YELLOW SQUASH CASSEROLE

Serves 6-8

3 pounds yellow squash
½ pound bacon, crisp-fried, crumbled
2 small onions, chopped

½ cup (2-ounces) grated Cheddar cheese
½ cup seasoned bread crumbs

Wash squash, cut into pieces, and cook in water until tender. Drain and slightly mash. Crisp-fry bacon, and crumble. Combine squash, bacon, onions, grated cheese and ½ of the bread crumbs, spoon into a baking dish. Top with the remaining bread crumbs. Bake uncovered at 350° until hot, about 20-25 minutes.

Nancy Chamberlain

CHEDDAR ZUCCHINI BAKE

Serves 6-8

6 cups sliced zucchini (¼-inch slices)
1 cup sour cream
2 eggs, separated
2 tablespoons flour

2 strips bacon, crisp-fried
2 cups (16-ounces) grated Cheddar cheese
½ cup Ritz cracker crumbs
1 tablespoon butter, melted

Spray 13"x9"x2" casserole dish with non-stick cooking spray. Place one-half of the sliced zucchini in the dish. Mix sour cream, egg yolks and flour. Beat egg whites until stiff, fold into sour cream mixture. Pour one-half of the sour cream mixture over zucchini. Crumble bacon; sprinkle half the bacon and 1 cup cheese on top of sour cream. Repeat, layering zucchini, then sour cream mixture, then bacon and cheese. Combine cracker crumbs with melted butter, top casserole with crumbs. Bake at 350° for 30-40 minutes.

Jane Ray

FESTIVE SQUASH CASSEROLE

Serves 8

1½ pounds small yellow squash, grated
1½ medium carrots, grated
1 small onion, grated
1 cup sour cream
1 (10¾-ounce) can condensed cream of chicken soup

1 (2-ounce) jar chopped pimiento
½ cup (1 stick) butter or margarine
1 (8-ounce) package seasoned stuffing mix

Grate and parboil squash and carrots; drain. Mix onion, sour cream, soup, carrots, squash and pimiento. Melt butter and toss with stuffing mix. Use ½ of the stuffing mixture to line the bottom of a 13"x9"x2" baking dish. Add vegetable mixture, and top with remaining stuffing mixture. Bake at 350° for 30-40 minutes.

Binnie Bauml

PECAN-CARROT CASSEROLE

Serves 10-12

3 pounds carrots, sliced
²/₃ cup sugar
½ cup (1 stick) butter or
  margarine, softened
½ cup chopped pecans, toasted
¼ cup milk
2 large eggs, lightly beaten

3 tablespoons flour
1 tablespoon vanilla extract
1 teaspoon grated orange rind
¼ teaspoon ground nutmeg
Carrot curls and fresh parsley for
  garnish (optional)

In medium saucepan, cook carrots in small amount of boiling water 12-15 minutes or until tender. Drain carrots; mash. Stir in sugar, butter, pecans, milk, eggs, flour, vanilla, orange rind and nutmeg. Spoon into a lightly greased 2-quart baking dish. Bake at 350° for 40 minutes. Garnish with carrot curls and fresh parsley, if desired.

Susan Laver

SAUTÉED JULIENNE CARROTS

✓ *Quick to fix*   *Serves 4*

1 tablespoon butter or margarine
1 tablespoon olive oil
3-4 medium carrots, sliced in
  thin lengthwise strips
1 small green pepper, sliced in
  thin lengthwise strips

½ teaspoon salt
Pepper to taste
Dillweed or dill seeds to taste
Pinch of sugar

Melt butter in large skillet, add oil. Stir in remaining ingredients and cook, stirring occasionally, for 5 minutes or until carrots are crisp-tender.

Janice Keller

CHEESY CARROTS

Serves 6

2 pounds carrots, sliced
¼ cup (½ stick) margarine
1 (8-ounce) package Velveeta
  cheese

½ cup chopped onion
1½ cups crushed potato chips

Cook carrots just until tender, being careful not to overcook. Drain, and place in greased 2-quart baking dish. Cube Velveeta and place cheese, butter and onion on top of carrots. Top with crushed chips. Bake at 375° for 30 minutes.

Jo Ann Brown

GOLDEN CROWN CAULIFLOWER

Serves 6-8

1 medium head cauliflower
1 cup water
½ cup mayonnaise

¼ teaspoon instant minced onion
1 teaspoon prepared mustard
½ cup shredded Cheddar cheese

Place cauliflower and water in 2-quart saucepan. Cover, cook on high heat until cauliflower steams. Reduce heat to low, and continue cooking 20 minutes. Meanwhile, combine mayonnaise, onion and mustard; mix well. Place cooked cauliflower in shallow baking dish. Spread mayonnaise mixture over the top, and sprinkle with cheese. Bake in preheated oven at 375° for 10 minutes.

Nancy Standlee

CAULIFLOWER-GREEN BEAN CASSEROLE

Serves 4-6

1 head cauliflower, chopped
½ cup chopped celery
½ cup chopped onion
½ pound fresh mushrooms, sliced
2 (10-ounce) packages frozen green beans

2 (10¾-ounce) cans cream of mushroom soup
1 cup seasoned croutons
2 tablespoons butter
1 cup (4-ounces) shredded Cheddar cheese

Mix together cauliflower, celery, onion, mushrooms, green beans, soup and croutons. Dot with butter. Bake at 350° for 30 minutes. Remove casserole from oven, sprinkle with cheese. Return to oven for 8 minutes.

Linda Cullitan

*~ **Nutrition tip:** Increasing your intake of complex carbohydrates — fresh fruits and vegetables plus whole grains — can improve your body's energy stores and help fill you up with fewer calories.*

SESAME BROCCOLI

✓ *Quick to Fix*   *Serves 4*

1 pound fresh broccoli
1 tablespoon vinegar
1 tablespoon soy sauce
1 teaspoon sugar

1½ teaspoons vegetable oil
1½ teaspoons water
1 tablespoon toasted sesame
  seeds

Trim large leaves from broccoli, and remove tough ends of stalk. Wash well, and separate into spears. Cook broccoli in small amount of water for 8-10 minutes, or until tender-crisp. Drain. Combine vinegar, soy sauce, sugar, oil, water and sesame seeds in a small saucepan; bring to a boil. Pour over broccoli. Toss and serve.

Ruth Seiwell

CREAMY BROCCOLI BAKE

Serves 6-8

2 (10-ounce) packages frozen
  broccoli spears or flowerets
1 (10¾-ounce) can condensed
  cream of mushroom soup
¼ cup milk

½ cup (2-ounces) shredded
  Cheddar cheese
1 cup Bisquick baking mix
¼ cup (½ stick) firm margarine
  or butter

Cook broccoli according to package directions, and drain. Place in ungreased 1½-quart round casserole. Heat oven to 400°. Beat soup and milk with hand beater until smooth, pour over broccoli. Sprinkle with cheese. Mix baking mix and margarine until crumbly. Sprinkle over cheese. Bake until crumbs are light brown, about 20 minutes.

If using fresh broccoli: Trim large leaves and remove tough ends of stalk from 1½ pounds fresh broccoli. Heat 1-inch salted water (½ teaspoon salt to 1 cup water) to boiling. Add broccoli. Cover and heat to boiling. Cook until stems are almost tender, about 10-12 minutes; drain.

Roberta Hemphill

~ *Buying broccoli: Since broccoli is actually a flower stalk, the broccoli buds indicate both freshness and nutrition. The buds should be closed, and dark brown or purplish — not yellow.*

RICE-CORN CASSEROLE

Serves 8

½ cup (1 stick) margarine
½ cup celery, chopped
1 medium onion, chopped
1 bell pepper, chopped
2 cups cooked rice
2 (17-ounce) cans cream-style corn
1 (16-ounce) can whole kernel corn
1 tablespoon sugar
1 chopped jalapeño pepper, if desired
1 cup (4-ounces) Cheddar cheese, grated

Sauté celery, onion and bell pepper in margarine. Add cooked rice, both kinds of corn, sugar and jalapeño pepper if desired. Pour into 13"x9"x2" baking dish. Top with Cheddar cheese, and bake at 350° for 30 minutes.

Kay Wright

EGGPLANT SUPREME

Serves 6

1 large eggplant, cubed
2 ribs celery, sliced
1 large onion, chopped
1 small bell pepper, diced
¼ cup (½ stick) butter
1 cup (4-ounces) grated sharp Cheddar cheese,
1 cup chopped black olives
1 teaspoon Worcestershire sauce
Dash hot sauce
Salt to taste
1 cup cracker crumbs

Cube eggplant, and steam in a little water on low heat until tender. Sauté celery, onion and bell pepper in butter. Add eggplant, cheese and olives. Season with Worcestershire sauce, hot sauce and salt to taste. Spoon into a baking dish, and top with cracker crumbs. Bake at 375° for 30 minutes.

Jackie Brewer

~ **Freezer friendly:** *Rice freezes well, and can be frozen plain or in combination with other foods. It will keep in the freezer for 6-8 months.*

YAM CASSEROLE

Serves 8-10

4 cups cooked, mashed yams
   OR 2 (29-ounce) cans, drained
2 cups granulated sugar
1 cup (2 sticks) butter, softened
1 cup evaporated milk

4 eggs
2 tablespoons vanilla extract
1 teaspoon nutmeg
1 teaspoon cinnamon

Topping:

1½ cups crushed corn flakes
1 cup brown sugar

½ cup (1 stick) butter, melted
1 cup chopped pecans

Mix mashed yams, sugar, butter, evaporated milk, eggs, vanilla, nutmeg and cinnamon with mixer. Pour mixture into ungreased 13"x9"x2" baking dish. To make topping, mix together corn flakes, brown sugar, melted butter and chopped pecans. Spread on top of yam mixture. Bake uncovered at 350° for 30 minutes.

Susan Plowman

COCONUT-SWEET POTATO CASSEROLE

Serves 12

1 (29-ounce) can or 3 cups
   sweet potatoes
1 cup granulated sugar
½ cup (1 stick) butter or
   margarine

1 teaspoon vanilla extract
2 eggs, beaten
⅓ cup condensed milk

Coconut Topping:

1 cup light brown sugar
½ cup flour
⅓ cup margarine

1 cup chopped pecans
1 cup coconut

Mix sweet potatoes, granulated sugar, ½ cup margarine, vanilla, eggs and condensed milk with mixer; spoon into baking dish. Mix topping ingredients and crumble on top of the sweet potatoes. Bake at 350° for 25 minutes.

Sherrie Ezell

TEXAS PARTY POTATOES

Serves 12-16

1 (32-ounce) bag frozen hash
   browns, thawed
½ cup (1 stick) melted butter
   plus 3 tablespoons butter,
   divided
1 (8-ounce) carton sour cream
1 (10¾-ounce) can condensed
   cream of chicken soup
½ cup chopped onion

2 cups (8-ounces) grated
   Cheddar cheese
1 teaspoon salt
¼ teaspoon pepper
1 pound bacon (optional)
1 (8-ounce) can sliced water
   chestnuts, drained (optional)
2 cups crushed cornflakes

In large bowl, combine potatoes, ½ cup butter, sour cream, soup, onion, cheese, salt and pepper. Cook and crumble bacon, add to mixture if desired. Add water chestnuts if desired. Spread mixture in large casserole. Sauté cornflakes in 3 tablespoons butter; sprinkle on top of mixture. Bake at 350° for 40 minutes.

Note: This dish is a good choice for buffets or "covered dish" suppers.

*Cindy Cathcart/ Delight Fails/ Schelli Martin
Bonnie Novosad/ Carol Ann Adam*

FESTIVE MASHED POTATOES

Serves 12

12 medium potatoes, cooked,
   peeled, cubed
1 (8-ounce) package cream
   cheese
1 (16-ounce) carton sour cream
2-3 tablespoons chopped chives
   (or to taste)

Salt and pepper to taste
1 tablespoon garlic powder
½ teaspoon paprika
¼ cup (½ stick) margarine
½ cup milk

Mash the potatoes. Add all other ingredients except for paprika. Spoon into large baking dish, and sprinkle with paprika. Heat in 350° oven until hot, about 30 minutes.

Note: This dish is a great crowd pleaser!

Christy Spence

GRILLED POTATOES

Serves 4-6

4-6 medium potatoes, pared and sliced thin
1 large onion, sliced thin
½ teaspoon garlic salt
½ teaspoon seasoned salt
½ teaspoon celery seed
½ cup (1 stick) margarine
1 cup (4-ounces) grated cheese

Prepare a disposable pan made from a double thickness of heavy-duty aluminum foil to fit layers of potatoes. Mix together garlic salt, seasoned salt and celery seed. Layer some of the sliced potatoes and onions in foil boat and sprinkle with salt mixture. Dot with pats of margarine. Add another layer of potatoes, salt and margarine. Repeat until all potatoes are used. Top with cheese and seal foil. Cook on grill at medium heat for 45 minutes or until potatoes are done. Increase proportions of all ingredients to make a larger amount.

Ruth Seiwell

MIRELLA'S POTATOES AU GRATIN

Serves 6-8

2 pounds (6-8 medium) potatoes, cooked, diced, seasoned
¼ cup (½ stick) butter or margarine plus 2 tablespoons butter, divided
¼ cup sifted all-purpose flour
1 teaspoon salt
⅛ teaspoon pepper
2 cups milk
1 cup (4-ounces) freshly grated sharp Cheddar cheese
10-12 crushed saltine crackers
1 tablespoon minced parsley

Cook potatoes, dice and season to taste with salt and pepper. Grease a 1½-quart (or 13"x9"x2") casserole dish. Preheat oven to 375°. Melt ¼ cup butter in saucepan, add flour, salt and pepper; cook over low heat, stirring until smooth. Add milk gradually, stirring constantly. Gradually add grated cheese. Cook about 5 minutes or until sauce thickens.

Combine cheese sauce and diced potatoes. Place in prepared casserole dish. Melt remaining 2 tablespoons of butter, combine with crushed crackers and parsley. Sprinkle on top of potato mixture. Bake at 375° for 20 minutes, or until browned and thoroughly hot.

Cindy Williams

SPEEDY SCALLOPED POTATOES

Serves 6

5 cups boiled, sliced potatoes
½ cup milk
1 (10¾-ounce) can condensed
 cream of mushroom soup
1 tablespoon minced onion
Salt and pepper to taste
1 cup (4-ounces) grated cheese

Boil and slice potatoes. Blend soup and milk in a saucepan, and bring to a boil. Add onion, salt and pepper. Arrange a layer of potatoes in a greased baking dish. Pour in half the soup. Repeat layers, and sprinkle top with cheese. Bake at 350° for 30 minutes.

Dina Dornburg

SEASONED RED POTATOES

Serves 4

2 pounds red potatoes
1 purple onion
1 medium green pepper
1 medium red pepper
½ cup prepared garlic-herb salad
 dressing

Cut potatoes, onion and peppers into chunks. Arrange in a single layer in a baking dish. Pour salad dressing over vegetables, mixing to coat evenly. Bake in preheated 400° oven for 45 minutes, stirring occasionally to brown evenly.

♥ *Heart healthy hint: Use fat-free dressing and enjoy a heart-healthy potato dish.*

Kathy Carr

BAKED NEW POTATOES

Serves 6

2½ pounds new potatoes,
 unpeeled and quartered
¼ cup (½ stick) butter or
 margarine
2 tablespoons vegetable oil
½ teaspoon salt
½ teaspoon dried whole thyme

Arrange potatoes in 13"x9"x2" baking dish. Melt butter; combine with remaining ingredients; pour over potatoes, turn potatoes to coat. Bake, uncovered, at 350° for 35 minutes or until tender. The cooking time will vary, depending on size of potatoes.

Donna Schwertner

MY DIET BAKED POTATO

♥ *Heart Healthy*   *Serves 1*

1 baking potato
1 (¼-inch) slice of onion
1 slice of bell pepper

Garlic salt and pepper to taste
1 tablespoon defatted chicken
   broth (optional)

Cut potato in half lengthwise. Put slice of onion between potato halves. Sprinkle with garlic salt and pepper. Add slice of bell pepper. Wrap potato in foil and bake for 1 hour. Add 1 tablespoon chicken broth to potato if desired to make it more moist.

Note: *This recipe supplies great flavor without using butter or sour cream. Increase the number of potatoes and "fixings" as needed for additional servings.*

Polly Galloway

BAKED POTATO CASSEROLE

                                                     Serves 6-8

6 medium potatoes, cooked and
   chopped
1½ teaspoons salt
1 cup sour cream

6-8 green onions, chopped
1 cup (4-ounces) grated Cheddar
   cheese
½ cup (1 stick) butter, melted

Combine potatoes, salt, sour cream, green onion and cheese in a large bowl; mix gently. Spoon into a 2-quart casserole. Pour butter over top, and bake at 400° for 30 minutes or until lightly browned on top.

Note: *This recipe can be doubled. It is a great alternative to traditional baked potatoes.*

Jo Ann Brown

*~ **Nutrition tip:** Many of a root vegetable's minerals are concentrated in and directly under its skin. When you peel potatoes, carrots or beets, these minerals are lost. Try scrubbing instead whenever possible.*

Grains, Eggs and Cheese

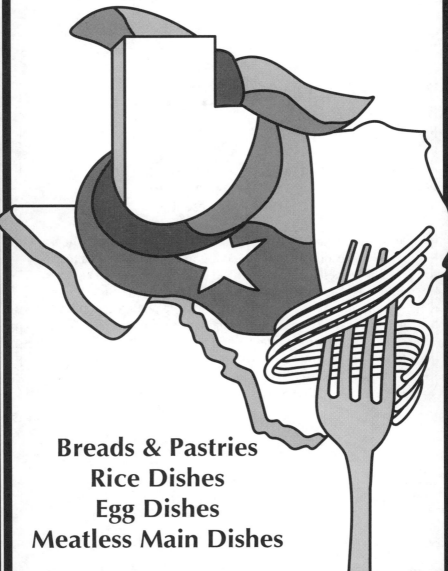

Breads & Pastries
Rice Dishes
Egg Dishes
Meatless Main Dishes

A TROUPE OF DISABLED
AND NON-DISABLED PUPPETS

KIDS ON THE BLOCK
1982 - to present

Friendly puppets with names like Renaldo and Mandy help
teach Brazosport-area third and fourth graders about the real-
life challenges of living with handicaps. Junior Service League
volunteers present the puppet shows twice each year at every
Brazosport Independent School District elementary school and
at two private schools. The entertaining but thought-provoking
shows spotlight the obstacles and feelings of physically-chal-
lenged and learning-disabled students.

QUICK AND EASY BISCUITS

Serves 12

2 cups self-rising flour　　　**½ cup oil**
1 cup milk

Preheat oven to 400°. Combine flour, milk and oil; mix well. Spoon into well-greased muffin tins. Bake at 400° for 20 minutes. Serve slathered in butter.

Jenny Pennington

FRONTIER BISCUITS

Serves 12

1 cup butter or margarine,　　　**1 cup sour cream**
softened　　　　　　　　　　　　**2 cups self-rising flour**

Mix softened butter and sour cream together. Stir in self-rising flour. Pinch off chunks of mixture and put in well-greased mini-size muffin tin. Use larger amounts of dough for full-size muffins. Bake at 425° for 10-15 minutes.

Kim Gary

MINI SAUSAGE MUFFINS

Yields 5 dozen

1 pound pork or turkey sausage　　**½ teaspoon red pepper**
⅔ cup chopped green onions　　　**1 cup milk**
(tops too)　　　　　　　　　　　　**1 cup (4-ounces) grated Cheddar**
1 (12-ounce) package biscuit mix　　**cheese (or more, to taste)**
1 teaspoon dry mustard

Cook sausage and green onions in skillet; drain. Combine biscuit mix, dry mustard and red pepper; add milk, stirring just until moistened. Stir in sausage mixture and cheese. Grease mini muffin pans or coat with non-stick spray; spoon in batter. Bake at 400° for 12-14 minutes, or until golden. Remove from pans immediately, and serve warm. Recipe can be doubled or tripled. Freeze cooled muffins in sealed freezer bags. To reheat, wrap frozen muffins in a paper towel and microwave for a few seconds.

Lisa Baker

ORANGE MARMALADE MINI MUFFINS

Yields 2-3 dozen

1 naval orange, peeled and
   chopped
2 teaspoons orange zest
¾ cup sugar
¾ cup corn oil
2 eggs
2 cups flour

1 teaspoon baking powder
½ teaspoon baking soda
½ teaspoon salt
½ cup orange marmalade
¼ cup orange liqueur
¼ cup chopped pecans

Peel and chop orange. Reserve peel for 2 teaspoons finely chopped zest. Blend sugar, oil and eggs in food processor. Sift flour, baking powder, baking soda and salt. Add dry ingredients to food processor items. Process with "off-on" switch only until moist. Add marmalade and liqueur; process with "off-on" switch until smooth. Add pecans, chopped orange pieces and orange zest. Mix until blended. Spoon batter into buttered mini muffin tins, filling ½ way. Bake at 375° until lightly golden, about 15 minutes. Muffins can be frozen.

Sandra Frazier

FRENCH MINI PUFFS

Yields 2 dozen

½ cup sugar
1½ cups flour
1½ teaspoons baking powder
½ teaspoon salt

½ teaspoon nutmeg
1 egg
⅓ cup oil
½ cup milk

Topping:
½ cup (1 stick) butter, melted
½ cup sugar

1 teaspoon cinnamon

Grease mini-muffin tins. Mix together ½ cup sugar, flour, baking powder, salt and nutmeg. Blend in egg, oil and milk. Fill muffin pans and bake in preheated 350° oven for 10 minutes. While muffins cook, mix together melted butter, sugar and cinnamon. When muffins have baked, remove from oven and, while still warm, roll in sugar-cinnamon mixture.

Note: *These are nice for a quick breakfast served with fresh fruit.*

Sharon Shaver

PEACH MUFFINS

Yields 10-12 muffins

1½ cups flour
¾ teaspoon salt
½ teaspoon baking soda
1 cup sugar
2 eggs

½ cup vegetable oil
1 (16-ounce) can peaches, well
   drained, chopped
½ teaspoon vanilla extract
¼ teaspoon cinnamon

Combine flour, salt, soda and sugar. Stir in eggs and oil. Add chopped peaches, vanilla and cinnamon. Bake in greased muffin tins at 350° for 20-25 minutes.

Penny Daigle

BANANA-NUT MUFFINS

Yields 24-30 muffins

2½ cups sugar
4 mashed bananas
1 cup (2 sticks) margarine
4 eggs
4 tablespoons buttermilk

2 teaspoons soda
2 teaspoons vanilla
¼ teaspoon salt
3 cups flour
1 cup chopped nuts (optional)

Grease and flour muffin tins (or use paper liners). Cream sugar, bananas and margarine. Add remaining ingredients. Fill muffin cups ¾ full. Bake in preheated 325° oven for about 22 minutes, or until toothpick comes out clean. Do not over-bake.

Janis Warny

TEXAS PECAN OATMEAL MUFFINS

Yields 12 muffins

1 cup quick-cooking oatmeal
1 cup buttermilk
½ cup (1 stick) margarine
¾ cup brown sugar
2 eggs

1 cup flour (half or all whole-
   wheat)
1 teaspoon baking powder
½ teaspoon salt
½ teaspoon soda
½ cup chopped pecans

Soak oatmeal in buttermilk for 1 hour. Beat together margarine and brown sugar; add to buttermilk mix. Beat in eggs. Sift flour, baking powder, salt and soda; add to buttermilk mixture. Add pecans. Fill greased muffin pans ⅔ full. Bake at 400° for 20 minutes.

Sherrie Ezell

GOOD MORNING MUFFINS

Yields about 30 muffins

4 cups all-purpose flour
2½ cups sugar
4 teaspoons baking soda
4 teaspoons cinnamon
1 teaspoon salt
4 cups coarsely grated carrot
1 cup raisins

1 cup chopped pecans
1 cup shredded coconut
2 tart apples, peeled and grated
6 large eggs
2 cups canola oil
2 teaspoons vanilla extract

Preheat oven to 350°. Sift together flour, sugar, baking soda, cinnamon and salt. Stir in grated carrot, raisins, pecans, coconut and grated apple. In a bowl, whisk together eggs, oil and vanilla. Add egg mixture to flour mixture, and stir batter until just combined. Spoon batter into paper-lined or well-buttered muffin tins. Bake at 350° for 30-35 minutes. Let muffins cool for 5 minutes; transfer to a rack to finish cooling. Muffins can be frozen.

Christy McConnell

BATTER BREAD

Serves 6

1 package dry yeast
¾ cup warm water
2 tablespoons sugar
1 egg, beaten
1 tablespoon water

1½ teaspoons salt
¼ cup non-fat dry milk
¼ cup melted butter
2¼ cups flour
Sesame seeds

Dissolve yeast in warm water in large mixing bowl. Stir in sugar, egg, 1 tablespoon water, salt, dry milk and melted butter. Add flour; mix well. (Mixture will be sticky.) Place dough in greased 8"x8" pan, sprinkle with sesame seeds. Cover with light cloth, let rise until double (about 2 hours). Bake at 400° for 15-20 minutes, until golden brown. Brush with melted butter, cut into squares to serve.

Karen Moran

~ **Muffins for a crowd:** *Instead of making dozens of individual muffins, spread the batter in round baking pans. Cut in wedges to serve.*

SOUR CREAM ROLLS

Serves 6-8

½ cup (1 stick) butter
½ cup sugar
1 (8-ounce) carton sour cream
2 envelopes dry yeast
½ cup warm water (105°-115°)

2 eggs
4 cups flour
1 teaspoon salt
Melted butter

Melt butter in saucepan, bring to a boil. Remove from heat. Stir in sugar and sour cream, cool to lukewarm. Meanwhile, dissolve yeast in warm water in large bowl. Add sour cream mixture and eggs to yeast. Add flour and salt, blend well. Place in lightly greased bowl; cover. Let rise overnight in refrigerator. Next day, knead and roll to ½-inch thickness to cut out or shape into clover-leaf rolls. Top with melted butter. Bake at 350° for 15-20 minutes. Rolls can be frozen and reheated, but are best served right out of the oven.

Note: *This is a great recipe to use during busy holiday cooking, since the rolls are started the day before.*

Eva Kinney

BEST REFRIGERATOR ROLLS

Yields 5 dozen

1 package dry yeast
¾ cup lukewarm water
6 tablespoons sugar
¾ teaspoon salt

½ cup (1 stick) butter
¾ cup boiling water
2 eggs, beaten
4½ cups flour

Dissolve yeast in lukewarm water. Mix sugar, salt and butter. Add boiling water to dissolve. Cool; stir in eggs and yeast mixture. Add flour to make soft dough. Cover bowl with damp cloth and refrigerate at least 4 hours. With greased hands, pinch off dough for rolls, and place on greased baking pan. Cover and let rise to double in bulk. Bake at 425° for 10-12 minutes.

Hint: *For a warm place to let dough rise, place dough inside oven and crack oven door just enough for light to come on. The heat from the light bulb will be enough to rise bread.*

Lana Booher

PUMPKIN ROLLS

Yields 15 rolls

1 (16-ounce) package hot roll
   mix
⅓ cup warm water (105°-115°)
1 cup canned or cooked mashed
   pumpkin
1 egg

2 tablespoons granulated sugar
2 tablespoons melted butter or
   margarine
½ cup sugar
1½ teaspoons pumpkin pie spice
⅓ cup raisins

Icing Drizzle:

1 cup sifted powdered sugar
1 tablespoon plus 1 teaspoon
   milk

¼ teaspoon vanilla extract

Dissolve yeast packet for hot roll mix in warm water. Let stand 5 minutes. Combine pumpkin, egg and 2 tablespoons granulated sugar; mix well. Add yeast. Stir in flour packet to form a stiff dough. Place dough in well-greased bowl, turning to grease top. Cover, and let rise in a warm place (85°) for 45 minutes or until doubled in bulk.

Turn dough out on floured surface; knead 12 times. Roll dough into a 15"x12" rectangle. Spread with 2 tablespoons melted butter, sprinkle with sugar and pie spice, top with raisins. Beginning at the long side, roll up dough jellyroll fashion. Press edges and ends together securely. Cut into 1-inch slices; place rolls, cut-side down, in a greased 13"x9"x2" baking pan. Cover and let rise in a warm place free from drafts, for about 30 minutes or until doubled in bulk. Bake at 375° for 20 minutes or until golden brown. Combine powdered sugar, milk and vanilla; drizzle over warm rolls.

Sandy Carlberg

ORANGE BISCUITS

Serves 10-12

2 cans refrigerator biscuits
1 cup sugar
3 teaspoons grated orange rind

¼ cup (½ stick) butter or
   margarine

Grease Bundt pan with butter. In bowl, mix sugar with orange rind. Melt ¼ cup butter. Dip each biscuit in butter and roll in sugar mixture. Stand biscuits on edge in Bundt pan. Bake at 350° for 30 minutes. Invert pan on rack after baking.

Kristi Abild

BUTTERY PAN ROLLS

Yields 15 rolls

2 packages active dry yeast
½ cup warm water (about 110°)
¼ cup sugar
1 teaspoon salt
4½ cups flour, divided

10 tablespoons (1¼ sticks)
  butter, melted and cooled
1 egg
1 cup warm milk (about 110°)

In large bowl, dissolve yeast in water and let stand until bubbly, about 15 minutes. Stir together sugar, salt and 2 cups flour until well mixed. Add 6 tablespoons melted butter, egg, yeast mixture and milk. Beat about 5 minutes to blend well. Gradually beat in remaining 2½ cups flour. Cover bowl and let batter rise in a warm place until doubled, about 45 minutes.

Pour 2 tablespoons of the remaining melted butter into a 13"x9"x2" baking pan, tilting pan to coat bottom. Beat down batter and drop by spoonfuls into buttered pan; making about 15 rolls. Drizzle remaining butter over dough. Cover lightly and let rise in a warm place until almost doubled, about 30 minutes. Bake at 425° (400° if using a glass pan) for 12-17 minutes, or until lightly browned. Serve hot.

Janice Keller

BUTTERHORNS

Yields 24-36 rolls

1 package dry yeast
½ cup very warm water (105°-
  115°)
1 beaten egg
½ cup milk

½ cup (1 stick) butter
⅓ cup sugar
¾ teaspoon salt
4 cups flour, divided

Mix dry yeast and warm water until dissolved. Add beaten egg. Heat milk, dissolve butter in milk. In a large bowl, mix sugar and salt. Pour milk-butter mixture over sugar-salt, stir until dissolved. Cool to lukewarm. Add yeast and egg mixture to bowl. Add 2 cups flour, beat with electric mixer. Add remaining 2 cups flour, knead lightly to mix. Set in greased bowl to rise 1 hour. Divide into 2 or 3 portions. Roll out portion into pie shape, then cut pizza-style into 12 wedges. Roll wedges, starting at large end. Rolls may be frozen at this point. Let dough rise for 1 hour (if frozen, thaw and let rise.) Bake at 350° for 8-10 minutes.

Lisa Baker

CHARLENE'S TOMATO CHEESE BATTER BREAD

Yields 1 loaf

¼ teaspoon baking soda
1 (10¾-ounce) can condensed
  tomato soup
½ cup Cheez Whiz
2 tablespoons butter
¼ cup water

3 to 3¼ cups flour
2 tablespoons sugar
1 teaspoon salt
2 packages active dry yeast
1 egg

Warm baking soda, soup, cheese, butter and water in a pan. Cool to lukewarm. In a bowl, combine 2 cups flour, sugar, salt and yeast. Add lukewarm liquid to flour mixture. Add egg; beat 2 minutes with mixer at medium. By hand, gradually stir in remaining flour to form a stiff batter. Cover, let rise in warm place until light and doubled in size (45-60 minutes). Stir vigorously (35 strokes). Pour into well-greased 1½- to 2-quart casserole dish. Cover and let rise for 30-45 minutes. Bake at 350° for 35-40 minutes (until deep brown and loaf sounds hollow when tapped). Remove from dish immediately.

Note: *These rather unusual ingredients combine to create a very flavorful bread.*

Dee Eddins

HERB BREAD

Serves 8-10

1 thick loaf sliced French bread
  (or 2 small)
1 package sliced Swiss cheese
1 cup (2 sticks) butter or
  margarine (or less, to taste)
1 tablespoon prepared mustard

½ teaspoon Beau Monde
  seasoned salt
2 tablespoons minced onion
1 tablespoon poppy seed
2 teaspoons lemon juice

Melt butter; stir in mustard, seasoned salt, onion, poppy seed and lemon juice. Place 1 slice of Swiss cheese between each bread slice. Position bread on foil; pour mustard mixture over bread, and wrap in foil. Bake at 350° for 30 minutes. Serve immediately. Mustard sauce can be prepared ahead, and reheated before using.

Hint: *If bread loaf is thin, reduce amount of butter used. Add thinly sliced roast beef or ham between bread slices with cheese to make a main dish.*

Jo Ann Brown/ Patti Hosack/ Schelli Martin

HEARTY BEEF MEXICAN CORNBREAD

Serves 6

1 pound ground beef
1 medium onion, chopped
6 jalapeño peppers, chopped
   (use more or less, to taste)
1½ cups (6-ounces) grated
   rat cheese (use more or less,
   to taste)
1 cup yellow cornmeal
1 cup milk

½ teaspoon baking soda
1 teaspoon salt
2 eggs
⅓ cup solid shortening
1 (17-ounce) can cream-style
   corn
Cooking grease
Sprinkling of cornmeal

Brown ground beef; drain. Chop onion and jalapeño peppers. Grate cheese. In a large bowl, mix together cornmeal, milk, baking soda, salt, eggs, shortening and corn. Heat grease in iron skillet. Brown a sprinkling of cornmeal in hot grease; then pour in half the prepared cornmeal mixture. Next layer cheese, ground beef, onions and jalapeño peppers. Pour last half of cornmeal mixture on top. Bake in skillet, at 350° about 45 minutes.

Gwen Williams

JALAPEÑO JELLY

Yields 2 cups

¾ cup ground green bell pepper
½ cup ground jalapeño and
   green banana peppers
1½ cups cider vinegar

6 cups sugar
6 ounces liquid pectin
Red food coloring

Remove seeds and stems from all peppers. Grind green pepper with vinegar in blender, adding peppers there is ¾ cup of ground bell pepper. Repeat process with jalapeño and green banana peppers to obtain ½ cup ground chile peppers. Put pepper-vinegar mixture in large saucepan with 6 cups sugar. Boil for one minute, cool slightly. Add liquid pectin, and food coloring to desired color. Strain, and place in 5 clean, boiled pint jelly jars. Seal tops with paraffin.

Hint: *This jelly is good with Colby or Longhorn cheese on crackers.*

Susan Plowman

FIRECRACKER BREAD

Serves 8-10

2 French bread baguettes

Pepper Butter:

**1 cup (2 sticks) unsalted butter,
at room temperature**
**1 (7-ounce) jar roasted red bell
peppers, drained**
1 tablespoon tomato paste

1½ teaspoons brown sugar
¼ teaspoon cayenne pepper
¼ teaspoon hot pepper sauce
Salt to taste

Bring butter to room temperature. Place butter, red bell peppers, tomato paste, brown sugar, cayenne pepper and hot pepper sauce in food processor; blend to combine. Season to taste with salt. Preheat broiler. Cut baguettes into ¾-inch slices. Place slices on cookie sheet, broil tops until light brown. Turn slices over, spread with pepper butter. Broil until bubbling. Serve hot.

Note: *Pepper butter can be made up to 3 days in advance. Store in refrigerator. Bring pepper butter to room temperature before using in recipe.*

Sandra Frazier

JALAPEÑO CORNBREAD

Serves 16

1 cup cornmeal
½ teaspoon salt
½ teaspoon baking soda
⅓ cup oil
2 eggs
1 cup creamed corn

⅔ cup buttermilk
**1 cup (4-ounces) grated Cheddar
cheese**
**6 medium jalapeño peppers,
chopped**
¼ to ½ cup chopped onion

Combine cornmeal, salt and baking soda; mix well. Stir in oil. Add eggs; mix well. Stir in corn and buttermilk. Spoon one-half of mixture into greased 9x12x2-inch pan. Sprinkle cheese, peppers and chopped onion over mixture. Add remaining batter. Bake at 375° for 25 minutes.

Linda Jordan

HOT WATER CORNBREAD

Serves 6

2 cups water
½ cup chopped green onion
  (optional)
1 teaspoon salt
1 teaspoon sugar
1 teaspoon ground pepper
1 cup yellow cornmeal
1 cup white cornmeal
Oil for frying

Add green onion, salt, sugar and pepper to water in saucepan; bring to a boil. Turn off heat. Combine cornmeals, and add ⅓ of the mixture to water in thin stream, stirring constantly until very thick. Vigorously stir in remaining cornmeal. Cool to room temperature. Form cornmeal mixture into 3-inch rounds ½-inch thick. Heat oil in deep-fryer or large saucepan to 350°. Fry cornbread rounds in batches, cooking until golden brown, about 1 minute per side. Transfer to paper towels with slotted spoon.

Jackie Brewer

BROCCOLI CORNBREAD

Serves 8-10

2 (8½-ounce) boxes cornbread
  mix
¾ to 1 cup (1½ to 2 sticks)
  butter
1 large onion, chopped
1 (10-ounce) box frozen
  chopped broccoli, thawed
1 (12-ounce) carton cottage
  cheese
4 eggs, beaten
1 teaspoon salt (optional)

Mix all ingredients; pour into greased 13"x9"x2" pan. Bake at 350° for 45 minutes.

Hint: *Substitute fresh broccoli, if desired. Use Texas 1015 sweet onions when available for a special flavor treat.*

Sharon Shaver/ Susan Laver

SKILLET BROCCOLI CORNBREAD: Cook 2 cups chopped broccoli until tender-crisp, drain. Mix ½ cup (1 stick) margarine, 1 (8-ounce) package cornmeal muffin mix, ⅓ cup milk and 2 eggs. Add cooked broccoli, 1 cup chopped onion and 1 cup (4-ounces) grated Cheddar cheese. Mix well; pour into greased 10-inch iron skillet. Bake at 350° for 30 minutes.

Delores Smith

POPPY SEED BREAD

Yields 3 small or 2 large loaves

3 cups flour
½ teaspoon salt
1½ teaspoons baking powder
2¼ cups sugar
1½ tablespoons poppy seeds
1½ teaspoons almond extract

3 eggs
1½ cups milk
1 cup plus 2 tablespoons
  vegetable oil
1½ teaspoons vanilla extract
1½ teaspoons butter

Glaze:

¼ cup orange juice
½ teaspoon butter flavor extract
½ teaspoon almond extract

½ teaspoon vanilla extract
¾ cup sugar

Mix all bread ingredients for 1-2 minutes, using hand mixer. Pour into 3 small or 2 large greased and floured loaf pans. Bake at 350° for 1 hour. Cool five minutes in pans, then remove loaves from pans. Combine all glaze ingredients. Brush loaves with glaze, making sure to coat all sides. Wrap in foil to keep moist. This recipe freezes well.

Barbara Lundahl

POPPY SEED BRUNCH CAKE

Yields 1 Bundt cake

1 (18.25-ounce) box yellow
  butter cake mix
½ cup (1 stick) butter or
  margarine
½ cup sugar

¾ cup vegetable oil
4 eggs
1 cup sour cream
¼ cup poppy seeds
Sugar

Combine dry cake mix, softened butter, sugar and oil. Add eggs, one at a time. Fold in sour cream, mix well. Add poppy seeds. Oil a large Bundt pan and sprinkle with sugar. Bake at 350° for 1 hour.

Note: *This is very moist, delicious cake, good for breakfast and a favorite with men!*

Peggy McKnight

LEMON BREAD

Yields 1 loaf

½ cup (1 stick) butter
1 cup sugar
2 eggs
1½ cups flour
½ cup milk

½ cup chopped pecans
1 teaspoon baking powder
½ teaspoon salt
Grated rind of one lemon

Glaze:

½ cup sugar

Juice of one lemon

Cream butter and 1 cup sugar. Add eggs, flour, milk, pecans, baking powder, salt and lemon rind; mix well. Pour into greased loaf pan. Bake at 325° for 50-60 minutes. Remove from oven, cool 5 minutes. Combine ½ cup sugar and lemon juice for glaze; drizzle glaze over bread and cool thoroughly.

Barbara Allen

LEMON-BLUEBERRY POPPY SEED BREAD

Yields 1 loaf

1 (23.5-ounce) box Duncan
 Hines bakery-style blueberry
 muffin mix
2 tablespoons poppy seeds

1 egg
¾ cup water
1 tablespoon grated lemon peel

Icing Drizzle:

½ cup powdered sugar

1 tablespoon lemon juice

Combine dry muffin mix and poppyseed. Add egg and water, stir until moist. Drain blueberries from muffin mix, fold blueberries and lemon peel into batter. Pour batter into loaf pan, and sprinkle with topping from muffin mix. Bake at 350° for 1 hour. Cool 10 minutes in pan, then remove loaf; let cool completely. Mix powdered sugar and lemon juice to make icing, and drizzle over loaf.

Penny Daigle

~ ***Full of zest:*** *The outer rind of citrus fruits is full of low-calorie flavor that adds zing to soups, salads, entrees and desserts. Start with cold, firm fruit and gently cut away a thin layer of rind, avoiding the bitter white pith beneath. A zester is the best tool for the job, or use a vegetable peeler. After peeling, julienne the strips into tiny pieces.*

PUMPKIN BREAD

Yields 4 coffee-can loaves

3 cups sugar
1 cup vegetable oil
²/₃ cup water
4 eggs
2 cups canned pumpkin
3½ cups flour
2 teaspoons baking soda

1 teaspoon salt
1 teaspoon cinnamon
½ teaspoon nutmeg
1 cup chopped pecans
1 (8-ounce) package chopped
  dates

Grease and flour four 1-pound coffee cans. Mix together sugar, oil and water, beat in eggs. Stir in canned pumpkin. Combine flour, baking soda, salt, cinnamon and nutmeg; add to pumpkin mix. Stir in pecans and dates; mix dough well. Half-fill cans, bake at 350° for 1 hour.

Nancy Chamberlain

QUICK BANANA BREAD

Yields 1 loaf

3-4 ripe bananas
1 cup sugar
1 egg
1½ cups flour

¼ cup (½ stick) butter, melted
1 teaspoon baking soda
1 teaspoon salt

Mash bananas with fork. Stir in sugar, egg, flour, melted butter, soda and salt. Pour batter into greased loaf pan, bake at 325° for one hour.

Susie Hanchey

COFFEE-CAN BANANA BREAD

Yields 3 coffee-can loaves

1 cup (2 sticks) butter
3 cups sugar
8 tablespoons buttermilk
2 teaspoons baking soda
3 cups flour

4 eggs, separated
5 very ripe bananas
2 teaspoons vanilla extract
½ teaspoon salt
1 cup chopped pecans

Cream butter and sugar; add milk with soda, alternating with flour. Add beaten egg yolks. Mash bananas; add to mixture with vanilla, salt and pecans. Fold in stiffly beaten egg whites. Fill greased 1-pound coffee cans half-full; bake at 350° for 40 minutes. Cool 10-15 minutes before removing from cans.

Linda Cullitan

WHOLE-WHEAT BANANA BREAD

Yields 1 loaf

½ cup (1 stick) butter, softened
¾ cup brown sugar
1 egg
1 cup unsifted whole wheat flour
½ cup unsifted unbleached
    white flour

1 teaspoon baking soda
¾ teaspoon salt
1¼ cups mashed ripe bananas
    (2 large or 3 small)
¼ cup buttermilk OR non-fat
    plain yogurt

Cream butter and sugar together until very light and creamy; beat in egg. In a separate bowl, sift together whole wheat flour, white flour, baking soda and salt. In a third bowl, combine mashed bananas and buttermilk, stirring just to mix. Add dry ingredients and banana mixture alternately to butter mixture, stirring just enough to combine well. Pour batter into oiled 9"x5" loaf pan. Bake at 350° for 50-60 minutes, or until done. Cool in pan 10 minutes, then remove from pan and finish cooling on rack.

Note: *My children have enjoyed helping make this recipe since they were toddlers. It makes a good rainy-day cooking project, with delicious results!*

Cynthia Lancaster

MARY ANN'S BANANA-NUT BREAD

Yields 1 loaf

⅓ cup shortening
½ cup sugar
2 eggs
1¾ cups sifted all-purpose flour
1 teaspoon baking powder

½ teaspoon baking soda
½ teaspoon salt
1 cup mashed ripe banana
½ cup chopped walnuts

Cream together shortening and sugar; add eggs and beat well. Sift together dry ingredients; add to creamed mixture alternately with banana, blending well after each addition. Stir in nuts. Pour into well-greased 9½x5x3-inch loaf pan. Bake at 350° for 40-45 minutes or until done. Remove from pan, cool on rack.

Mary Ann Sosebee

~ Nutrition tip: *Good sources of Vitamin E include whole grain breads and cereals, wheat germ, nuts, safflower and sunflower oils, and green leafy vegetables.*

FRESH FRUIT BREAD

Yields 2 large loaves

1 cup (or more) chopped fresh
   fruit
2 cups flour
2 teaspoons baking powder
1 teaspoon ground cinnamon

1 teaspoon salt
2 eggs
1 cup milk
1 cup vegetable oil
¾ cup sugar

Use food processor or finely chop by hand your choice of fresh fruit. Combine flour, baking powder, cinnamon and salt; mix well. Beat eggs lightly; stir in milk, oil and sugar. Quickly stir egg mixture into dry ingredients; carefully stir in fresh fruit. Spoon into two greased loaf pans. Bake at 300° for 60 minutes.

Hint: Try pineapple, strawberries, blueberries, peaches, apples, pears or bananas. For a delicious accompaniment to Italian food, use peeled tomatoes and substitute dry spaghetti seasoning for cinnamon.

Lisa Baker

GRANDMA'S CHRISTMAS BUTTER

Yields 1½ cups

2 cups fresh cranberries
1 cup (2 sticks) real butter

Juice of ½ lemon
3 cups powdered sugar

Wash cranberries. Let butter soften slightly, put in blender with lemon juice and cranberries. Blend until cranberries are well diced. Add powdered sugar gradually, continuing to blend until all sugar is added. Serve with any bread.

Hint: Fill three decorative 8-ounce jars with butter for gift-giving.

Delight Fails

~ Fiber facts: To add fiber to your diet for better nutritional health:

~ ...Sprinkle cereals, casseroles, baked goods with wheat germ or bran.

~ ...Choose whole-grain baked products over those using refined flour.

GREAT AUNT OLGA'S BLITZKUCHEN

Serves 6-8

1 cup sifted flour
½ cup sugar plus ⅓ cup sugar, divided
1½ teaspoons baking powder
½ teaspoon salt

½ cup (1 stick) butter plus 2 tablespoons butter, divided
1 egg, well beaten
½ cup milk
1½ teaspoons cinnamon
⅓ cup chopped pecans

Sift flour, then measure 1 cup. Mix flour with ½ cup sugar, baking powder and salt. Cut in stick of butter, using a pastry blender or two crossed knives, until pieces are size of rice kernels. Make a well in the center of the flour, and add one well-beaten egg mixed with ½ cup milk. Stir only enough to moisten dry ingredients, about 15 strokes. Pour batter evenly into greased 8"x8"x2" baking pan. To make topping, mix ⅓ cup sugar, cinnamon, chopped pecans and 2 tablespoons melted butter. Sprinkle topping over bread batter, cutting some into the batter with a knife if desired. Pat down topping with the back of a spoon to form a layer. Bake cake at 375° for about 20 minutes or until brown.

Cary Rosenbohm

SOUR CREAM COFFEE CAKE

Serves 16

1 cup (2 sticks) margarine
2 cups sugar
2 eggs
2 cups flour
1 teaspoon baking powder
½ teaspoon salt

1 teaspoon vanilla
1 cup sour cream
1 cup chopped pecans
4 tablespoons brown sugar
1 tablespoon cinnamon

To make cake batter, cream margarine and sugar. Add eggs, mix well. Add dry ingredients. Mix. Add vanilla and sour cream. Mix. To make topping, mix together pecans, brown sugar and cinnamon. Grease a tube or Bundt pan well. Dust the sides of the pan with one-third of the topping mixture. Add one-half of the batter. Sprinkle one-third of the topping over the batter. Add remaining batter, then top with remaining topping. Bake in 350° oven for 50 minutes. Cool in pan 15 minutes.

Linda Jordan

MRS. JERABEK'S KOLACHES

Yields 3-4 dozen

2 packages dry yeast
¼ cup lukewarm water
1 teaspoon sugar
⅔ cup margarine
⅔ cup sugar
2 egg yolks

2 teaspoons salt
6 cups flour
1 (14-ounce) can evaporated
  milk
Hot water
Butter

Topping (Posipka):

1 cup sugar
½ cup flour

¾ teaspoon cinnamon
2 tablespoons butter, melted

To make Posipka topping, mix sugar, flour, cinnamon and melted butter until mixture resembles coarse meal. Set aside. (Mixture will keep well in refrigerator.)

To make pastry, dissolve dry yeast in ¼ cup lukewarm water; then sprinkle mixture with 1 teaspoon sugar. In large mixer bowl, cream margarine and ⅔ cup sugar. Add yolks and salt, mix well. Add the dissolved yeast and about ½ cup of the flour; mix slowly with mixer. Combine evaporated milk with hot water to make 2 cups. Add milk to batter. Next, continue adding remaining flour, using mixer or stirring by hand with wooden spoon until dough is glossy. Cover; let rise in warm place until double in bulk, about one hour.

After dough has risen, pinch off portions of dough about the size of an egg. Use a tablespoon to shape dough into balls; place on greased baking sheets about an inch apart. Butter dough well; let rise until light. When dough has risen, make an indentation in each piece; and fill with cheese or fruit filling of choice. Sprinkle on Posipka topping; then bake at 375° for 15 minutes. Brush with butter after removing from oven, and move kolaches to a wire cooling rack.

Note: *Filling recipes appear on the next page.*

Lisa Ondrey

KOLACHE FILLINGS

Cheese filling:

2 cups (1 pint) small-curd
    cottage cheese
1 (8-ounce) package cream
    cheese
Pinch of salt

1 egg yolk
½ cup sugar
Grated rind from one lemon
½ teaspoon lemon extract
Cream of wheat cereal, if needed

Press liquid from cottage cheese, drain. Mix cottage cheese with cream cheese, salt, egg yolk, sugar, lemon rind and lemon extract. If filling is too moist, add a small amount of cream of wheat to absorb excess liquid. (Fills about 2 dozen kolaches.)

Prune filling:

1 pound dried prunes
½ teaspoon cinnamon

Heat prunes very slowly in just enough water to cover; cook until prunes are soft and tender. Let prunes cool, remove pits. Add ½ teaspoon cinnamon to prunes, and mix well by hand or with mixer. Do not over-mix or prunes will lose color. (Fills about 3 dozen kolaches.)

Apricot filling:

1 (10-ounce) package dried
    apricots
1½ to 1¾ cups sugar

Heat apricots slowly in just enough water to cover; cook until apricots are soft and water has been cooked out. Do not overcook or fruit will turn dark. Add sugar, and mash with potato masher until well blended. (Fills about 2 dozen kolaches.)

Note: Kolache recipe appears on the preceding page.

Lisa Ondrey

SOPAPILLAS DELIGHT

Serves 8-10

1¾ cups all-purpose flour
2 teaspoons baking powder
1 teaspoon salt
2 tablespoons shortening

¾ cup cold water
Oil for frying
Powder sugar
Honey

Sift flour, baking powder and salt in mixing bowl. Cut in shortening. Add cold water gradually; mix just enough to hold together. Place dough on floured board; knead until very smooth. Cover, and let dough rest for 5 minutes. On a floured board, roll dough out to about ⅛" thickness and cut into 3" squares. Drop sopapillas into deep fryer, 1 or 2 at a time. When they surface, fan with hot oil until dough begins to rise. Turn sopapillas, repeat on underside. Remove from oil when sopapillas turn light brown; drain on paper. Sprinkle with powdered sugar and serve with honey.

Delight Fails

BUÑUELOS (Mexican Pastry)

Serves 12

2 cups flour
1 teaspoon salt
⅛ teaspoon baking powder
⅓ cup shortening

½ cup hot water
Oil for frying
Cinnamon-sugar mixture, or
    powdered sugar

Combine flour, salt and baking powder. Add shortening, and use hands to evenly distribute within mixture. Add hot water, kneading well as quickly as possible, until dough rounds into a ball and bowl is clean. If mixture seems dry, add a little more warm water and knead well.

Form dough into balls about the size of golf-balls. Roll each ball out on floured surface until very thin, almost transparent. Stretch further by hand if necessary. (The thinner the dough, the crisper the buñuelo will be.) Place each buñuelo in hot oil; cook until golden brown, turning once. Drain on paper towel. Sprinkle buñuelos with cinnamon-sugar mixture or powdered sugar while still hot.

Leah Martin

OVEN-BAKED HERB RICE

Serves 8

3 tablespoons margarine
½ cup chopped onion (about 1 medium onion)
⅛ teaspoon cayenne pepper (or 4 drops hot pepper sauce)
2 cups uncooked rice
3 cups chicken broth

2 teaspoons salt (if saltless broth used)
2-3 parsley sprigs
1 bay leaf
4 sprigs fresh thyme (or ½ teaspoon dried)

Preheat oven to 400°. Make bouquet garni: place parsley sprigs, bay leaf and fresh thyme on cheesecloth or coffee filter. Gather edges together to form a bundle; secure with piece of string. Heat margarine in large oven-proof saucepan (2½-quart or larger). Add onion, sauté until translucent. Add rice; stir until grains are completely coated. Add salt (if needed), cayenne pepper and chicken broth. Place bouquet garni on top of rice. Let rice broth mixture come to a boil over high heat. Cover, place in preheated oven; bake 17 minutes. For drier rice, bake an additional 5 minutes. Discard bouquet garni before serving.

Note: *This dish has a nice, subtle flavor.*

Christy McConnell

PARMESAN OVEN-BAKED RICE

Serves 4

3 tablespoons butter or margarine
⅔ cup uncooked long grain rice
1 (14½-ounce) can chicken broth

¼ cup grated Parmesan cheese
2 tablespoons snipped parsley
½ teaspoon salt
Dash pepper

In medium skillet, melt butter over low heat. Add rice, cook and stir until rice is coated and light brown. Remove from heat; add chicken broth, Parmesan cheese, parsley, salt and pepper. Spoon into a greased 1-quart baking dish. Bake, covered, at 350° for 50 minutes, stirring after 30 minutes.

Becky Gilliland

MUSHROOM RICE CASSEROLE

Serves 8

½ cup (1 stick) margarine
1 medium onion, chopped
1 (4-ounce) can mushroom bits
  and stems, drained
1 tablespoon Worcestershire
  sauce

1 cup uncooked rice
1 (10¾-ounce) can consommé
  soup
1 soup can water

Sauté onion and mushrooms in margarine, add Worcestershire sauce. Add rice, soup and water. Mix together, place in glass dish; bake covered at 350° for 1 hour.

Patti Hoffmann

RICE DRESSING

Serves 8

4 cups cooked rice
2 tablespoons butter
1 cup chopped onion
1 cup chopped celery
1 tablespoon parsley
1 teaspoon sage
1 teaspoon thyme

1 cup milk
2 (10¾-ounce) cans condensed
  cream of mushroom soup
1 tablespoon salt
1 teaspoon pepper
1 cup chopped pecans

Sauté onions, celery, parsley, sage and thyme in butter. Mix all ingredients. Place in large baking dish; bake at 350° for 30 minutes.

Jan Davis

MEXICAN RICE

Serves 6

1 cup uncooked rice
¼ cup cooking oil
½ cup chopped onion
½ bell pepper, chopped
1 large tomato, peeled and
  chopped

1 teaspoon garlic salt
1 teaspoon salt
¼ teaspoon black pepper
2 cups hot water
2 teaspoons instant bouillon

Brown rice in hot oil. Mix onion, bell pepper, tomato, garlic salt, salt and pepper; add to rice. Cook for 1 minute. Dissolve bouillon in hot water, add broth to rice. Stir once, then reduce heat to simmer. Cover and cook for 30 minutes, or until rice is tender.

Leah Martin

EASY DIRTY RICE

Serves 10

1 pound ground beef
1 beef bouillon cube
¼ cup hot water
1 medium bell pepper, chopped
1 (10¾-ounces) can French
   onion soup

1 (10¾-ounce) golden
   mushroom soup
1 cup uncooked white rice
¼ cup parsley flakes
1 can mushroom steak sauce
Dash red pepper

Brown beef. Dissolve bouillon cube in water. Combine all ingredients and mix well; place in a 13"x9"x2" casserole dish. Cover dish with foil; bake at 350° for 1 hour, or until rice is cooked.

Lisa Solis

JALAPEÑO RICE

Serves 10-12

1 cup uncooked rice
¼ cup (½ stick) butter
⅓ cup chopped green onions
¼ teaspoon oregano

⅛ cup grated Parmesan or
   Romano cheese
½ roll of jalapeño cheese, diced
Salt to taste

Cook rice according to package directions. Melt butter, add onions and simmer until soft. Add oregano and Parmesan cheese. Dice jalapeño cheese and add to mixture. Pour over rice and toss lightly with fork. Bake at 400° about 25 minutes, or until cheese melts. This dish may be prepared a day in advance.

Jackie Brewer

JONSI'S BROCCOLI CASSEROLE

Serves 8-10

2 (10-ounce) packages frozen
   chopped broccoli
1 cup cooked rice
2 eggs, beaten
2 cups mayonnaise

2 (10¾-ounce) cans condensed
   cream of mushroom soup
1½ cups (6-ounces) grated sharp
   Cheddar cheese
1½ cups sliced almonds

Prepare broccoli according to directions; drain. Mix all ingredients; bake in a 13"x9"x2" buttered baking dish at 350° for 45 minutes. This casserole freezes well.

Jonsi Elam

BOILED EGG CASSEROLE

Serves 12-15

18 boiled eggs
½ pound bacon, fried and
    crumbled
¼ cup (½ stick) butter
¼ cup flour
1 cup half-and-half cream
1 cup milk
4 cups (1-pound) grated sharp
    Cheddar cheese
¼ teaspoon salt
Dash pepper
½ teaspoon oregano
1 clove garlic, crushed
¼ teaspoon thyme
¼ teaspoon chopped parsley
1½ cups buttered bread crumbs
    (or more, to taste)

Boil eggs, peel and slice. Fry and crumble bacon. Melt butter in saucepan, add flour to make paste. Slowly add half-and-half and milk, stir constantly until sauce thickens. Add cheese, stir until melted. Add seasonings and parsley. Put sauce in a 13"x9"x2" baking dish. Layer sliced eggs over sauce; sprinkle bacon over eggs. Top with buttered crumbs. Bake at 350° for 20-30 minutes. This dish can be prepared a day in advance.

Kathy Carr

MEXICAN BREAKFAST CASSEROLE

Serves 10-12

1 pound ground sausage
2 dozen large eggs
2 (16-ounce) containers sour
    cream
1 cup picante sauce
2 cups (8-ounces) shredded
    Cheddar cheese
2 cups (8-ounces) shredded
    Monterey Jack cheese
¼ cup fresh chopped cilantro
2 large tomatoes, cut in wedges

Crumble and brown sausage in skillet; drain grease. Arrange sausage in a 13"x9"x2" baking dish. Layer ½ of the Cheddar cheese and ½ of the Monterey Jack cheese on top of the sausage; pour picante sauce on top. Mix eggs and sour cream until smooth; lightly scramble in a skillet over low heat. Pour egg mixture on top of picante sauce. Cover with remaining cheese. Garnish with cilantro and tomato wedges. Bake at 350° for 1 hour.

Hint: *Serve with a fruit salad to make an easy meal for a large crowd.*

Karen Johnson

GIGI'S SCRAMBLED EGG CASSEROLE

Serves 12-15

1 cup cubed ham or Canadian
  bacon
¼ cup chopped green onions
7 tablespoons butter or
  margarine, divided

1 dozen eggs, beaten
1 (4-ounce) can sliced
  mushrooms, drained
2¼ cups soft bread crumbs
⅛ teaspoon paprika

Cheese Sauce:

2 tablespoons butter or
  margarine
2½ tablespoons all-purpose flour
2 cups milk

¼ teaspoon salt
⅛ teaspoon pepper
1 (4-ounce) package shredded
  process American cheese

Make cheese sauce: melt 2 tablespoons butter in heavy saucepan over low heat. Blend in flour, and cook 1 minute. Gradually add milk; cook over medium heat until thickened, stirring constantly. Add salt, pepper and cheese, stirring until cheese melts and mixture is smooth. (Yields 2½ cups.) Use large skillet to sauté ham and green onions in 3 tablespoons butter until onion is tender. Add eggs; cook over medium-high heat; stirring to form soft curds. When eggs are set, stir in drained mushrooms and cheese sauce. Spoon eggs into a greased 13"x9"x2" baking pan. Combine 4 tablespoons (¼ cup) melted butter and bread crumbs, mixing well. Spread topping evenly over egg mixture. Sprinkle with paprika. Cover, and chill overnight. Uncover, and bake at 350° for 30 minutes or until heated through.

Note: *Since this dish is prepared the night before, it makes meal-time less hectic when company is visiting. It is great for brunch or a holiday breakfast.*

Peggy McKnight

HASHBROWN SCRAMBLE

Serves 6-8

1 pound sausage
2 cups frozen hash browns
1 cup (4-ounces) grated Cheddar
  cheese

6-8 eggs
2 cups milk
1 teaspoon salt

Brown sausage; drain. Cook hash browns according to package directions. Layer sausage, potatoes and cheese in a 2-quart casserole dish. Mix eggs, milk and salt; pour over other ingredients. Bake at 350° for 45 minutes. This dish can be prepared ahead of time and refrigerated until ready to bake.

Deani Farrar

ARLETTE'S QUICHE LORRAINE

Serves 4-6

1 (8-inch) pastry shell, partially
  cooked
8 ham slices
3 eggs
1 cup whipping cream

Dash of salt, white pepper
Pinch of nutmeg
1 cup (4-ounces) grated Swiss
  cheese
2 tablespoons butter

Partially cook shell at 350° for 10 minutes. Dice ham; place in bottom of pastry shell. In a bowl, beat eggs, cream and seasonings with a wire whisk. Add grated cheese and mix well. Pour into pastry shell, and dot with butter on top. Put in upper third of oven and bake at 375° for 45 minutes or until quiche has puffed and is golden. Do not cut quiche while it is hot. Wait 10 minutes before slicing.

Note: *Milk can be used instead of cream, and cheese can be omitted. Seafood, vegetables or bacon can be substituted for ham. This recipe comes from a cooking class taught by Arlette Hardoin.*

Jody Epps

SHRIMP QUICHE

Serves 6

¾ pound cooked shrimp,
  chopped
1 cup fresh sliced mushrooms
¼ cup chopped green onions
¼ cup (½ stick) margarine,
  melted
4 eggs, well beaten

1½ cups half-and-half cream
1 teaspoon salt
⅛ teaspoon dry mustard
Pinch nutmeg
1 cup (4-ounces) grated
  mozzarella cheese
1 unbaked 9-inch pie shell

Cook and chop shrimp. In a small saucepan, cook mushrooms and green onions in margarine until tender. In large bowl, combine eggs, cream, salt, dry mustard, nutmeg and cheese. Fold in shrimp. Pour mixture into pie shell. Bake at 400° for 15 minutes. Reduce heat to 300° and continue to bake for 30 minutes or until knife inserted in center comes out clean. Let stand for 5 minutes before serving.

Polly Galloway

RICOTTA LASAGNA ROLLS

Serves 6-8

1 (8-ounce) package lasagna, cooked and drained
1 (8-ounce) package cream cheese, softened
¼ cup (½ stick) butter or margarine
1 egg, slightly beaten

1 (16-ounce) carton ricotta cheese
¼ cup chopped parsley
½ teaspoon salt
⅛ teaspoon pepper
½ pound mozzarella cheese, sliced into thin strips
¼ cup grated Parmesan cheese

Tomato Sauce:

2 (6-ounce) cans tomato paste
3 cups water
2 tablespoons chopped parsley
1½ teaspoons salt

1 teaspoon sugar
½ teaspoon oregano
½ teaspoon basil
⅛ teaspoon pepper

Heat sauce ingredients in saucepan, stirring to blend well. Simmer for 20 minutes, stirring occasionally.

While sauce is cooking, prepare lasagna rolls. Cream together cream cheese and butter. Stir in egg, ricotta cheese, parsley, salt and pepper; blend thoroughly. Spread 2-3 tablespoons of filling on each cooked lasagna noodle. Starting at narrowest end, lightly roll up each piece. Place rolls open-side down in greased shallow baking pan. Pour sauce over rolls, top with mozzarella and Parmesan cheeses. Bake uncovered at 350° for 50-60 minutes.

Kristi Abild

~ Storing cheese: Store cheese tightly wrapped in the coldest part of the refrigerator. Double-wrap strong cheeses so their flavor doesn't spread to other foods.

~ Keep heat low: Cheese, like any protein food, becomes tough and stringy if overcooked. Use low to medium heat, and heat just until the cheese melts.

SPINACH SOUFFLÉ

Serves 4-5

1 (10-ounce) package frozen
    chopped spinach
2 eggs, beaten
½ cup milk
½ package dry onion soup mix

¼ cup (½ stick) butter, melted
1 cup (4-ounces) grated sharp
    Cheddar cheese
Salt and pepper to taste

Cook and drain spinach. Mix well with all remaining ingredients. Bake uncovered in greased 1½-quart casserole at 350° for 40-45 minutes, or until center "sets."

Bonnie Novosad

ONION PIE

Serves 6

4 tablespoons plus 2 teaspoons
    butter, divided
1 cup finely chopped Ritz
    cracker crumbs
2 cups sweet onion, thinly sliced
2 eggs
¾ cup milk

¾ teaspoon salt
¾ teaspoon pepper
¼ cup (1-ounce) grated Cheddar
    cheese
Paprika
Fresh parsley

Melt 4 tablespoons butter in a small saucepan; mix in cracker crumbs. Press crumbs into pie plate to make crust. In large skillet, melt 2 teaspoons butter. Sauté onions until clear but not brown. Spoon onion mixture into crust. In a small bowl, beat eggs with milk, salt and pepper. Pour over onions. Top with cheese and paprika. Bake in preheated 350° oven 30 minutes. After baking, sprinkle parsley on top.

Karen Parrett

~ **Cooking tip:** *To help prevent foods from sticking, try first heating the pan over low heat. Next heat the oil or butter, then add the food.*

BROCCOLI WITH ANGEL HAIR

✓ *Quick to fix* *Serves 4*

1 head of broccoli florets
1 package fresh angel hair pasta
4 tablespoons butter
⅓ cup olive oil

1 clove garlic, sliced
1 cup white wine
Parmesan cheese, freshly grated

Blanch broccoli for 3 minutes; remove from heat and rinse under cold water to stop cooking. Set aside. (This step can be done in advance.)

Cook pasta according to package directions. In a large, heavy skillet, melt butter with olive oil. Sauté garlic for 1 minute. Add wine, and cook 3 minutes. Add broccoli to wine sauce, and toss with hot pasta. Serve with freshly grated Parmesan cheese.

Hint: *This dish is so easy, and makes a great fast meal. For a light summer meal, serve with an avocado half filled with French dressing, and fresh-sliced strawberries.*

Ruth Bondurant

SPINACH-GARLIC FETTUCCINE

Serves 6

4 cups fresh spinach
6 ounces fettuccine
¼ cup olive oil
3 large or 4 small cloves garlic,
   mashed and peeled

Salt and freshly ground white
   pepper to taste
Dash freshly grated nutmeg
¼ cup freshly grated Parmesan
   cheese (or to taste)

Wash and dry spinach, remove stems and tear leaves into bite-size pieces. Cook fettuccine in large pot of boiling salted water until just tender; drain well. Keep warm. Heat oil in large skillet over medium heat; sauté garlic until tender, about 5 minutes or until oil is fragrant. Add prepared spinach to oil, and cook over medium heat about 5 minutes or until limp and tender, stirring occasionally. Season with salt, white pepper and nutmeg. Add spinach to cooked fettuccine.

Katy Engen

BEAN CHALUPAS

Serves 5

10 corn tortillas
¼ cup cooking oil
1 (16-ounce) can refried beans
¾ cup (3-ounces) grated
  Cheddar and/or Monterey
  Jack cheese

1 cup lettuce, shredded or torn
  into bite-size pieces
1 tomato, finely chopped

Heat oil in small frying pan, fry tortillas one at a time until crisp. (Turn tortilla several times. Tortilla will stop sizzling when it is crisp.) Drain tortillas on paper towels. Heat refried beans in microwave or stove; spread hot beans on each tortilla. Top with cheese and place under broiler just long enough to melt cheese. Top with lettuce and tomato.

Note: Create a deluxe chalupa by adding extra toppings such as picante sauce, taco meat, sliced olives, sour cream or guacamole.

Leah Martin

LEMON AND OIL CHALUPA DRESSING

✓ *Quick to fix*   *Serves 4*

¼ cup salad oil
¼ cup lemon juice

2 teaspoons garlic salt
1 teaspoon salt

Mix all ingredients in a salad dressing bottle; shake well to mix. Use on tacos and chalupas; or as a dressing for lettuce salads.

Leah Martin

~ Healthy tradition: Granola was eaten as a health food more than 100 years ago. Back then, "granula" was a mixture of crumbly grains. Today there are many versions. Make your own by combining your favorite grains, fruits and nuts.

Soups, Stews
and Beans

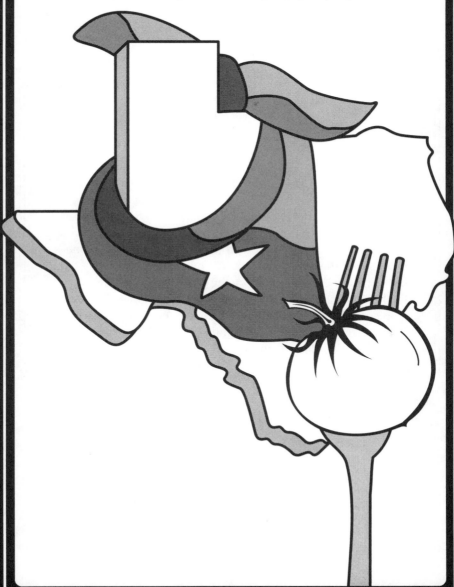

TOY SALE
1984 - to present

The children of needy families can enjoy happier holidays thanks to the annual Junior Service League Toy Sale. Originally this was a Bargain Box Project with all members contributing toys and time towards this project. In 1988 this became a Provisional (first-year) project. All members still donate toys but pricing and preparations for the early December sale are left to the Provisionals. Invitations, issued in cooperation with elementary school nurses, and churches who know local needs first-hand, go to hundreds of families who might otherwise be unable to provide Christmas toys for their children.

FRENCH ONION SOUP

Serves 4

4 medium onions, sliced
2 tablespoons margarine or
  butter
2 (10¾-ounce) cans condensed
  beef broth
1½ cups water
1 bay leaf

⅛ teaspoon pepper
⅛ teaspoon dried thyme leaves
4 slices French bread, ¾-1 inch
  thick
1 cup (4-ounces) shredded Swiss
  cheese
¼ cup grated Parmesan cheese

Cook onion in margarine in covered 3-quart saucepan over low heat, stirring occasionally, until tender (20-30 minutes). Add beef broth, water, bay leaf, pepper and thyme. Heat to boiling; reduce heat. Cover and simmer 15 minutes. Set oven control to broil and/or 550°. Place bread slices on cookie sheet; broil with tops about 5 inches from heat until golden brown. Place bread in 4 ovenproof bowls. Add broth, top with Swiss cheese. Sprinkle with Parmesan cheese. Place bowls on cookie sheet. Broil with cheese about 5 inches from heat just until cheese is melted and golden brown, 1-2 minutes.

Sandy Carlberg

CREAM OF ONION SOUP

Serves 6

4 large white onions
¼ cup (½ stick) margarine
¼ cup flour
4 cups chicken broth

1 cup light cream
¼ teaspoon white pepper
1 cup (4-ounces) grated mild
  Cheddar cheese

Slice peeled onions. Place in saucepan, cover with water and cook until tender. Drain water from onions. Puree onions in blender. Melt margarine in a large pan. Stir in flour and cook 3 minutes, stirring constantly (do not brown). Gradually stir in chicken broth. Bring to a boil; add pureed onions. Simmer 15 minutes, then add light cream. Season with white pepper. Heat soup until hot, but not boiling. Sprinkle with grated cheese.

Marty Dunn

EASY ONION CHEESE SOUP

✓ *Quick to fix* *Serves 4-6*

1 cup chopped onion	**Dash pepper**
3 tablespoons butter	**4 cups milk**
3 tablespoons flour	**2 cups shredded American**
½ teaspoon salt	**cheese**

Cook chopped onion in butter until tender but not brown. Blend in flour, salt and pepper. Add milk and heat to boiling, stirring constantly. Remove from heat; add shredded cheese and stir soup until cheese is melted.

Susie Hanchey

CREAMY CHEESE SOUP

Serves 8-10

⅓ cup chopped carrots	**4 cups chicken broth**
⅓ cup chopped celery	**4 cups milk**
1 cup chopped green onion	**1 (15-ounce) jar Cheez Whiz**
2 cups water	**Salt and pepper to taste**
1 medium white onion, chopped	**½ teaspoon cayenne pepper**
½ cup (1 stick) margarine	**1 tablespoon prepared mustard**
1 cup flour	

Boil carrots, celery and green onion in 2 cups water for 5 minutes. Sauté white onion in ½ cup of margarine. Add flour, and blend well. In separate pan, heat milk and chicken broth. Stir briskly into flour paste, using wire whisk. Add Cheez Whiz, salt, pepper and cayenne pepper. Stir in mustard and the boiled vegetables, including water the vegetables cooked in. Bring to a boil; then serve immediately. Serve with whole wheat crackers.

Debbie Gentry

CHEDDAR CHEESE SOUP

Serves 10

1 cup finely chopped onion
1 cup grated carrot
1 cup finely chopped celery
2 quarts water
2 ounces chicken base
1 (12½-ounce) can chicken stock
1 cup flour

1 cup (2 sticks) margarine, melted
1 (12-ounce) can evaporated milk
2 cups (8-ounces) shredded Cheddar cheese
White pepper to taste

Add water and vegetables in pot; cook until tender. Add chicken stock and base; cook for 30 minutes. Mix flour and melted butter, add to vegetables. Add milk, cheese and pepper; cook until cheese melts.

Polly Galloway

SHARON'S CHEESE SOUP

Serves 8-10

3 cups chopped potatoes
2 cups water
1 cup chopped celery
½ cup carrot slices
½ cup chopped onion
2 teaspoons parsley flakes

2 chicken bouillon cubes
1 teaspoon salt
Dash pepper
3 cups milk
4 tablespoons flour
1 pound Velveeta cheese, cubed

In a large saucepan, combine potatoes, water, celery, carrots, onion, parsley flakes, bouillon cubes and seasonings. Mix well and cover. Simmer 15-20 minutes or until vegetables are tender. Gradually add milk to flour, mixing until well blended. Add milk mixture to vegetables. Cook until thickened. Add Velveeta cheese cubes and stir until melted. Do not overcook.

Sharon Shaver

VEGETABLE-CHEESE SOUP

Serves 10

1½ pounds potatoes, cubed
1 cup sliced carrots
1 cup sliced celery
1 cup coarsely chopped onion
5 ounces frozen chopped
   broccoli
½ head cabbage, shredded
1 envelope butter substitute
   buds
5 chicken bouillon cubes
8 cups water, divided
1 pound Velveeta cheese

Cube potatoes, slice and chop other vegetables. In an 8-quart Dutch oven, dissolve butter buds in 1 cup of water. Add remaining ingredients except cheese, and cook over medium heat for 1½ hours. Cube Velveeta cheese. Lower heat to simmer, add cubed Velveeta. Continue stirring until cheese melts and soup thickens.

Lisa Solis

YANCY'S CHEESE SOUP

Serves 6-8

1 carrot, diced
1 potato, diced
½ cup diced onion
½ cup chopped bell pepper
4 tablespoons butter
2 cups chicken broth
1 cup water
1 cup milk
1 tablespoon parsley flakes
4 tablespoons flour
¼ cup milk
1 (8-ounce) package Velveeta
   cheese

Sauté diced carrot, potato, onion and bell pepper in butter in large pan. Add chicken broth, water and 1 cup milk. Cook until vegetables are tender, about 20 minutes. Mash vegetables slightly. Add parsley. Dissolve flour in ¼ cup milk and add to mixture. Add cheese and cook until cheese melts.

Dee Eddins

SWISS CHEESE-BROCCOLI SOUP

Yields 2 quarts

2 cups chopped broccoli
3 medium carrots sliced
1 medium onion, chopped
1 small clove minced garlic
1 (12½-ounce) can chicken
    broth

2 cups water
1 teaspoon salt
½ teaspoon pepper
1½ cups milk
1½ cups flour
2 cups diced Swiss cheese

Combine all but the milk, flour and cheese in a 3-quart saucepan. Bring to a boil, reduce heat and cover. Simmer for about 15 minutes. Combine ½ cup of milk and the flour until well blended. Gradually add to soup with the rest of the milk. Continue cooking over medium high until thick, stirring constantly to prevent sticking. Mix in the diced cheese until melted. Let stand 5 minutes before serving.

Sue Allen

BROCCOLI CHEESE SOUP

Serves 12

3 cups chopped broccoli
6 tablespoons butter
6 tablespoons flour
Salt and pepper to taste

3 cups milk
2 tablespoons dehydrated onion
¾ pound Velveeta cheese

Cook and drain broccoli. Melt butter, stir in flour, salt and pepper. Add milk; stir constantly until thickened. Add chopped broccoli and onion. Stir and heat almost to boiling. Turn off heat and add cheese. Reheat soup over low heat after cheese has melted.

Dina Dornburg

BROCCOLI CHOWDER

Serves 6-8

2 pounds fresh broccoli
2 (12½-ounce) cans chicken
   broth
3 cups milk
1 cup chopped cooked ham
2 teaspoons salt

¼ teaspoon pepper
1 cup light cream
2 cups (8-ounces) grated Swiss
   cheese
¼ cup (½ stick) butter

Pour 1 can of chicken broth into large Dutch oven; cook broccoli, covered, in broth for about 7 minutes or until tender. Remove broccoli from broth, cool and chop coarsely. Add remaining can of chicken broth, milk, ham, salt and pepper to broth in the Dutch oven. Bring to a boil over medium heat, stirring occasionally. Stir in cream, cheese, butter and chopped broccoli. Heat to serving temperature. Do not boil.

Note: *This is not a thick soup. Cheese will be stringy.*

Cheri McBurnett

QUICK CHICKEN AND CORN CHOWDER

✓ *Quick to fix* *Serves 4*

1 tablespoon butter
1 medium onion, finely chopped
1 large potato, diced
1 cup chicken broth
1 cup cooked diced chicken

1 (17-ounce) can cream-style
   corn
2 cups milk
Salt and pepper to taste

Cook onion in butter until yellowed. Add potato and chicken broth; boil gently, covered. Cook until potato is soft (about 10 minutes). Stir in chicken, corn and milk. Add salt and pepper to taste. Reheat over medium heat. Do not boil. Recipe can be doubled or tripled easily.

Marilyn Woody

~ **Cooking tip:** *Use a blender to smooth a lumpy gravy or white sauce. Start with about ½ cup in the blender, then gradually add remaining gravy or sauce.*

MOTHER-IN-LAW CORN CHOWDER

Serves 12

4 slices bacon, diced
1 large onion, chopped
3 cups chopped potatoes
3 cups water
3 tablespoons butter or
  margarine, melted
¼ cup flour

2 cups whole milk
2 (16-ounce) cans whole kernel
  corn
2 cups diced cooked ham
2 teaspoons parsley
2 teaspoons salt
¼ teaspoon pepper

In a large pot, fry bacon until crisp; add onion and sauté until tender. Add potatoes and water, cook until fork-tender. In a medium mixing bowl combine butter, flour and milk. Empty milk mixture, corn, ham, parsley, salt and pepper into potato pot. Cook over medium heat, but do not boil. Serve hot.

Note: *Use whole milk for thicker consistency. Soup can be frozen.*

Linda St. Lawrence

CREAMY CORN SOUP

Makes 6 cups

2 tablespoons margarine
1 medium celery stalk, chopped
1 small onion, chopped
2 (10-ounce) packages frozen
  whole kernel corn

2 chicken flavor bouillon cubes
½ teaspoon salt
2 cups water
1 cup half-and-half cream

In a 3-quart saucepan over medium heat, cook celery and onion in hot margarine until very tender, stirring occasionally. Add corn, bouillon, salt and water, heat to boiling. Reduce heat to low, cover and simmer 5 minutes.

With slotted spoon, remove ¾ cup corn mixture to medium bowl. Spoon remaining corn mixture, ⅓ at a time, into blender; cover and blend at low speed until smooth. Pour mixture into bowl with reserved corn mixture. Return corn mixture to saucepan; stir in cream. Heat over medium heat. Garnish with parsley, if desired.

Hint: *Serve as the first course in a Mexican meal of burritos or fajitas.*

Carol Bohley

ERWTENSOEP (Dutch Split Pea Soup)

Serves 6-8

1 (16-ounce) box dry split peas
1 pound beef, cubed for stew
8 cups water (or more, if desired)
2 beef bouillon cubes
6-7 medium potatoes, peeled and cubed

1½ cups finely chopped vegetables (carrots, cauliflower, cabbage, etc.)
2 leeks, chopped
1 pound smoked sausage, cut in 1-inch chunks

Wash peas well. In a very large saucepan, combine peas, beef, water and bouillon; cook over medium heat. While beef cooks, chop vegetables (in food processor, if desired). Add potatoes, vegetables and leeks to soup; simmer gently for 1-2 hours. Ten minutes before serving, add sausage; heat thoroughly.

Note: *Serve with crusty bread, or follow the Dutch tradition of serving with "pannekoeken," a thick crêpe.*

Carol Bohley

GET-WELL-SOON LENTIL SOUP

Serves 6-8

1 (16-ounce) package dried lentils
½ pound Polish sausage
½ pound pan sausage
4 cups (1 quart) canned tomatoes
1 onion, chopped
3 quarts water

2 beef bouillon cubes
1 teaspoon dried parsley
1 teaspoon salt
½ teaspoon black pepper
¼ teaspoon white pepper
¼ teaspoon garlic powder
⅓ cup red wine

Wash lentils. Brown sausage and drain. Mix all ingredients, except wine, in a large pot. Bring to a boil; cook over high heat for 15 minutes. Reduce heat; simmer, covered, for about 1½ hours. Add wine during the last 15-20 minutes. Left-over pork roast can be substituted for sausage.

Note: *Members of my family always ask for my lentil soup when they're sick. Served with Broccoli Cornbread, it makes a great cold-weather supper.*

Delores Smith

GAZPACHO ANDALUZ

Serves 6

5 tablespoons olive oil
2 cloves garlic, minced
½ small onion, chopped
1 (30-ounce) can tomatoes,
    undrained (or equivalent fresh
    tomatoes)
½ green pepper, diced

1 small cucumber, peeled and
    chopped
¼ cup red wine vinegar
1 (14-ounce) can tomato juice,
    chilled
Salt and pepper to taste

Condiments:

Green pepper, finely chopped
Cucumber, peeled and chopped
Onions, chopped

Tomatoes, chopped
Hard-cooked eggs, chopped
Croutons

In a blender, combine oil, garlic, onion, tomatoes, green pepper, cucumber and vinegar. Whirl until smooth. Pour mixture into 2½-quart bowl. Stir in tomato juice, add salt and pepper to taste. Chill until ready to serve. Use chilled bowls. Sprinkle each serving of soup with croutons and other condiments, according to taste of person being served.

Note: *I collected this authentic gazpacho recipe while living in Spain. Serve with an omelet or salad and French bread for a wonderful summer supper.*

Judy Robinson

PANTRY SOUP

Serves 6-8

1½ pounds ground chuck
1 medium onion, chopped
3 (19-ounce) cans minestrone
    soup
2 (15-ounce) cans ranch-style
    beans

1-2 (10-ounce) cans of tomatoes
    with green chilies (to taste)
1 (28-ounce) can whole
    tomatoes, chopped, undrained

Sauté onion with meat. Drain excess fat; add remaining ingredients and simmer 1½ to 2 hours.

Terrie Lumsden

PESTO MINESTRONE SOUP

❤ *Heart healthy*   *Serves 8*

1 tablespoon plus 1 teaspoon
  olive oil
10 ounces potatoes, pared and
  cubed
1 medium onion, thinly sliced,
  separated into rings
1 cup chopped tomatoes

½ cup green beans
½ cup diced celery
½ cup diced carrot
6 cups water
1 cup chicken broth
1½ ounces small pasta shells

Pesto:

¾ cup fresh basil leaves or fresh
  spinach, packed
¼ cup chopped parsley

1 tablespoon plus 1 teaspoon
  olive oil
1 tablespoon Parmesan cheese
1 garlic clove

In a 4-quart saucepan, heat oil and add potatoes, onion, tomatoes, beans, carrots and celery. Cook, stirring frequently, 4-6 minutes or until just tender. Add 6 cups water and broth; bring to a boil. Reduce heat to low and simmer 45 minutes. Stir in pasta shells; cook 8-10 minutes, until pasta is tender. Combine Pesto ingredients and add to soup. Simmer 5 minutes.

Janice Keller

BAKED POTATO SOUP

Serves 4

6 large potatoes, peeled and
  cubed
1 small onion, chopped
Salt and pepper to taste
1 (12-ounce) can evaporated
  milk

½ cup (1 stick) margarine
¼ cup (1-ounce) grated Cheddar
  cheese
Chopped green onion
Bacon or bacon bits
Sour cream

Combine potatoes and onion in large saucepan or Dutch oven. Cover with water by ½ inch, and boil until potatoes are tender. Add evaporated milk and margarine. When ready to serve, place 1 tablespoon grated cheese in each bowl. Pour soup over cheese and top with green onions, bacon and sour cream to taste.

Tonya Heard

RUTH'S POTATO SOUP

Serves 4

3-4 medium potatoes, chopped
¼ cup chopped onion
1 teaspoon garlic salt (or to
 taste)
½ teaspoon celery salt (or to
 taste)

¼ teaspoon pepper
1½ tablespoons flour
1 cup milk
2 tablespoons margarine
1 tablespoon parsley

Chop potatoes into small pieces, place in large saucepan. Add chopped onion; cover with water. Add garlic and celery salt. Bring to a boil and cook potatoes until tender. Mix flour in a small amount of water; add milk and blend. Add flour-milk blend to pot when potatoes are tender. Add margarine, and simmer until thickened. Sprinkle with parsley for color.

Ruth Seiwell

CHEESE-POTATO SOUP

Serves 6-8

6-7 medium potatoes, cubed
3 carrots, sliced
1 celery stick, chopped
1 onion, chopped
Salt and pepper to taste
1 teaspoon parsley
5 cups water

2 chicken bouillon cubes
⅔ stick unsalted margarine
1 pound Velveeta cheese, cubed
1 (13-ounce) can evaporated
 milk
1 clove crushed garlic (optional)

Combine potatoes, carrots, celery, onion, salt, pepper, parsley, water and bouillon cubes; cook over medium heat until vegetables are tender. Add margarine, stir to dissolve. Remove pan from burner; add cubed cheese and evaporated milk. Season with garlic, if desired. Simmer to melt cheese, stirring constantly.

Barbara Allen

~ Cooking tip: Use a lid on pans to trap steam, retain vitamins and conserve energy.

HASHBROWN SOUP

Serves 12

1 (32-ounce) package frozen hashbrowns
1 (16-ounce) can Veg-All mixed vegetables
4 cups water
1½ tablespoons dried parsley flakes
3 tablespoons chicken bouillon granules
2 cups (1 pint) half-and-half cream
2 heaping tablespoons cornstarch
2 cups (8-ounces) grated Cheddar cheese

Put hashbrowns, vegetables, water, parsley flakes and bouillon granules in a large pot; bring to a boil. Boil for 5 minutes. Mix together the cream and cornstarch; add to soup. Stir constantly until thickened. Serve topped with grated cheese.

Tammi Blevins/ Barbara Monical

TACO SOUP

Serves 4-6

1 pound lean ground beef
1 envelope taco seasoning mix
1 onion, chopped
1 (16-ounce) can pinto beans, undrained
1 (16-ounce) can kidney beans, undrained
1 (16-ounce) can golden hominy, undrained
1 (17-ounce) can cream-style corn
1 (14-ounce) can diced stewed tomatoes, undrained
1 (10-ounce) can diced tomatoes with chiles (optional)
1 envelope Ranch-style dressing mix
Tortilla chips
1 cup (4-ounces) grated Cheddar or Monterey Jack cheese

Brown ground beef and chopped onion; drain. Add taco seasoning, mix thoroughly. Add without draining the cans of beans, hominy, corn and tomatoes. Stir in the dry Ranch dressing mix. Simmer over low heat until bubbly. Serve over tortilla chips and top with grated cheese.

Note: *Replace meat with 1 cup cooked rice, if desired.*

Marilyn Matthews/ Julie Zimmerman

TORTILLA SOUP

Serves 6

1 onion, chopped
1 jalapeño pepper, chopped
2 cloves garlic, minced
1 (14-ounce) can stewed
   tomatoes
4 cups chicken or beef stock
1 (10¾-ounce) can condensed
   tomato soup
1 teaspoon cumin
1 teaspoon chili powder

Salt and pepper to taste
½ teaspoon lemon pepper
2 teaspoons Worcestershire
   sauce
4 corn tortillas, sautéed lightly
1 avocado, peeled, cubed
¾ cup (3-ounces) grated
   Cheddar or Monterey Jack
   cheese
6 tablespoons sour cream

Sauté onion, jalapeño pepper, garlic and tomatoes in large kettle for several minutes. Add all remaining ingredients except tortillas, avocado, sour cream and cheese. Simmer 1 hour. About 10-20 minutes before serving, tear sautéed tortillas into bite-size pieces; add to soup. Place cubed avocado and grated cheese in bowls and ladle soup on top. Top with sour cream.

Note: *Chicken can be added to soup. Substitute canned tomatoes with green chiles for stewed tomatoes and jalapeños, if desired. This dish tastes great the next day.*

Janet Steffler

KATHY'S CHILI

Serves 8-12

2 pounds cubed beef or venison
1 large onion, chopped
2-4 tablespoons vegetable oil
2 (10-ounce) cans tomatoes with
   green chiles
½ teaspoon cumin

1 tablespoon oregano
1 clove garlic, minced
½ bottle Gebhardt chili powder
   (or less, to taste)
Salt and pepper to taste

Sauté onions in oil. Add meat, and brown. Add tomatoes, cumin, oregano, garlic, chili powder, salt and pepper. Cook over low heat for 2 hours.

Kathy Creel

SEAFOOD BISQUE

Serves 4-6

½ pound raw shrimp, peeled and deveined
1 (6-ounce) can crab meat
3 tablespoons minced celery
3 tablespoons chopped green onions and tops
2 tablespoons minced bell pepper
½ cup (1 stick) margarine, melted

1 (10¾-ounce) can condensed cream of shrimp soup
1 (13-ounce) can evaporated milk
½ cup milk
½ teaspoon salt
⅛ teaspoon pepper
½ teaspoon thyme
2 tablespoons dry sherry or cooking sherry

Cut large shrimp in half. Remove any remaining shell or cartilage from crab meat. Cook celery, onions and bell pepper in margarine until tender. Add shrimp and crab. Cook over low heat until shrimp turn pink. Add remaining ingredients and heat to a near boil. Serve immediately.

Polly Galloway

CREAMY SHRIMP AND AVOCADO BISQUE

Serves 10

2 (10¾-ounce) cans condensed cream of asparagus soup
2 (10¾-ounce) cans condensed cream of potato soup
1 teaspoon curry powder
2 soup cans of milk

2 soup cans of half-and-half cream
2 cups cooked shrimp
1 avocado, peeled, chopped
2 tablespoons minced chives

Combine soups and curry in a large, heavy saucepan. Stir in milk and cream. Set over low heat until thoroughly heated, stirring occasionally. Mix in shrimp and heat thoroughly. Do not boil. Pour into soup tureen. Gently stir in avocado. Sprinkle with chives. Serve at once.

Christy Spence

~ **How to select fish:** *When buying whole, fresh fish, look for bright, clear, bulging eyes; and elastic flesh that springs back when pressed.*

QUICK AND EASY GUMBO

✓ *Quick to fix*   *Serves 6*

½ cup chopped onion
½ cup chopped green pepper
1¾ cups water, divided
1 (28-ounce) can tomatoes
½ teaspoon minced garlic
¼ teaspoon dried rosemary,
  crushed

¼ teaspoon paprika
¼ teaspoon pepper
1 (6¼-ounce) double-packet
  quick-cooking long grain
  rice/wild rice mix
1 pound shrimp, peeled

In a large saucepan, combine onion, green pepper and ¼ cup water. Bring to a boil, then reduce heat, cover, and simmer for 3-5 minutes. Cut up tomatoes and add undrained to onion mixture along with garlic, rosemary, paprika and pepper. Stir in 1½ cups water and both packets of rice mix. Bring mixture to boiling. Add shrimp, return to boiling, then reduce heat. Cover; simmer for 4-5 minutes or until rice is cooked and shrimp turns pink.

Nancy Germano

SEAFOOD CHOWDER

Yields 12 cups

4 medium onions, chopped
1 large green pepper, chopped
¼ cup vegetable oil
2 tablespoons all-purpose flour
3 (14½-ounce) cans stewed
  tomatoes, undrained
1 tablespoon celery salt
1 teaspoon garlic powder
1 teaspoon sugar

1 teaspoon hot sauce
½ teaspoon pepper
2 pounds fresh medium shrimp,
  cleaned
½ pound crab meat
½ pint oysters, drained
1 large fish fillet, cut in bite-size
  pieces (optional)

Sauté onion and green pepper in a large saucepan until tender. Add flour, stirring until smooth. Cook 1 minute, stirring constantly. Stir in next 6 ingredients; bring to a boil. Cover, reduce heat, and simmer 15 minutes. Add remaining ingredients; cover and simmer an additional 15 minutes. Serve with or over rice, if desired.

Note: *Imitation crab meat can be substituted for genuine crab.*

Janet Steffler

ITALIAN TORTELLINI SOUP

Yields 5 quarts

4 (14½-ounce) cans beef broth
7 cups water
1 pound sweet Italian sausage, cut in ½-inch pieces
1 (9-ounce) box tortellini
1 (9-ounce) box spinach tortellini
½ pound cabbage, shredded

1 small green bell pepper, cored and diced
1 medium zucchini, sliced
1 small red onion, chopped
1 tablespoon chopped fresh basil
Salt and freshly ground pepper to taste
Freshly grated Parmesan cheese (optional)

Combine all ingredients except cheese in large pot; season with salt and pepper. Bring to slow boil over medium-high heat. Reduce heat and simmer until vegetables are tender, about 15 minutes. Ladle soup into bowls and serve immediately. Top with Parmesan cheese if desired.

Note: *Soup can be prepared a day ahead, covered and refrigerated.*

Lisa Baker

HEARTY VEGETABLE SOUP

♥ *Heart healthy*   *Yields 2 quarts*

1 (10-ounce) package frozen corn
½ (10-ounce) package frozen green beans
½ cup uncooked rice
⅓ cup dried kidney beans
½ cup dried garbanzo beans
1 (8-ounce) can tomatoes, undrained
½ cup chopped celery

¾ cup chopped onion
1 tablespoon dried parsley flakes
1½ teaspoons salt
½ teaspoon pepper
¾ teaspoon dried sweet basil
¼ teaspoon dried rosemary
⅛ teaspoon cayenne pepper
1 tablespoon brown sugar
½ teaspoon red pepper sauce
3 cups water

Combine all ingredients in a large saucepan and cover. Simmer 4-5 hours, adding water as necessary. Refrigerate 24 hours to allow flavors to blend. Reheat to serve. Serve with crusty bread.

Carol Bohley

BEEF SOUP SUPREME

Serves 6-8

½ cup chopped onion
1½ pounds ground beef
1 (10-ounce) can beef
  consommé
1 package dry cream of leek
  soup
4 cups water

3 sliced carrots (or more, to
  taste)
1 cup chopped celery leaves
¼ teaspoon pepper
Salt to taste
1 (12-ounce) can tomatoes,
  undrained
Shredded Cheddar cheese

In a large saucepan, brown beef and onions. Drain fat; add consommé, dry leek soup mix, water, carrots, celery leaves, pepper and salt. Simmer, covered, for 20 minutes. Add tomatoes (can be sieved or pureed, if desired) and simmer 10 more minutes. Pour soup into individual serving bowls, sprinkle with shredded Cheddar cheese to taste. Serve with a tossed salad and crusty bread.

Carol Bohley

OVEN STEW

Serves 6-8

1½ pounds lean stew meat,
  cubed
1 onion, cut in large pieces
3-4 ribs celery, chopped
3-4 carrots, sliced
4 medium white potatoes, cubed
1 rutabaga, cubed (optional)

1 (12-ounce) can V-8 vegetable
  juice
1 teaspoon salt
Pepper to taste
2 tablespoons brown sugar
2-3 tablespoons instant tapioca
½ cup red wine (optional)

Clean vegetables, cut into large bite-size pieces. Layer vegetables with meat in greased baking dish. Mix together V-8 juice, salt, pepper, brown sugar, tapioca and wine. Pour this sauce over vegetables and meat. Cover; bake in preheated oven at 275° for 4-5 hours, or at 325° for 3-4 hours.

Note: *Slower cooking gives an excellent flavor blend.*

Helen Baker

AUNT WILLETTE'S BRUNSWICK STEW

Yields 2 gallons

1 (2½-3 pound) broiler fryer
1½ pounds beef for stewing, cut
 in 1-inch squares
1 pound pork tenderloin
6 medium potatoes, peeled and
 cubed
4 cups chopped onion
2 cups sliced carrots
1 cup chopped cabbage
3 medium jalapeño peppers,
 seeded and chopped
3 (16-ounce) cans whole
 tomatoes, chopped, undrained

4 cups frozen lima beans
2 cups frozen sliced okra
1 cup frozen green peas
1 (16-ounce) package frozen
 white shoepeg corn
1 (6-ounce) can tomato paste
3 tablespoons Worcestershire
 sauce
2 tablespoons lemon juice
1 tablespoon sugar
2 teaspoons salt
½ to 1 teaspoon pepper

Place broiler-fryer in a Dutch oven, cover with water. Bring to a boil, cover, reduce heat and simmer 1 hour. Remove chicken from broth, reserve broth and let chicken cool. Debone chicken and coarsely chop meat; set aside.

Place beef and pork in a Dutch oven, cover with water, and bring to a boil. Cover, reduce heat and simmer 2 hours. Remove meat from broth, reserving broth. Let meat cool. Coarsely chop meat, set aside.

Combine chicken and beef-pork broths. Reserve 6-7 cups of broth mixture (Or for thicker stew, use 5 cups.) Combine broth, chopped meat and all ingredients except Worcestershire sauce, lemon juice, sugar, salt and pepper in a large Dutch oven. Bring to a boil, cover, reduce heat, and simmer 2 hours. Add remaining ingredients, and mix well.

Barbara Allen

~ Freezer wraps: Meat should be properly wrapped to prevent freezer burn. Use moisture-proof wraps such as heavy aluminum foil, heavily waxed freezer paper or plastic freezer bags. Wrap the meat tightly, eliminating all air if possible. Use double thicknesses of waxed paper between cuts to prevent sticking. Seal packages well, and date them. The rule in using frozen meat: First in, first out.

BEACH HOUSE BEANS

Serves 12-18

1 pound bacon, chopped
3 large red onions, chopped
6 (15-ounce) cans pinto beans
   with jalapeños, drained
3 (12-ounce) bottles dark beer

3 cups canned beef broth
3 large tomatoes, chopped
1½ cups fresh cilantro, chopped
1 tablespoon sugar
Salt and pepper to taste

Fry bacon until crisp. Remove bacon, leaving grease in skillet. Add onions to grease and cook until tender. Add fried bacon, beer, beef broth, tomatoes, cilantro and sugar. Season with salt and pepper. Bring to boil and reduce heat. Simmer about 1½ hours until slightly thickened, stirring occasionally.

Note: *There are never any left-overs with this dish. It is sure to become a favorite!*

Sandra Frazier

HILL COUNTRY BAKED BEANS

Serves 6-8

5 slices bacon
¼ green pepper, seeded and
   chopped
½ medium onion, chopped
2 (15-ounce) cans baked beans

½ cup ketchup
1½ teaspoons prepared mustard
⅓ cup hickory-smoke barbecue
   sauce
½ cup brown sugar, packed

Crisply cook bacon, and crumble. Chop green pepper and onion. Drain baked beans; do not rinse. Thoroughly mix bacon, beans, green pepper, onion, ketchup, mustard, barbecue sauce and brown sugar. Place in casserole dish and bake at 400° for 1 hour.

Maureen Schefsky

THREE-BEAN CASSEROLE

Serves 6-8

8 slices bacon
1 green pepper, chopped
1 medium onion, chopped
½ teaspoon garlic powder
1 cup brown sugar
½ teaspoon dry mustard
1 teaspoon salt

1 tablespoon Worcestershire
   sauce
½ cup vinegar
1 (16-ounce) can green beans,
   drained
1 (16-ounce) can baked beans
1 (16-ounce) can kidney beans

Fry bacon in large skillet. Remove bacon from pan, reserving 1 table-spoon grease. Sauté green pepper, onion, spices, Worcestershire sauce and vinegar in skillet for 10 minutes. Add beans to skillet mixture, then transfer to a casserole dish. Crumble bacon and sprinkle on top. Bake at 300° for 1 hour.

Karen Parrett

BARBECUE BAKED BEANS

Serves 6-8

1 pound lean ground beef
1½ onions, chopped
2 (16-ounce) cans pork and
   beans

1⅛ cups (8-ounces) firmly
   packed brown sugar
¼ cup liquid smoke
½ cup barbecue sauce
1 tablespoon dry mustard

Brown meat and onions, drain well. Add pork and beans, brown sugar, liquid smoke, barbecue sauce and dry mustard; mix well. Put in casserole dish, bake at 350° for 1 hour.

Note: *Everyone will love these beans, especially men! Add more meat if desired for a main-dish meal.*

Peggy McKnight

~ **Nutrition tip:** *Add garbanzo beans (chickpeas), lentils or kidney beans to rice dishes for added fiber and flavor.*

OLD SETTLERS BAKED BEANS

Serves 8

½ pound bacon
1 pound ground beef
1 cup diced onion
½ cup granulated sugar
½ cup brown sugar
½ cup barbecue sauce
¼ cup ketchup
2 tablespoons molasses
2 tablespoons prepared mustard

1 teaspoon liquid smoke
  (optional)
½ teaspoon chili powder
1 teaspoon salt (optional)
½ teaspoon pepper
1 (16-ounce) can kidney beans
1 (16-ounce) can pork and beans
1 (16-ounce) can butter beans

Cut bacon into medium strips, cook with ground beef and onion until brown. Meanwhile, mix together: granulated sugar, brown sugar, barbecue sauce, ketchup, molasses, mustard, liquid smoke, chili powder, salt and pepper. Drain the three cans of beans; combine in a 13"x9"x2" baking dish. Add sauce mixture and meat mixture to beans; mix well. Bake at 350° for 1 hour.

Kathy Carr

DUANE'S CAJUN BEANS

Serves 8

1 pound dry pinto beans
1 onion, chopped
Salt and pepper to taste

1 pound smoked sausage, cut in
  bite-size pieces
2 pods garlic

Wash beans, bring to a boil. Add chopped onion, salt and pepper. Cut sausage into bite-size pieces; add to beans. Add garlic. Continue cooking until beans are tender. Serve with rice and cornbread.

Gwen Williams

~ **Switching beans:** *Dried beans are interchangeable in most recipes, although flavor will vary.*

JOHN'S FAMOUS BEANS

Serves 6-8

1 pound dry pinto beans
10 cups water
2 teaspoons vegetable oil
1 onion, diced
4 cloves garlic, crushed
1 (16-ounce) can stewed
  tomatoes
2 tablespoons mild picante sauce
¼ cup Worcestershire sauce

¼ teaspoon chili powder
1 teaspoon salt
1 teaspoon comino
1 teaspoon cilantro
1 pound seasoned, cooked lean
  ground beef (optional)
1 cup (4-ounces) grated sharp
  Cheddar cheese (optional)

Pick over dry beans, remove stones. Soak beans in water overnight, or use quick-soak method. Drain beans, place in large pot. Add water and oil. Bring to a boil, then lower heat and simmer uncovered for 1½ hours. Add onion, garlic, tomatoes, picante sauce, Worcestershire sauce, chili powder, salt, comino and cilantro. Simmer for an additional 1½ hours.

Stir 1 pound seasoned, cooked lean ground beef into finished beans for a heartier main dish meal. Top with grated cheese in individual serving bowls if desired.

Quick soak method: Put beans in large pot with a lid. Add enough water to cover beans by several inches. Bring to a boil, and boil for 2 minutes. Remove from heat and let stand, covered, for 1 hour.

❤ *Heart healthy hint: Omit the meat and cheese to enjoy a low-fat, heart healthy dish.*

Cynthia Lancaster

~ Love me tender: Beans should be cooked almost tender before adding any acidic ingredients such as tomatoes, lemon juice or wine. To find out if the beans are tender enough, stick the point of a sharp knife in a sample bean or two.

Main Dishes

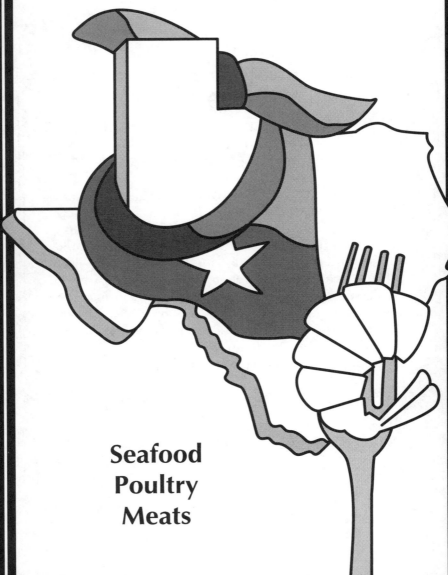

Seafood
Poultry
Meats

CPR
1976 - to present

Students learn a variety of life-saving techniques for victims of all ages at cardiopulmonary resuscitation (CPR) courses taught each year by members of Junior Service League. Hundreds of high school students receive the invaluable training during courses taught by JSL volunteers in Brazosport Independent School District high schools during the regular school year and during summer school. JSL also schedules courses for the general public. All members of Junior Service League receive CPR training during their provisional (first) year. League members who choose CPR instruction as their service project undergo additional training to gain instructor certification.

EASY SCAMPI

✓ *Quick to fix* *Serves 4*

¾ cup (1½ sticks) unsalted
   butter
¼ cup finely chopped onion
3-4 garlic cloves, crushed
4 parsley sprigs, chopped

1 pound medium shrimp, peeled,
   deveined
¼ cup dry white wine
2 tablespoons fresh lemon juice
Salt and freshly ground pepper

Melt butter in medium skillet over low heat. Add onion, garlic and parsley; sauté until golden, about 10 minutes. Add shrimp and cook just until pink. Remove shrimp and place in oven-proof dish. Cover lightly and keep warm. Add wine and lemon juice to skillet, simmer 2-3 minutes. Season to taste with salt and pepper, pour over shrimp.

Mary Ann Sosebee

HEAVENLY RED SNAPPER

✓ *Quick to fix* *Serves 6*

2 pounds snapper filets
2 tablespoons lemon juice
½ cup grated Parmesan cheese
¼ cup (½ stick) butter or
   margarine, softened

3 tablespoons mayonnaise or
   salad dressing
3 tablespoons chopped green
   onion
¼ teaspoon salt
⅛ teaspoon hot pepper sauce

Skin filets, cut into serving size portions. Place on well-greased broiling pan. Baste fish with lemon juice and let stand for 10 minutes. Broil approximately 4 inches from heat source for 4-5 minutes. Turn carefully and continue broiling 4-5 minutes until fish flakes easily. Combine Parmesan cheese, butter, mayonnaise, green onions, salt and hot sauce. Spread sauce evenly over fish. Broil 2-3 minutes longer or until lightly brown.

💗 *Heart healthy hint:* Make this dish low-fat by using diet margarine and non-fat mayonnaise.

Barbara Lundahl

~ *Flaky fish:* Fish is cooked when it loses its transparent look and flesh flakes easily when tested with a fork.

SHRIMP AND VEGETABLE STIR FRY

❤ Heart healthy, ✓ Quick to fix   Serves 6

2 tablespoons peanut oil
2 (¼-inch) slices fresh ginger
  root, peeled and minced
1 clove garlic, chopped
1½ cups broccoli flowerets
1½ cups thinly sliced carrots
1 small onion, sliced
1 small green pepper, cut into
  long, thin strips
¾ cup low-salt chicken stock
1 teaspoon salt
½ pound large shrimp, shelled
1 tablespoon cornstarch
2 tablespoons cold water
1 (8-ounce) can sliced water
  chestnuts, drained
1 cup sliced mushrooms
2 tablespoons oyster sauce

Heat oil in wok until hot. Add ginger root and garlic; stir-fry 15 seconds. Add broccoli, carrots, onion and green pepper; stir-fry 1 minute. Add chicken stock and salt, toss to combine. Cover; cook until carrots are tender-crisp, 2-3 minutes. Uncover, add shrimp; stir-fry 1 minute or until pink. Dissolve cornstarch in 2 tablespoons cold water; add to wok along with drained water chestnuts, mushrooms and oyster sauce. Stir-fry 30-45 seconds or until heated thoroughly. Serve immediately.

Penny Daigle

GRILLED TERIYAKI SHRIMP KABOBS

Serves 6

2 pounds (about 3 dozen) fresh
  raw jumbo shrimp
1 tablespoon chopped fresh
  garlic
1½ tablespoons chopped fresh
  ginger root
½ cup brown sugar
1 teaspoon sesame oil
1 cup premium soy sauce
1 (8-ounce) can chunk pineapple
¼ cup pineapple juice from
  canned pineapple
1 medium onion, diced

Peel shrimp, set aside. Combine garlic, ginger root, brown sugar, sesame oil, soy sauce, pineapple, pineapple juice and onion in large shallow dish; stir well. Add shrimp to marinade mixture, tossing gently to coat. Cover and marinate in refrigerator at least 2 hours. Remove shrimp from marinade; thread tail and neck of each shrimp onto six 14-inch skewers (arrange shrimp to lie flat). Alternate shrimp with pineapple chunks. Grill over medium to hot coals 3-4 minutes each side, until shrimp turns pink. Baste with marinade while grilling. Kabobs can also be cooked under a broiler.

Christy Spence

EASY MARINATED SHRIMP

Serves 3-4

2 pounds medium or large
  shrimp
½ cup (1 stick) butter, melted

1 (8-ounce) bottle zesty Italian
  dressing

Thaw shrimp, if frozen. Remove shells and devein. Put shrimp in roasting pan or 13"x9"x2" pan. Pour melted butter and Italian dressing over shrimp. Cover pan; bake at 325° for 30-45 minutes. Serve shrimp with a small dip bowl of drippings from the pan, if desired.

Tonya Heard

RICE SHRIMP PARTY PIE

Serves 6-8

2 tablespoons minced parsley
2 tablespoons minced pimiento
1 tablespoon grated onion
¼ teaspoon salt

⅛ teaspoon pepper
2 tablespoons butter
3 cups cooked rice

Shrimp Filling:

1½ pounds cleaned raw shrimp
2 tablespoons butter
1 (10¾-ounce) can condensed
  cream of mushroom soup

1 teaspoon lemon juice
¼ teaspoon pepper
1 cup (4-ounces) grated
  mozzarella cheese

To make crust: Mix parsley, pimiento, onion, salt, pepper, butter and hot rice until butter melts. Press evenly around sides and bottom of a 10-inch pie plate.

To make filling: Brown shrimp in butter and put into rice shell. In same skillet, heat soup, lemon juice and pepper. Stir until smooth and heated through; pour over shrimp. Sprinkle with cheese. Bake at 350° for 30 minutes or until lightly brown.

Karen Parrett

*~ **Add a garnish:** Garnish fish with orange slices, twists or wedges; hard-cooked egg slices or wedges; paprika sprinkled sparingly; radishes; watercress; mint, or chives.*

SHRIMP-CRAB AU GRATIN

Serves 6

¼ cup (½ stick) butter or
   margarine plus 1 tablespoon
   butter, divided
½ pound fresh mushrooms,
   sliced
1 clove garlic, minced
2 tablespoons finely minced
   shallots
¼ cup flour
½ teaspoon pepper
¾ cup milk

⅔ cup dry white wine
1 pound shrimp, cooked
2 (6-ounce) cans crab meat,
   flaked and drained
1 (10-ounce) package frozen
   artichoke hearts, cooked,
   drained (or use canned)
2½ cups (10-ounces) grated
   Cheddar cheese, divided
2 tablespoons bread crumbs

Melt ¼ cup butter in skillet; add mushrooms, garlic and shallots. Sauté for 5 minutes. Remove from heat; stir in flour, pepper and milk. Slowly bring to a boil, stir, and remove from heat. Stir in wine. Combine sauce, shrimp, crab, artichokes and 1½ cups grated cheese. Pour into a buttered 2-quart casserole dish. Combine bread crumbs and 1 tablespoon melted butter; sprinkle on top of casserole. Top with remaining cheese. Bake uncovered at 375° for 30 minutes, or until bubbly and lightly browned.

Helen Baker

SHRIMP RICE

Serves 8-10

2 (10¾-ounce) cans beef broth
   soup
1 (10¾-ounce) can onion soup
1 (4-ounce) can sliced
   mushrooms

2 cups uncooked rice
2 pounds cocktail shrimp or crab
   meat

In a large saucepan, combine broth soup, onion soup and mushrooms; bring to a boil. Remove from heat, add rice and shrimp. Pour into covered casserole dish; bake at 350° for 30 minutes. Remove lid, bake 10 minutes longer.

B. J. Smith

SEAFOOD CASSEROLE FOR A CROWD

Serves 30

3 pounds shrimp, cooked and
  chopped
3 pounds crab meat (imitation or
  genuine crab)
2 cups finely chopped celery
1 large bell pepper, chopped
1 large onion, chopped

1 tablespoon Worcestershire
  sauce
2 cups (1 pint) mayonnaise
Dash of hot pepper sauce
2 cups bread crumbs
½ cup (1 stick) margarine or
  butter, melted

Combine shrimp, crab, celery, bell pepper, onion and Worcestershire sauce; mix well. Spoon mixture into greased extra-large (18"x14"x3") casserole dish. Mix mayonnaise with dash of hot pepper sauce, mix bread crumbs with melted butter; combine mayonnaise and bread mixtures. Spoon over shrimp mixture. Bake at 350° for 30 minutes.

Janis Warny

SHRIMP-RICE FIESTA

Serves 6-8

2 cups boiled, peeled shrimp
2 tablespoons cooking oil
3 tablespoons flour
1 cup chopped onion
½ cup chopped bell pepper
1 (10-ounce) can diced tomatoes
  with chiles (or regular
  tomatoes)

1 teaspoon salt
1 teaspoon Accent
1 teaspoon black pepper
1 (10¾-ounce) can condensed
  cream of mushroom soup
3 cups hot, cooked rice

Boil, peel shrimp. Brown flour in oil. Add onion, bell pepper, tomatoes and spices; cook until onion and pepper are tender. Add shrimp and soup, cook over medium heat for 30 minutes. Serve over hot rice.

❤ *Heart healthy hint: Make this dish low-fat by using fat-free cream of mushroom soup.*

Dee Swope

~ *Fish servings: For whole fish, plan on 1 pound per person. Dressed fish, ½ pound per person; fillets, steaks or sticks, ⅓ pound.*

DIANE'S SEAFOOD PIZZA

Serves 6

1 pound shrimp, peeled and
  deveined
½ pound lump crab meat
1 pint oysters
1 cup sliced onions
2 cloves garlic, minced
2 tablespoons butter

Sliced green olives for garnish
1 pound sliced provolone cheese
1 cup (4-ounces) shredded
  mozzarella cheese
½ cup grated Romano cheese
½ cup grated Parmesan cheese

Pizza Sauce:

1 (8-ounce) can tomato sauce
1 (6-ounce) can tomato paste
1 teaspoon sugar

1 teaspoon Italian seasoning
1 teaspoon garlic powder

Brioche Pizza Crust (Recipe on
  following page)

2 tablespoons olive oil

Prepare Brioche crust according to directions on following page. Spray two 12-inch pizza pans with non-stick vegetable spray. Spread dough in pans. Baste with olive oil to completely cover crusts. Mix all ingredients for sauce, spread evenly on crusts. Cover with provolone cheese slices. In large skillet, sauté onion and garlic in butter. Add peeled, deveined shrimp, oysters and crab. Cook until shrimp are pink. Distribute evenly on pizza crusts. Add olives. Top with mozzarella, Parmesan and Romano cheese. Bake at 425° for 18-20 minutes.

Diane Hill

BRIOCHE PIZZA DOUGH

Yields two12-inch crusts

1 teaspoon dry active yeast
2 tablespoons warm water
(105°-115°)
2¼ cups sifted bread flour,
divided
4½ teaspoons sugar, divided
½ teaspoon salt

¾ cup (1½ sticks) unsalted
butter, well-chilled, cut in
small pieces
3 eggs, room temperature
¼ cup half-and-half cream, room
temperature

Sprinkle yeast over water in small bowl; stir to dissolve. Mix in 3 tablespoons flour and pinch of sugar. Seal bowl in plastic bag. Let stand until mixture doubles, 15-20 minutes.

Blend remaining flour, sugar and salt in food processor for 5 seconds. Arrange butter in circle atop dry ingredients and process until butter is indistinguishable, stopping once to scrape down sides of work bowl, about 30 seconds. Place eggs in circle atop dry ingredients. Pour cream over eggs; add yeast mixture. Process until ball forms, then breaks down into evenly dispersed, very sticky batter, 20 to 25 seconds (do not stop machine until batter forms).

Transfer dough to medium bowl, using rubber spatula. Place plastic directly atop dough, and seal bowl in plastic bag. Let rise at room temperature until doubled, 2½- 3 hours.

Stir dough down. Cover with plastic and seal in plastic bag. Chill overnight. (Can be made up to 3 days ahead. Store in refrigerator.)

Note: *Use this crust with Seafood Pizza recipe, previous page.*

Diane Hill

HERBED SHRIMP AND PASTA

Serves 2

1 pound fresh medium shrimp
4 ounces uncooked angel hair
  pasta
½ cup (1 stick) butter
2 cloves garlic, minced

1 cup half-and-half cream
¼ cup chopped fresh parsley
1 teaspoon dried dillweed
¼ teaspoon salt
⅛ teaspoon pepper

Peel and devein shrimp, set aside. Cook pasta according to package directions, drain and set aside; keep warm. Melt butter in a heavy skillet over medium-high heat; add shrimp and garlic. Cook 3-5 minutes, stirring constantly; remove shrimp and set aside, reserving garlic and butter in skillet. Add cream to skillet; bring to a boil, stirring constantly. Reduce heat to low; simmer about 15 minutes or until thickened, stirring occasionally. Add shrimp, parsley and seasonings; stir until blended. Serve over angel hair pasta.

Hint: *Serve with steamed or sautéed red, green and yellow pepper strips.*

Julie Zimmerman

CRAB MEAT-SHRIMP CASSEROLE

Serves 8

½ pound shrimp, boiled
1 (15-ounce) can boneless crab
  meat, drained, flaked
1 (8-ounce) package shell pasta
  or egg noodles
1 cup (2 sticks) butter

½ pound processed pimiento
  cheese (or 1 large jar Cheez
  Whiz mixed with canned
  pimiento)
1 cup half-and-half cream

Boil shrimp; drain and flake crab meat. Cook noodles in boiling water according to package directions, drain. Melt butter and cheese in double boiler, or use microwave. Add cream. Stir in crab meat, shrimp and cooked, drained noodles. Bake in casserole dish at 350° for 30 minutes.

Note: *For extra seasoning, add a little curry and Greek seasoning salt. Everyone loves this casserole!*

Alexa Kincannon

SEAFOOD FETTUCCINE WITH ALFREDO SAUCE

Serves 4

1 (8-ounce) package fettuccine
1 pound seafood (shrimp, crab, or mixture)
3 tablespoons butter
1 clove garlic, crushed

2 teaspoons fresh-squeezed lemon juice
¼ cup dry white wine
Chopped parsley (optional)

Alfredo Sauce:

4 tablespoons butter
¼ cup grated Parmesan cheese
¼ cup grated Romano cheese

½ cup half-and-half cream
Salt and pepper to taste

Cook fettuccine according to package directions; drain. While fettuccine is cooking, make Alfredo Sauce: In saucepan, whisk together all sauce ingredients; cook on low heat until blended, set aside. In large skillet, sauté seafood in butter and garlic on medium heat until cooked. Add lemon juice and wine; cook on high heat 3 minutes. Add Alfredo Sauce, cook on low heat 3-5 minutes. Pour over noodles. Top with parsley or additional cheese, if desired. Grilled chicken can be used in place of seafood.

Sherrie Ezell

CRAWFISH FETTUCCINE

Serves 4-6

1 pound fresh or frozen crawfish tails, peeled
½ cup (1 stick) butter
1 bunch green onions, chopped
8-10 ribs of celery, chopped
1 large bell pepper, seeded and chopped
1 medium white onion, chopped

1 (10¾-ounce) can condensed cream of mushroom soup
2 cups (8-ounces) Monterey Jack cheese with jalapeños
½ cup heavy cream
Salt and pepper to taste
1 (12-ounce) package fettuccine

Thaw crawfish tails if frozen. Melt butter in saucepan, add green onions, celery, bell pepper and white onion; sauté until soft. Add soup and cheese; stir until cheese is melted. Stir in heavy cream. Add crawfish tails; simmer over medium heat until warm, about 20 minutes. Add salt and pepper to taste. Cook fettuccine as directed on package. Serve sauce over warm noodles.

Sandra Frazier

SHRIMP IMPERIAL

Serves 8

1 pound shrimp, cleaned and
  deveined
1 (6-ounce) can crab meat
½ cup (1 stick) margarine plus
  2 tablespoons margarine,
  divided
1 (8-ounce) package cream
  cheese
1 onion, diced
2 ribs celery, sliced
1 bell pepper, diced

1 teaspoon hot pepper sauce
½ teaspoon red pepper
¼ teaspoon garlic salt
¾ cup rice, cooked
1 (10¾-ounce) can condensed
  cream of mushroom soup
1 (4-ounce) can sliced
  mushrooms
Grated Cheddar cheese to taste
Bread or cracker crumbs to taste

Clean and devein shrimp; drain and flake crab meat. Melt ½ cup margarine, mix with cream cheese. Sauté shrimp, onion, celery and bell pepper in 2 tablespoons margarine; combine with cream cheese. Season with hot pepper sauce, red pepper and garlic salt. Stir in cooked rice, soup, crab and mushrooms. Place mixture in casserole dish, top with cheese and crumbs to taste. Bake at 350° for 30-35 minutes.

Note: *This dish is very rich. Serve with just a salad for a full meal.*

Donna Schwertner

SHRIMP VICTORIA

Serves 4

1 pound shrimp, peeled and
  deveined
½ cup finely chopped onion
¼ cup (½ stick) margarine
1 (6-ounce) can sliced
  mushrooms

1 tablespoon flour
¼ teaspoon salt
Dash of cayenne pepper
1 cup sour cream
1½ cups cooked rice

Sauté shrimp and onion in margarine for 5 minutes, or until shrimp are tender. Add mushrooms, cook for 2-3 minutes more. Sprinkle in flour, salt and pepper. Stir in sour cream; cook gently for 10 minutes, being careful not to boil mixture. Serve over rice.

Karen Johnson

PETE'S ROYAL SEAFOOD CASSEROLE

Serves 8-10

3 pounds fresh shrimp
1 (7½-ounce) can crab meat
2 (10¾-ounce) cans condensed
　cream of shrimp soup
½ cup mayonnaise
1 small onion, grated
¾ cup milk plus 2 tablespoons
　milk if needed, divided
3 tablespoons minced parsley

⅛ teaspoon cayenne pepper (or
　more, to taste)
½ teaspoon ground nutmeg
Salt and pepper to taste
1½ cups uncooked rice
1 (5-ounce) can water chestnuts,
　sliced
1½ cups diced celery
Paprika
Slivered almonds (optional)

Boil and peel shrimp, drain and flake crab meat; set aside. In a large bowl, blend soup and mayonnaise. Add onion, ¾ cup milk, parsley, cayenne pepper, nutmeg, salt and pepper; blend well. Cook rice until dry and fluffy (If cooking rice in chicken broth, reduce added salt.) Combine soup mixture, rice, water chestnuts, cooked shrimp, crab meat and celery. Taste for seasoning — there should be a subtle nutmeg flavor and cayenne pepper "zing" to taste. Mixture should be moist — add a few tablespoons of milk if too dry. Spoon mixture into a 13"x9"x2" buttered casserole dish. Sprinkle with paprika and slivered almonds. (Stir extra almonds into mixture, if desired.) Bake uncovered at 350° for 30 minutes, or until hot and bubbly. Casserole can be prepared a day ahead and refrigerated until baking time.

Note: *This makes an excellent buffet dish for brunch or dinner.*

Marilyn Woody

CHEESE-RICE SHRIMP CASSEROLE

Serves 6-8

2 pounds shrimp, cleaned, boiled
　and chopped in bite-size
　pieces
2 cups cooked rice
2 cups grated Velveeta cheese
2 (10¾-ounce) cans condensed
　cream of mushroom soup

¼ cup (½ stick) butter or
　margarine
6 tablespoons lemon juice
1 small bell pepper, chopped
1 (2-ounce) jar diced pimientos
1 teaspoon pepper
Dash of garlic powder

Prepare shrimp. Mix all ingredients; spoon into 13"x9"x2" baking dish. Bake at 350° for 40-50 minutes. Dish can be prepared ahead.

Cheryl Whitten

AU-SEASON SHRIMP

Serves 4

1 pound medium shrimp
2 tomatoes, peeled, quartered
1 bell pepper, sliced
1 medium onion, sliced

½ cup (1 stick) butter
½ pound fresh mushrooms
Salt, pepper and garlic to taste
2-3 cups cooked rice

Peel and devein shrimp, set aside. Peel tomatoes and slice into quarters, set aside. Slice bell pepper and onion, sauté in butter until tender. Add whole mushrooms and peeled shrimp, sauté until shrimp turns pink. Season to taste with salt, pepper and garlic. Turn off stove. Place tomato quarters on top of shrimp mixture, cover pan with lid, and steam tomatoes for 3-5 minutes. Serve over a bed of rice.

Serena Andrews

BAKED SEAFOOD CASSEROLE

Serves 8

2 (6-ounce) cans crab meat,
    drained and flaked
1 pound shrimp, cooked
1 (4-ounce) can sliced
    mushrooms
½ bell pepper, chopped
½ cup chopped onion
1 cup chopped celery
½ jar (1-ounce) diced pimiento

1 cup Miracle Whip dressing
1 cup milk
1 cup cooked rice
1 tablespoon Worcestershire
    sauce
½ teaspoon salt
⅛ teaspoon pepper
Bread crumbs to taste

Mix crab meat, shrimp, mushrooms, bell pepper, onion, celery and pimiento. In a separate bowl, combine Miracle Whip, milk, cooked rice, Worcestershire sauce, salt and pepper. Blend the two mixes together; place in 2-quart buttered casserole dish. Top with bread crumbs to taste. Bake at 375° for 30 minutes.

❤ *Heart healthy hint:* Use skim milk and non-fat Miracle Whip for a low-fat seafood casserole.

Jan Davis

SAUCY SHRIMP SQUARES

Serves 4-6

2 cups cooked shrimp, cut in
  small pieces
2 (10-ounce) packages frozen
  Green Giant rice medley
1/4 cup sliced celery
1/4 cup diced green pepper
1/4 cup minced onion
2 tablespoons butter or
  margarine
1 cup (4-ounces) grated sharp
  Cheddar cheese

1 (10¾-ounce) can condensed
  cream of mushroom soup
2 tablespoons diced pimiento
1 tablespoon Worcestershire
  sauce
1 teaspoon dry mustard
1/2 teaspoon curry powder
Salt and pepper to taste
Dash of Accent

Sauce:

1 (10¾-ounce) can condensed
  cream of shrimp soup
1 (8-ounce) carton sour cream
1/4 cup dry white wine

1 tablespoon diced pimiento
Dash of dry mustard
Dash of curry powder

Cook, chop shrimp. Prepare rice medley according to package directions. Sauté celery, green pepper and onion in butter (do not brown). Mix with all other main ingredients; pour into 8"x8" casserole dish. Bake at 350° for 30-45 minutes, until bubbly. Mix sauce ingredients, heat well but do not allow to boil. Cut casserole into squares to serve, spoon sauce over individual servings.

Binnie Bauml

SHRIMP-BROCCOLI CASSEROLE

Serves 8-12

3 cups shrimp, cooked, peeled
1/2 cup chopped celery
1 medium onion, chopped
6 tablespoons (¾ stick) butter
1 (10-ounce) package frozen
  chopped broccoli, cooked
1 (8-ounce) jar Cheez Whiz

1 (10¾-ounce) can condensed
  cream of chicken soup
Dash of hot pepper sauce
1 (8-ounce) can sliced water
  chestnuts
2 cups cooked rice
Crumbs from 5 bread slices

Cook and peel shrimp. Sauté celery and onion in butter. Add broccoli, Cheez Whiz, soup, hot pepper sauce, water chestnuts, cooked rice and shrimp. Pour into 13"x9"x2" baking dish; top with crumbs. Bake at 350° for 30 minutes.

Becky Lowery

SHRIMP CREOLE

Serves 4

1 pound shrimp, peeled and
  deveined
⅓ cup shortening
¼ cup flour
1 garlic bud, minced
½ cup minced onion
2 tablespoons minced parsley
½ cup chopped bell pepper

1 cup water
2 teaspoons salt
2 bay leaves
½ teaspoon cayenne pepper
1 (8-ounce) can tomato sauce
½ teaspoon monosodium
  glutamate (MSG)
3 cups cooked rice

Peel and devein shrimp, set aside. Melt shortening in heavy skillet over high heat. Add flour, stir until it is light brown. Lower heat, add shrimp; cook 3 minutes or until pink. Add garlic, onion, parsley and bell pepper, cook 2 minutes longer. Raise heat; gradually add water. Add salt, bay leaves, cayenne pepper, tomato sauce and MSG. Bring to a boil, then simmer, covered, for 20-30 minutes. Serve very hot over fluffy rice.

Cary Rosenbohm

SHERMAN SHRIMP CREOLE

Serves 4-6

2 pounds medium or small
  shrimp, peeled and deveined
¼ cup (½ stick) butter
1 large white onion, chopped
1 small green pepper, diced
1 stalk celery, sliced
1 teaspoon curry
Juice of one lemon
2 teaspoons sugar
½ cup tomato cocktail sauce

1 (16-ounce) can green beans,
  drained
1 (4-ounce) can sliced
  mushrooms, drained
1 (16-ounce) can stewed
  tomatoes
20 drops soy sauce
1 tablespoon cornstarch
3 cups cooked rice

Peel and devein shrimp, set aside. Melt butter and sauté chopped onion, green pepper and celery until slightly brown. Stir in curry, lemon juice and sugar. Add cocktail sauce, green beans, mushrooms, tomatoes and peeled shrimp. Cover pan with lid; simmer for 50 minutes to 1 hour. Add soy sauce and thicken with cornstarch. Simmer uncovered for 15 minutes. Serve over rice.

Cindy Williams

BOB'S SHRIMP CREOLE

Serves 8-10

5 pounds shrimp, peeled and deveined
1 cup (2 sticks) butter
1 large onion, chopped
1 medium bell pepper, chopped
3 stalks celery, coarsely chopped
1 (14-ounce) can stewed tomatoes
1 (10-ounce) can diced tomatoes with chiles
1 (10-ounce) can tomato sauce
2 dashes of Worcestershire sauce
2 dashes of hot pepper sauce
1 bay leaf
1-1½ tablespoons cornstarch
Salt to taste
8 cups cooked rice
1 cup chopped green onion

Peel and devein shrimp. Melt butter in a large pot, sauté onion, bell pepper and celery until tender. Add stewed tomatoes, diced tomatoes with chiles, tomato sauce, Worcestershire sauce, hot pepper sauce and bay leaf. Simmer for about 20 minutes. Add shrimp, cook on medium heat about 10 minutes or until shrimp are done. Add enough cornstarch to thicken as desired. Serve over rice, and garnish with chopped green onions.

Hint: *Use peeled, garden-fresh tomatoes in place of stewed tomatoes for an outstanding taste difference.*

Barbara Franklin

CRAWFISH ETOUFFEE

Serves 4-6

1 pound crawfish tails, peeled
¼ cup (½ stick) margarine or butter
1 cup finely chopped onion
½ cup chopped bell pepper
2 cups water plus ½ cup water, divided
½ cup chopped green onion tops
2 cloves garlic, crushed
½ teaspoon paprika
2 teaspoons cornstarch
Chopped parsley or parsley flakes
6 cups cooked rice

Clean, peel crawfish tails. Melt margarine in pot over low heat. Add onions and bell pepper, cook until onions are clear. Add 2 cups water and bring to a boil. Add crawfish tails and green onion. Cook over low heat for 5 minutes, stirring occasionally. Add garlic and paprika to taste. Dissolve cornstarch in half-cup water; pour into crawfish broth. Simmer 15 minutes, stirring occasionally. Remove from heat; sprinkle with parsley. Stir; let set a few minutes. Serve over rice.

Alexa Kincannon

PAELLA À LA VALENCIANA

Serves 4-6

½ cup olive oil
¼ cup cubed ham
1 chicken, cut into pieces,
   OR 6 chicken legs
1 clove garlic, minced
¾ cup shrimp, shelled and
   deveined
½ cup crawfish or crab, fresh
   or frozen
1 cup mussels or small clams,
   fresh or canned

1 cup tomato sauce
2 cups uncooked rice
1 quart boiling water
½ teaspoon saffron
1 teaspoon salt
½ cup green peas, freshly boiled
   or canned
3 tablespoons chopped
   pimientos

Heat olive oil in a large, heavy skillet (or in a paellera, a special paella cooking pan found in every kitchen in Spain). When oil is hot, add ham, chicken and garlic; sauté until all ingredients are golden. Remove chicken, set aside. Add the seafoods; stir and sauté for 5 minutes. Pour tomato sauce into skillet, stir another minute. Add rice; and while stirring constantly with a fork, pour in the boiling water. Add saffron and salt. Return chicken to skillet; simmer until chicken and rice are tender. Add peas and pimientos near end of cooking time; mix gently into rice mixture. When liquid is absorbed, turn off heat; cover, and keep on warm burner for 5 minutes before serving.

Note: *This authentic Spanish recipe makes a wonderful meal with a green salad and French bread. My Spanish cook taught me to make this dish when I was living in Rota, Spain.*

Judy Robinson

~ *Cooking yields for rice:*

1 cup uncooked regular white rice yields 3 cups cooked

1 cup uncooked parboiled or brown rice yields 3-4 cups cooked

1 cup precooked "instant" rice yields 1-2 cups

DURANGO CHICKEN

Serves 4-6

4 chicken breasts, split
  (or 1 frying chicken cut into
  serving pieces)
½ cup (1 stick) butter, melted
Juice of 2 lemons

1 teaspoon garlic salt
1 tablespoon paprika
1 tablespoon oregano
Salt and pepper to taste

Mix together melted butter, lemon juice, garlic salt, paprika, oregano, salt and pepper to taste. Marinate chicken in sauce for 3-4 hours, or overnight. Place chicken in baking dish, skin-side up, and bake uncovered at 325° for 45 minutes or until done.

Note: *This is the solution for dinner on a busy day! Prepare the dish the night before and it will be ready to cook when you need it the next day.*

Peggy McKnight

GOURMET LEMON CHICKEN

✓ *Quick to fix*   *Serves 3*

3 boneless, skinless chicken
  breasts
⅓ cup olive oil

¾ cup flour
Salt and pepper to taste

Lemon Sauce:

4 tablespoons real butter
Juice of 1 lemon

2 tablespoons fresh chopped
  parsley

Pound chicken breasts flat with mallet. Heat olive oil in large skillet. Put flour in plastic bag; coat chicken. Cook chicken in hot oil, approximately 3 minutes per side. Season with salt and pepper to taste. Remove to platter and keep warm.

To make sauce, add butter to skillet; heat until melted, scraping brown bits left from chicken into the butter. Remove pan from heat, add lemon juice and parsley. Pour sauce over chicken to serve.

Note: *This dish is a family favorite. It goes well with Gourmet Filled Tomatoes.*

Ruth Bondurant

MARILYN'S LEMON CHICKEN

Serves 6-8

2 pounds boneless, skinless
   chicken breasts
Flour for dredging
Salt and white pepper to taste
2 eggs, beaten
2 tablespoons water
2 cups soft white bread crumbs

4 tablespoons vegetable oil,
   divided
6-8 tablespoons butter or
   margarine, divided
Juice of 1 lemon
1 tablespoon finely chopped
   parsley

Flatten chicken to about ⅛-inch. Season flour with salt and pepper; mix beaten eggs with water. Dredge chicken in seasoned flour, then in eggs, then in bread crumbs. Put on plate, cover loosely and refrigerate until ready to cook.

Heat large frying pan over moderate heat, add 2 tablespoons oil and 2 tablespoons butter. Sauté chicken 2-3 minutes each side, or until done. Add more oil and butter as needed. Place chicken on warm platter. In same skillet, heat lemon juice to boiling. Swirl in remaining butter (about 3 tablespoons), and chopped parsley. Drizzle sauce over chicken.

Note: *Veal may be used in place of chicken.*

Marilyn Matthews

BAKED LEMON BUTTER CHICKEN

Serves 6

6 boneless chicken breasts
½ pound fresh mushrooms,
   sliced
½ cup (1 stick) real butter
½ cup lemon juice

1-2 tablespoons Worcestershire
   sauce (to taste)
1 teaspoon dry mustard
Garlic salt to taste

Place chicken breasts in a 13"x9"x2" casserole dish. Top with sliced mushrooms. Melt butter; mix with lemon juice, Worcestershire sauce, dry mustard and garlic salt. Pour lemon butter over chicken; bake at 350° for 1 hour. Spoon lemon butter over chicken to serve.

Jonsi Elam

OVEN CHICKEN PARMESAN

Serves 4

1 fryer, cut up, or 4 chicken
   breasts
1 egg, beaten
2 tablespoons milk
¼ cup flour
½ cup Parmesan cheese

2 teaspoons paprika
½ teaspoon salt
½ teaspoon pepper
½ cup (1 stick) margarine,
   melted

Preheat oven to 350°. Combine egg and milk; mix flour with Parmesan cheese, paprika, salt and pepper. Dip chicken in egg-milk mixture; then dredge in seasoned flour. Place in shallow baking dish. Pour melted margarine over chicken. Bake at 350° for 1¼ hours.

Jenny Pennington

CHICKEN BREASTS PARMESAN

Serves 4

4 skinless, boneless chicken
   breasts
½ cup biscuit or pancake mix
¼ teaspoon salt
⅛ teaspoon pepper

1 (10¾-ounce) can condensed
   cream of mushroom soup
⅓ cup dry onion soup mix
⅓ cup milk
½ cup grated Parmesan cheese
Parsley for garnish (optional)

Preheat oven to 375°. Combine pancake mix, salt and pepper in bowl; coat chicken pieces well. Place chicken in greased pan or 11"x7"x2" casserole dish. Combine mushroom soup, dry onion soup and milk in bowl; blend until smooth. Pour mixture over chicken. Cover dish tightly with foil and bake at 375° for 1 hour. Remove foil and sprinkle Parmesan cheese over chicken; return to oven and cook uncovered for 15 minutes. Garnish with parsley if desired.

Hint: *This dish tastes great with Mushroom Rice Casserole.*

Patti Hoffmann

❤ **Heart healthy tip:** *Removing the skin from chicken cuts the fat almost in half.*

CHICKEN-ITALIAN DRESSING BAKE

✓ *Quick to fix* *Serves 4*

4 split boneless, skinless chicken
  breasts
½ cup Italian-seasoned bread
  crumbs
¼ cup grated Parmesan cheese

⅛ teaspoon salt
¼ cup commercial Italian salad
  dressing
Non-stick vegetable cooking
  spray

Combine bread crumbs, cheese and salt in a plastic bag; shake to mix. Dip chicken in salad dressing then place one piece of chicken in bag, and shake to coat. Repeat with remaining chicken. Place in lightly greased pan. Bake at 400° for 15 minutes. Spray chicken with cooking spray, and bake an additional 5-10 minutes or until done.

💗 *Heart healthy hint: Use non-fat Italian dressing to reduce fat content.*

Julie Zimmerman

BAKED CHICKEN À LA LANCASTER

💗 *Heart healthy* *Serves 6*

6-12 chicken pieces
1 cup wheat germ
1 cup Italian-seasoned bread
  crumbs

½ cup grated Parmesan cheese
1 (8-ounce) carton non-fat plain
  yogurt
Diet margarine

Combine wheat germ, bread crumbs and Parmesan cheese in a jar with a lid; shake to mix well, set aside. Rinse chicken pieces, remove skin and visible fat; pat dry. Line baking sheet with foil, if desired, and spray surface with non-stick cooking spray. Preheat oven to 350°.

Scoop yogurt into a shallow bowl. Dip one chicken piece in yogurt, coating well. Pour about one-fourth of the breading mixture into a plastic bag. Add the yogurt-coated chicken piece; shake to coat well. Place chicken piece on prepared baking sheet, meatiest side up. Continue coating chicken pieces, dipping each into yogurt, then breading; and placing on baking sheet. Add more breading mixture to bag as needed. Place a thin sliver of margarine atop each chicken piece to prevent sticking. Bake at 350° for 1 hour, turning once.

Note: *Unused breading mixture can be stored in refrigerator for future use.*

Cynthia Lancaster

SWISS BAKED CHICKEN

Serves 8

8 boneless, skinless chicken
  breasts
8 slices Swiss cheese
2 (10¾-ounce) cans condensed
  cream of mushroom soup

¼ cup water
2 cups herb stuffing mix
½ cup (1 stick) melted butter

Place chicken breasts in a buttered 13"x9"x2" baking dish. Place a slice of Swiss cheese on top of each breast. Mix both cans of soup with ¼ cup water; spread over chicken. Sprinkle stuffing mix over all, and drizzle melted butter on top. Bake at 350° for 50 minutes, or until done.

Hint: This dish is great served with long grain and wild rice. The chicken may be assembled a day ahead, and baked before serving.

Roberta Hemphill

CHICKEN ALMOND

Serves 6-8

4 whole chicken breasts, split
1 clove garlic, minced
¼ cup (½ stick) margarine
1 tablespoon paprika
1 tablespoon lemon juice
¼ teaspoon salt
1 (10¾-ounce) can condensed
  cream of mushroom soup

¼ cup skim milk
1 (4-ounce) can mushrooms,
  drained
½ tablespoon Worcestershire
  sauce
½ cup light sour cream
½ cup slivered almonds

Place chicken, skin-side up, in 13"x9"x2" pan. Sauté garlic in margarine until tender; remove from heat. Add paprika, lemon juice and salt to garlic. Pour garlic-lemon sauce over chicken, and bake at 350° for 30 minutes.

Combine soup, milk, drained mushrooms, Worcestershire sauce and sour cream in bowl. Mix, and spoon over chicken. Sprinkle with almonds. Return to oven, bake 30 minutes longer. Place chicken on serving platter, and spoon sauce over chicken.

Katy Engen

EASY CHICKEN BREAST CASSEROLE

Serves 8

8 boneless chicken breasts
8 strips bacon
1 (2.25-ounce) jar dried beef
1 (8-ounce) carton sour cream

1 (10¾-ounce) can condensed
   cream of mushroom soup
Salt and pepper to taste

Place dried beef on bottom of a 13"x9"x2" baking dish. Wrap chicken breasts with bacon and secure with toothpick; set atop dried beef. Mix sour cream and soup; pour over chicken breasts. Sprinkle with salt and pepper. Cover dish with foil, and bake at 350° for 1 hour. Uncover, and bake another 15 minutes to brown.

Hint: *This dish is delicious served over wild rice. Add tossed salad and a vegetable for a delightful, easy dinner!*

Sharon Schwing

SOUR CREAM CHICKEN BREASTS

Serves 6

6 boneless chicken breasts
2 cups sour cream
½ cup lemon juice
4 teaspoons Worcestershire
   sauce
4 teaspoons celery salt

2 teaspoons paprika
4 teaspoons salt
½ teaspoon pepper
1-2 cups Ritz cracker crumbs
½ cup (1 stick) butter

A day in advance, cut chicken breasts in half. In large bowl, combine sour cream, lemon juice, Worcestershire sauce, celery salt, paprika, salt and pepper. Add chicken to mixture and refrigerate, covered, overnight. The next day, preheat oven to 350.° Remove chicken from cream mixture and roll in dry cracker crumbs. Arrange chicken in shallow baking pan. Melt butter; spoon over chicken. Bake, uncovered, for 1 hour.

Note: *This is an easy and delicious recipe that I make often for my family. It is good with rice or any kind of potatoes.*

Jo Ann Brown

CHICKEN IN CRANBERRY GRAVY

Serves 6-8

6-8 chicken breasts
Salt and pepper to taste
Flour for dredging
4-6 tablespoons vegetable oil
1 medium onion, sliced
   (optional)

2 (10¾-ounce) cans condensed
   cream of chicken soup
1 (16-ounce) can jellied
   cranberry sauce

Season chicken breasts with salt and pepper, and dredge in flour. Brown chicken in oil; set aside. Line bottom of 13"x9"x2" casserole dish with sliced onions, if desired. Mix soup and cranberry sauce, spoon into casserole dish. Add browned chicken breasts, and cover dish with foil. Bake at 350° for 45 minutes.

Hint: *The cranberry gravy is also good over rice, potatoes or dressing.*

Kathy Creel

CHICKEN AND DRESSING CASSEROLE

Serves 8

1 (8-ounce) package cornbread
   stuffing mix
½ cup (1 stick) margarine,
   melted
1 cup water
2½ cups diced cooked chicken
   (4 whole breasts)
¾ cup diced onion
½ cup diced celery

¾ teaspoon salt
½ cup real mayonnaise
2 eggs
1½ cups milk
1 (10¾-ounce) can condensed
   cream of mushroom soup
2 cups (8-ounces) grated
   Cheddar cheese

Mix melted margarine and water with dressing mix; toss lightly to mix well. Place half of the dressing in the bottom of a greased 12"x8"x2" dish. Mix together chicken, onion, celery, salt and mayonnaise. Spread mixture over layer of dressing. Add remaining dressing for top layer. Beat eggs and milk together; pour over casserole. Cover, and refrigerate overnight or for several hours. Remove 1 hour before baking, and spread soup over top. Bake uncovered at 325° for 40 minutes. Remove and sprinkle with grated cheese.

Doris Aldrich

EASY CHICKEN POT PIE

Serves 4-6

3 chicken breasts
3 potatoes, diced
3 carrots, diced
1 onion, chopped
1 cup frozen peas

2 (10¾-ounce) cans condensed
   cream of chicken soup
1 cup milk
¼ teaspoon pepper
1 can layered refrigerator
   biscuits

Boil chicken breasts, cool; debone and shred. Cook diced potatoes, diced carrots, chopped onion and peas in a small amount of water until just tender; drain. Mix soup and milk together; add pepper. Mix together chicken, vegetables and soup mixture; pour into a 13"x9"x2" pan that has been sprayed well with non-stick cooking spray. Tear layers of biscuits apart and layer on top of chicken mixture. Bake at 450° for 20 minutes, covering loosely with foil after 12 minutes.

Ruth Seiwell

THREE-SOUP CHICKEN POT PIE

Serves 6

3-4 chicken breasts, cubed
1 (10¾-ounce) can condensed
   cream of celery soup
1 (10¾-ounce) can condensed
   cream of potato soup

1 (10¾-ounce) can condensed
   cream of chicken soup
1 (16-ounce) can mixed
   vegetables, drained
2 ready-made pie crusts

Cut chicken breasts into bite-size pieces. Preheat oven to 400°. Mix chicken, soups and vegetables in a bowl. Press one pie crust to fit bottom of a 13"x9"x2" pan. Pour in soup mixture; top with remaining crust. Bake for 1 hour.

Note: *Cream of mushroom soup may be substituted for potato soup.*

Patti Hosack

HELEN'S BAKED CHICKEN CASSEROLE

Serves 10-12

4 whole chicken breasts, cooked and cubed
1 onion, quartered
1 carrot
1 bay leaf
2-3 ribs of celery (including leafy part)
1 cup mayonnaise
1 cup plain yogurt
3 eggs, hard-boiled and diced
1 (10¾-ounce) can condensed cream of chicken soup
2 cups chopped celery

1 (8-ounce) can sliced water chestnuts
½ cup sliced almonds
4 heaping tablespoons dried, minced onions
2 tablespoons fresh-squeezed lemon juice
1 teaspoon salt
¼ teaspoon pepper
1 cup (4-ounces) grated Cheddar cheese
1 can crushed onion rings

Place quartered onion, carrot and bay leaf in large pan. Add chicken and celery; cover with water. Bring to a boil, then simmer, covered, for 30 minutes. Cool chicken; then cube. Combine mayonnaise and yogurt in a small bowl; set aside. Mix together all other ingredients (except the Cheddar cheese and onion rings) in a large bowl. Spoon into a 13"x9"x2" baking dish. Cover with foil; bake at 350° for 30 minutes. Remove from oven; top with Cheddar cheese and onion rings. Return to oven, bake uncovered another 15 minutes.

Helen Baker

BARBECUPS

Serves 4

1 can refrigerator biscuits
Non-stick vegetable spray
1 pound ground turkey
½ cup chopped onion

Honey barbecue sauce
2 tablespoons brown sugar
2 cups (8-ounces) sharp Cheddar cheese

Spray muffin pan with non-stick vegetable spray. Press one biscuit into each muffin tin to make a shell. Spray skillet with non-stick oil. Brown turkey and onions. Add enough barbecue sauce to coat meat, but not be soupy. Add brown sugar, and stir. Put turkey mixture in prepared biscuit shells. Top with Cheddar cheese. Bake at 350° for 10 minutes.

Diane Hill

PECAN-CHICKEN CASSEROLE

Serves 6-8

1 stewing chicken or 3 pounds
   chicken pieces
1 cup chopped celery
1 cup chopped pecans
2 tablespoons minced onion
1 (10¾-ounce) can condensed
   cream of chicken soup

1 cup mayonnaise
2 tablespoons lemon juice
½ teaspoon salt
½ teaspoon red pepper
Bread crumbs to taste
Paprika
Butter

Steam chicken until tender. Remove meat, cut into bite-size pieces. Mix with all other ingredients except bread crumbs, paprika and butter. Spoon mixture into a well-greased 13"x9"x2" casserole dish. Top with bread crumbs and paprika. Dot with butter. Bake uncovered at 350° until bubbly, about 30 minutes. This dish freezes well.

Jonsi Elam

POPPYSEED CHICKEN

Serves 6

3 cups cooked, diced chicken
1 (10¾-ounce) can condensed
   cream of chicken soup
1 cup (8-ounces) sour cream

1 sleeve of Ritz crackers
½ cup (1 stick) butter or
   margarine, melted
Poppy seeds

Mix together soup and sour cream; add chicken. Place in a lightly oiled 2-quart casserole dish. Finely crush 1 sleeve of crackers; sprinkle on top. Melt butter; pour over cracker crumbs. Sprinkle with poppy seeds, and bake at 350° until hot and bubbly, about 45 minutes.

Hint: *Save time and mess by placing the crackers in a zipper-top plastic bag. Crush with a rolling pin to make crumbs. Chicken may be cooked and diced in advance, and stored covered in the refrigerator.*

Sharon Shaver

~ **Keep pecans cool:** *Refrigerate unshelled pecans to retain freshness. Shelled pecans in an air-tight container can keep 3 months in the refrigerator, 2 years in the freezer. Frozen pecans can be used without thawing, and any unused pecans can be returned to the freezer without loss of quality.*

CHICKEN CAVALOTTE

Serves 4-6

2 cups cooked, cubed chicken
½ cup chopped onion
½ cup (1 stick) margarine,
  divided
¼ cup flour
2 cups milk
1 teaspoon salt
¼ teaspoon pepper

1 teaspoon paprika
¼ teaspoon poultry seasoning
1 (4-ounce) can sliced
  mushrooms
2 hard-cooked eggs, sliced
2 cups cooked rice
1 cup (4-ounces) grated cheese

Sauté onions in ¼ cup margarine until transparent. Melt remaining ¼ cup margarine in heavy saucepan. Blend in flour until thick and smooth. Add milk, salt, pepper, paprika and poultry seasoning. Stir over medium heat until thickened. Remove from heat; add onion, chicken, mushrooms and eggs. Lightly press cooked rice into the bottom of a 2-quart baking dish. (If a rounded casserole is used, press the rice slightly up the sides, leaving a depression in the middle.) Pour chicken mixture over rice, top with cheese, and bake at 350° for 30 minutes or until bubbly and brown.

Note: *This dish is a family favorite that can go into the dining room for company!*

Carol Bohley

EASY CHICKEN-RICE CASSEROLE

Serves 6

6 skinless chicken breasts
3 cups uncooked rice
6 cups water
2 (10¾-ounce) cans condensed
  cream of mushroom soup

¼ cup (½ stick) margarine,
  melted
Salt and pepper to taste

Clean chicken breasts, remove skin. Put rice, water and soup in a large Dutch oven; stir to mix. Place raw chicken breasts on top of rice mixture. Melt margarine; drizzle over chicken. Season with salt and pepper to taste. Cover, and bake at 350° about 2 hours. (Baking time will vary depending on the depth of the rice.) When all water is absorbed, remove lid and let chicken brown slightly, about 10 minutes.

Note: *This recipe is easy, and very good!*

Carol Ann Adam

CURRIED CHICKEN CASSEROLE

Serves 6-8

4 cups cooked, chopped chicken
2 (16-ounce) cans whole green
  beans
1 (8-ounce) can sliced water
  chestnuts
2 (2.8-ounce) cans Durkee's
  onion rings

¼ cup Miracle Whip dressing
1 teaspoon curry powder
2 (10¾-ounce) cans condensed
  cream of chicken soup
2 tablespoons chicken stock

Boil chicken, chop meat to make 4 cups. Layer green beans, water chestnuts, chicken and half the onion rings in a greased 13"x9"x2" casserole dish. In a bowl, mix Miracle Whip, curry powder, soup and chicken stock. Spoon mixture over casserole layers; top with remaining onion rings. Bake at 325° for 30 minutes.

Hint: Boil the chicken ahead of time to speed preparation.

Susie Hanchey

CHICKEN CRUNCH

Serves 6

2 cups diced cooked chicken
1 cup finely diced celery
2 (10¾-ounce) cans condensed
  cream of mushroom soup
½ soup can of water

1 (3-ounce) can chow mein
  noodles
1 (8-ounce) can sliced water
  chestnuts

Mix all ingredients. Place in a lightly oiled 13"x9"x2" dish; bake at 350° for 30 minutes.

Kim Gary

~ Blender crumbs: Use a blender to make crumbs. Break 7 or 8 crackers or cookies in a blender container, cover and process until crumbed. The longer you blend, the finer the crumb.

CHICKEN-BROCCOLI CASSEROLE

Serves 6-8

1 (3-pound) fryer, cooked,
  deboned, chopped
1 (16-ounce) package frozen
  broccoli or mixed vegetables
2 (10¾-ounce) cans condensed
  cream of chicken soup
½ cup mayonnaise or salad
  dressing
¼ cup lemon juice
½ cup bread crumbs
2 tablespoons butter or
  margarine, melted
¼ cup (1-ounce) shredded
  Cheddar cheese

Bake chicken for 1 hour; debone and chop meat; set aside. Cook vegetables until crisp/tender; set aside. Stir together soup, mayonnaise and lemon juice; set aside. Mix bread crumbs and melted butter; set aside. Lightly grease a 13"x9"x2" pan. Layer chicken, vegetables, soup mixture and crumbs. Bake at 350° for 20 minutes. Sprinkle on cheese; bake 5 minutes more.

Dee Swope

WANDA'S CHICKEN DIVAN

Serves 6

2 (10-ounce) boxes frozen
  broccoli spears
1 cup mayonnaise or salad
  dressing
½ teaspoon lemon juice
6 chicken breasts
2 (10¾-ounce) cans condensed
  cream of chicken soup
½ teaspoon curry powder
½ cup (1 stick) butter
1½ cups bread crumbs (or less,
  to taste)

Cook broccoli, place in buttered casserole dish. Mix mayonnaise and lemon juice, spread over broccoli. Place chicken on top of broccoli. Mix curry powder and soup, pour over chicken. Slice butter, scatter across top. Sprinkle with bread crumbs. Bake at 350° for 1½ hours.

Note: *This dish can be prepared in advance, and refrigerated until ready to bake.*

Deani Farrar

EVELYN'S CHICKEN SPAGHETTI

❤ *Heart healthy*   *Serves 8-10*

1 chicken, boiled
1 large onion, chopped
1 bunch green onions, chopped
2 bell peppers, chopped
3 celery stalks, chopped
2 tablespoons cooking oil
1 clove garlic, chopped

1 (6-ounce) can tomato paste
¼ cup Worcestershire sauce
1 bay leaf
Salt to taste
Broth reserved from chicken,
    skimmed of fat
1 (16-ounce) package spaghetti

Boil chicken, chop meat. Skim fat from broth; reserve broth. In skillet, sauté onions, peppers and celery in oil until tender. Add garlic and tomato paste; cook over low heat until mixture turns dark. Add Worcestershire sauce, bay leaf and salt to taste; plus enough broth to float all ingredients. Let simmer 1 hour, adding broth as needed. Cook and drain spaghetti; ladle sauce over spaghetti.

Jan Davis

SPICY CHICKEN SPAGHETTI

Serves 4

1 small onion, diced
1 (4-ounce) can mushroom
    pieces
1 tablespoon margarine
1½ cups (8-ounces) cooked,
    diced chicken

3 ounces Mexican Velveeta
    cheese, cubed
2 cups cooked spaghetti
1 (10¾-ounces) can reduced-
    calorie cream of mushroom
    soup

In 4-quart saucepan, sauté onion and mushrooms in margarine until onion is tender. Add chicken, cubed cheese, cooked spaghetti and soup; mix well. Transfer mixture to 8"x8" casserole dish coated with non-stick cooking spray. Bake, uncovered, at 350° until cheese melts, about 30 minutes.

Lisa Solis

FIESTA CHICKEN SPAGHETTI

Serves 8-10

1 chicken, boiled and chopped
1 (16-ounce) box spaghetti, cooked
1 onion, chopped
1 green pepper, chopped
1 (16-ounce) can tomatoes
1 (10¾-ounce) can condensed cream of mushroom soup
1 (6-ounce) jar sliced mushrooms
1 pound Velveeta cheese, grated or melted

Boil chicken, reserve broth. Skin and debone chicken, cut into bite-size pieces. Cook spaghetti, set aside. Sauté onion and green pepper in some of the broth. Add tomatoes, soup and mushrooms to pan. Add cooked spaghetti and chicken to soup mixture. Cook over low heat until spaghetti is well seasoned; adding broth as necessary to keep from getting too dry. Before serving, add cheese; stir well.

Deani Farrar

CHICKEN SPAGHETTI SUPREME

Serves 12

3 whole chicken breasts, cooked (about 4 cups chicken)
6 slices bread
2 tablespoons butter
1 (12-ounce) package spaghetti , broken into 2-inch pieces
1 green bell pepper, finely chopped
3-4 stalks celery, chopped
2 cups reserved chicken broth
2 (10¾-ounce) cans condensed cream of mushroom soup
1 pound grated Velveeta cheese
1 (2-ounce) jar diced pimientos
¾ cup white wine
4 teaspoons parsley flakes
1 envelope (2 tablespoons) dry Italian salad dressing mix
Salt and pepper to taste

Cook chicken; cut meat into bite-size pieces. Reserve broth. Make buttered bread crumbs by buttering six slices bread. Put each slice into blender, and blend on high to make crumbs. Cook spaghetti in salted water according to package instructions. Sauté green pepper and celery in some of the reserved broth until tender. Combine all ingredients except buttered crumbs, and transfer to a 3-quart buttered casserole dish. Top with crumbs; bake at 350° for 30 minutes or until brown and bubbly.

Note: *This casserole can be prepared ahead and refrigerated or frozen. If frozen, allow to thaw, then bake about 45 minutes.*

Carol Ann Adam

CHICKEN TETRAZZINI

Serves 6

¼ cup (½ stick) margarine
¼ cup flour
½ teaspoon salt
¼ teaspoon pepper
1 cup chicken broth
1 cup whipping cream
1 (10¾-ounce) can condensed
    cream of mushroom soup

1 (10-ounce) package fettuccine,
    cooked
2 cups cooked chopped chicken
    or turkey
1 (4-ounce) can sliced
    mushrooms, drained
½ cup Parmesan cheese

Preheat oven to 350°. Melt butter in large saucepan over low heat; blend in flour, salt and pepper. Cook over low heat, stirring until mixture is smooth and bubbly. Remove from heat; stir in broth, cream and soup. Heat to boiling, stirring constantly; boil and stir 1 minute. Stir in noodles, chicken and drained mushrooms. Pour into greased 2-quart casserole dish; sprinkle with Parmesan cheese. Bake uncovered at 350° for 30 minutes or until bubbly.

Linda Cullitan

SOUR CREAM TETRAZZINI

Serves 6

1 (4-pound) hen, boiled and
    chopped
1 (12-ounce) package spaghetti
    or fettuccine
¼ cup (½ stick) butter
1 (4-ounce) can sliced
    mushrooms, drained

1 tablespoon parsley flakes
2 (10¾-ounce) cans condensed
    cream of chicken soup
1 cup sour cream
1 cup Parmesan cheese

Boil chicken, chop meat into bite-size pieces. Cook and drain noodles. Melt butter in skillet, add mushrooms and sauté until golden. Add parsley and cooked chicken; simmer for 10 minutes. Add soups and sour cream to skillet. Combine with cooked noodles; mix well. Place in buttered 2-quart casserole dish; sprinkle with cheese. Bake at 300° until hot, about 15 minutes.

Nancy Germano

CHICKEN FETTUCCINE ALFREDO

Serves 6

1 pound fettuccine, cooked
¼ cup (½ stick) margarine
¼ cup olive oil
1 pound boneless, skinless
  chicken breasts, cubed
½ cup chopped green onions
  with tops
3 cloves garlic, minced
1 cup whipping cream

1 package McCormick Pasta
  Prima alfredo sauce
12 ounces fresh mushrooms,
  sliced
1 (16-ounce) can tomatoes,
  drained and diced
1 teaspoon salt
½ teaspoon pepper
¼ cup parsley, chopped
½ cup Parmesan cheese

Cook fettuccine according to package directions, keep warm. Heat margarine and olive oil in large skillet over medium heat. Add chicken, onion and garlic; sauté until chicken is lightly browned. Stir in cream, sauce mix, mushrooms, tomatoes, salt and pepper. Bring to a boil over high heat. Reduce heat to medium; simmer 3-5 minutes or until sauce is slightly thickened. Stir in parsley; remove from heat. Toss pasta with sauce, and sprinkle with Parmesan cheese.

Jeanne Howard

CHICKEN NOODLE CASSEROLE

Serves 8

1 chicken, boiled and deboned
1 (10¾-ounce) can condensed
  cream of chicken soup
1 (10¾-ounce) can condensed
  cream of mushroom soup
1 (10¾-ounce) can condensed
  cream of celery soup

1 (8-ounce) package egg noodles
1 (4¼-ounce) can sliced black
  olives
Salt and pepper to taste
2 cups (8-ounces) grated
  Cheddar cheese

Boil chicken, chop meat into bite-size pieces. Use broth to cook noodles according to package directions. Spoon undiluted soups into greased 2-quart casserole dish. Add cooked noodles, chicken and sliced olives. Mix well, and season to taste. Cover with grated cheese; bake at 325° for 10-15 minutes.

Tammi Blevins

MONTEREY CHICKEN

Serves 4

¼ cup flour
1 (1¼-ounce) package taco
  seasoning mix

4 skinned chicken breasts
¼ cup (½ stick) margarine
1 cup crushed tortilla chips

Cheese Sauce:

2 tablespoons chopped onion
1 tablespoon vegetable oil
2 tablespoons flour
¼ teaspoon salt
1 (13-ounce) can evaporated
  milk

¼ teaspoon hot pepper sauce
1 cup (4-ounces) grated
  Monterey Jack cheese
¼ cup sliced olives
1 teaspoon lemon juice
Shredded lettuce

Combine flour and taco seasoning in a bag. Add chicken, shake to coat. Melt margarine in baking pan. Place chicken in pan, and turn to coat. Roll each piece in crushed chips and return to baking pan. Bake at 375° about 30 minutes. To make cheese sauce, cook onion in oil until tender but not brown. Stir in flour and salt. Add milk and hot pepper sauce. Heat, stirring constantly, until bubbly. Cook an additional 1-2 minutes. Stir in cheese, olives and lemon juice; cook until cheese melts. Serve chicken on shredded lettuce, and pour cheese sauce over top.

Ann Ragsdale

INSTANT CHICKEN ENCHILADAS

Serves 8

1 small onion, chopped
2 tablespoons butter
1 (4-ounce) can chopped green
  chiles (mild or hot, to taste)
4 (5-ounce) cans chicken meat
  with juice (or 1 cooked
  chicken, chopped)
1½ cups chicken broth

2 (10¾-ounce) cans condensed
  cream of chicken soup
1 cup sour cream
2 teaspoons cumin powder (or to
  taste)
1 (10-ounce) bag Dorito chips
1 cup (4-ounces) grated cheese
Chili powder (optional)

Sauté onion in butter. Add green chiles, cooked chicken, broth, soup and sour cream. Mix well. Add cumin powder, to taste. Place chips in a greased 13"x9"x2" glass pan. Pour chicken mixture over chips. Cover with grated cheese. Bake at 350° until thoroughly heated, about 20 minutes. Sprinkle top with chili powder if desired.

Note: *Nacho-cheese flavored chips work well in this recipe.*

Barbara Lundahl

ENCHILADA TORTE

Serves 3-4

1 pound ground turkey
1 large onion, chopped
¼ cup bell pepper, chopped
2 cloves garlic, minced
2 tablespoons vegetable oil
1 (8-ounce) can tomato sauce
½ cup picante sauce plus ¼ cup picante, divided
2 teaspoons chili powder

½ teaspoon ground cumin
2-3 chopped jalapeños (or to taste)
¾ cup pitted black olives
7-8 corn tortillas
1½ cups (6-ounces) grated Cheddar cheese
1½ cups (6-ounces) grated Monterey Jack cheese

Lightly sauté turkey, onion, bell pepper and garlic in oil. Add tomato sauce, picante, chili powder, cumin and jalapeños. Simmer 5 minutes. Add olives. Put 2-3 tortillas in bottom of lightly oiled 2-quart casserole. Top with ⅓ of meat mixture and ⅓ of mixed cheeses. Repeat layers 3 times, ending with cheese. Top with ¼ cup picante sauce (or to taste). Bake at 350° until heated through, about 20 minutes.

Note: *No one will realize this is turkey! Low-fat cheese can be substituted.*

Lisa Baker

TURKEY ENCHILADAS

Serves 4-6

½ medium onion, chopped
1 large garlic clove, chopped
2 tablespoons vegetable oil
1 pound ground turkey
1 (10-ounce) can Mexican-style stewed tomatoes
1 tablespoon chili powder

1 tablespoon cumin
Salt and pepper to taste
10 flour tortillas
2 cups (8-ounces) shredded Cheddar or Monterey Jack cheese

In a large skillet, sauté chopped onion and garlic in oil over medium heat. Add turkey, stir until cooked through. Add tomatoes; stir. Add chili powder, cumin, salt and pepper; cook about 2 minutes. Fill each tortilla with several spoonfuls turkey mixture, sprinkle with cheese, and roll up. (At this point, enchiladas can be baked or frozen.) To bake immediately, line enchiladas seam-down in a greased 13"x9"x2" casserole. Sprinkle remaining cheese on top. Bake in preheated 375° oven about 10 minutes. To freeze, put enchiladas on a cookie sheet in freezer. Once frozen, seal in plastic bags. Bake frozen enchiladas in preheated 325° oven 20-25 minutes, or until hot.

Jonsi Elam

SOUR CREAM CHICKEN ENCHILADAS

Serves 4-6

10 flour tortillas
3 cups cooked chopped chicken
1 onion, chopped

4 cups (1 pound) shredded
  Monterey Jack cheese

Sour Cream Sauce:

½ cup (1 stick) butter, melted
3 tablespoons flour
2 cups chicken broth

1½ cups sour cream
2 (4-ounce) cans diced green
  chiles

Combine chicken, cheese and onion; spoon ¹/₁₀ of mixture onto each tortilla. Roll up tortillas, and place in a 13"x9"x2" baking pan or glass dish. To make sauce, melt butter; stir in flour and chicken broth. Bring to a boil. Fold in sour cream and heat almost to boiling. Add green chiles. Pour sauce over assembled stuffed tortillas. Bake at 350° for 20 minutes.

Cheri McBurnett

KING RANCH CHICKEN

Serves 8

1 chicken, cooked and chopped
Reserved chicken broth
1 medium onion, chopped
2 stalks celery, chopped
⅔ cup chopped green pepper
¼ cup (½ stick) butter
1 dozen corn tortillas
1 (10¾-ounce) can condensed
  cream of mushroom soup

1 (10¾-ounce) can condensed
  cream of chicken soup
½ can (5-ounces) diced tomatoes
  with green chiles
1 teaspoon chili powder
2 cups (8-ounces) grated
  Cheddar cheese (or to taste)

Cook chicken, chop meat. Reserve broth. Sauté onion, celery and green pepper in butter. Soak tortillas in reserved broth, and layer on bottom of greased 13"x9"x2" pan. Mix chicken with vegetables; layer over tortillas. Mix tomatoes with chiles, soups and chili powder; heat. Pour over chicken. Cover with cheese. Bake at 350° for 30-40 minutes. Dish freezes well.

Gwen Williams

MARINATED GRILLED CHICKEN

Serves 6

6 boneless skinless chicken
  breasts
¼ cup soy sauce
¼ cup vegetable oil

1 tablespoon wine vinegar
2 tablespoons ketchup
¼ teaspoon pepper
2 cloves garlic, crushed

Combine soy sauce, oil, vinegar, ketchup, pepper and garlic; pour over chicken breasts. Refrigerate overnight. Remove chicken from marinade; grill over hot coals.

Note: *For fish or duck, add 1 tablespoon lemon juice to marinade.*

Mary Ann Sosebee

CHICKEN FAJITAS

Serves 6-8

4 whole boneless, skinless
  chicken breasts
12 warm flour tortillas

1 large onion, sliced
2 bell peppers, sliced

Chicken Fajita Marinade:

½ cup (4-ounces) fresh lime
  juice
½ cup (4-ounces) olive oil
2 tablespoons (1-ounce) top-
  quality Worcestershire sauce
2 whole cloves
1 bay leaf
1 teaspoon marjoram

1 tablespoon celery salt
1 tablespoon cumin
1 tablespoon brown sugar
2 cloves garlic, crushed or
  minced
1 tablespoon paprika
Chili powder to taste

Combine all marinade ingredients. Marinate chicken at least 4 hours, preferably all day. Grill chicken with onion and peppers to desired doneness. Slice chicken into thin strips; serve with warm flour tortillas and your favorite fajita fixings.

❤ **Heart healthy hint:** *If you are watching your diet, eat the chicken and grilled vegetables, but skip the high-fat fixings.*

Maureen Schefsky

~ **Kitchen tip:** *To soften tortillas or crêpes, wrap in a damp paper towel and microwave on high for 30 seconds.*

EVA'S BEEF FAJITAS

Serves 4-6

2½ pounds beef skirt steak

8-12 warm flour tortillas

Beef Fajita Marinade:

¼ cup pineapple juice
¼ cup orange juice
¼ cup lemon juice
¼ cup white wine
¾ cup water
¼ cup soy sauce

1 clove garlic, chopped
3 green chiles, chopped
Rind of lemon and orange
1 teaspoon pepper
3 tablespoons butter, melted

Combine all marinade ingredients, mix well. Marinate beef overnight, turning occasionally. Grill steak to desired degree of doneness. Slice meat into thin strips. Wrap the meat in warm flour tortillas.

Hint: Serve with sliced green peppers, red peppers and onions sautéed in small amount of cooking oil and wine. Garnish with salsa, sour cream and grated cheese, serve with guacamole and refried beans if desired.

Eva Kinney

ALL ABOUT MARINADES:

Marinades impart flavor, and in some cases tenderize tougher cuts of meat. Combine liquid ingredients such as fruit or vegetable juices, wine, water and oil with seasonings and herbs.

…To tenderize, marinade must contain an acidic ingredient such as lemon juice, wine, vinegar or yogurt. For flavor, marinade 15 minutes to 2 hours. To tenderize, marinate at least 6 hours or overnight.

…Always marinate in the refrigerator, never at room temperature. Discard marinade after one use to prevent contamination.

…Allow ¼ to ½ cup of marinade for each 1-2 pounds of meat. Select dishes in which the meat will fit snugly but lie flat. Turn meat occasionally so that all sides are equally exposed.

FABULOUS FAJITAS

Serves 10-12

**8 -10 pounds tenderized skirt or
flank steak**
12-24 warm flour tortillas

2 sliced onions
2 sliced bell peppers

Fajita Marinade:

1 cup soy sauce
¾ - 1 cup pineapple juice
½ cup brown sugar
½ cup Worcestershire sauce
½ cup Italian dressing

½ cup vinegar
1 teaspoon garlic powder
1 teaspoon salt
1 cup chopped onion

Mix together soy sauce, pineapple juice, brown sugar, Worcestershire sauce, Italian dressing, vinegar, garlic powder, salt and chopped onion. Trim excess fat from beef; place in marinade. Marinate meat in refrigerator overnight (or at least 10 hours). Grill over red hot coals with mesquite chips. While beef is cooking, sauté sliced onions and bell peppers until tender. Serve the beef sliced hot off the grill with sautéed vegetables, wrapped in flour tortillas.

Note: *The marinade will keep in the refrigerator for several weeks, provided chopped onions are not added until just prior to use. Divide marinade to use on smaller batches of meat at different times. Chicken breasts may be substituted for beef.*

Wendy Mathews

ORREN'S CROCKPOT FAJITAS

Serves 6-8

**5 - 6 pounds tenderized fajita
meat**
1 small jar liquid smoke
1 large onion, sliced

**Fiesta brand mesquite fajita dry
seasoning mix to taste (more is
better)**

Trim fat from meat, cut into strips, coat on both sides with Fiesta seasoning. Pour liquid smoke over coated meat; marinate in refrigerator 8 hours or overnight. Put into crockpot with sliced onion; cook for 6-7 hours. Serve with flour tortillas, sautéed onions and green peppers, and refried beans.

Marcie Allen

BARBECUED BRISKET

Serves 20

1 (7-pound) store-trimmed beef
  brisket
2 teaspoons onion salt
1 tablespoon celery salt
1 teaspoon garlic salt

4 teaspoons MSG or 2 teaspoons
  meat tenderizer
2 tablespoons Worcestershire
  sauce
1½ tablespoons liquid smoke

Optional Barbecue Sauce:

½ cup (1 stick) butter
¼ cup vinegar
¼ cup Worcestershire sauce
¼ cup sugar
2 teaspoons hot pepper sauce

2 cups ketchup
¼ cup lemon juice
½ cup water
1 large onion, chopped
Salt and pepper to taste

Rub brisket with onion salt, celery salt, garlic salt and meat tenderizer. Let stand about 30 minutes. Place in roaster, pour Worcestershire sauce and liquid smoke over surface of roast. Cover and refrigerate several hours, or overnight. Drain off marinade, wrap brisket fatty-side up in heavy-duty foil and seal. Bake at 300° for 5 hours. Allow to cool. Slice thinly across the grain.

To make sauce, combine all ingredients and simmer for 20 minutes over medium heat. (Yields 1 quart.) If desired, place sliced brisket in a baking dish, cover with barbecue sauce and bake at 325° for 20 minutes.

Linda Jordan

SEASONED SALT

✓ *Quick to fix*   *Yields about 3 cups*

3 cups salt
6 tablespoons paprika
8 teaspoons dry mustard
4 teaspoons thyme
4 teaspoons ground marjoram

4 teaspoons garlic salt
4 teaspoons curry powder
2 teaspoons onion powder
2 teaspoons celery salt

Place all ingredients into electric blender; process at medium speed until well blended. Pour into containers with shaker tops.

Hint: *Fill attractive containers with seasoned salt for clever gifts.*

Nancy Standlee

BUD'S SUMMER STEAK SALAD

Serves 4

1½ pounds top round steak
1 cup sour cream
1 cup mayonnaise
1 teaspoon curry powder
1 crisp Granny Smith apple,
   peeled and chopped

½ green pepper, chopped
1 avocado, peeled and chopped
1 bunch red-leaf lettuce, torn
   into bite-size pieces

To prepare sauce, mix sour cream, mayonnaise and curry powder. Peel apple, chop into bite-size pieces; add to mixture. Chop green pepper; peel avocado and cut into bite-size pieces. Add both to sauce; stir well. Place in refrigerator until serving time. Grill steak on a gas grill or barbecue pit until well done. Slice steak in very thin (¼-inch) strips across the grain. Place steak slices on a bed of red-leaf lettuce. Top with sauce.

Hint: *Add a loaf of hot French bread and a bottle of favorite red wine for a complete meal.*

Jody Epps

DEE'S PEPPER STEAK

Serves 6-8

1 pound round steak
1 tablespoon paprika
1 teaspoon salt
½ teaspoon black pepper
2 tablespoons oil
2 cloves garlic, crushed
1½ cups beef bouillon

1 cup sliced scallions
2 bell peppers, cut in strips
2 tablespoons cornstarch
¼ cup soy sauce
¼ cup water
2 fresh tomatoes, cut in ⅛ths
3 cups hot, cooked rice

Pound steak to ¼-inch thickness. Cut into ¼-inch wide strips. Sprinkle with paprika, salt and pepper, and let stand while preparing other ingredients. Brown meat in oil in Dutch oven or large pot. Add garlic and bouillon. Cover and simmer 30 minutes. Stir in peppers and onions. Cover and cook 5 minutes more. Blend cornstarch, water and soy sauce and stir into meat mixture. Stir and cook until thickened; about 5 minutes. Add tomato wedges, and serve over rice.

Dee Swope

BEEF STROGANOFF SUPREME

Serves 4-6

2 pounds beef tenderloin, cut in
   strips
½ cup flour
1 teaspoon salt
⅛ teaspoon pepper
½ cup finely chopped onion
¾ cup (1½ sticks) butter, divided

2 cups boiling water
3 cubes beef bouillon
1 cup (8-ounces) sour cream
3 tablespoons tomato paste
1 teaspoon Worcestershire sauce
½ pound fresh mushrooms,
   cleaned and sliced

Shake beef strips in a large plastic bag containing flour, salt and pepper. Heat ½ cup butter in large skillet, add beef and chopped onion. Brown slowly on all sides. Boil 2 cups water, add 3 bouillon cubes, and dissolve. When meat is browned, add beef broth, cover, and simmer 20-25 minutes. Sauté mushrooms in ¼ cup butter until lightly browned, and add to beef. Mix sour cream, tomato paste and Worcestershire sauce. Remove beef from heat, add small amounts of sour cream mixture until completely blended. Return to heat to rewarm — do not boil. Serve over rice or noodles.

Karen Moran

SECRET SURPRISE STROGANOFF

Serves 6-8

1½ to 2 pounds round steak
⅓ cup (⅔ stick) butter or
   margarine
2 (10¾-ounce) cans condensed
   chicken with rice soup

1 (16-ounce) carton sour cream
2 (4-ounce) cans sliced B&B
   mushrooms
1 (12-ounce) package wide egg
   noodles, cooked

Trim fat, and slice steak into thin strips. In a large skillet, melt butter and brown the steak. Stir in soup, cover, and simmer on medium-low heat for 15 minutes, stirring occasionally. Stir in sour cream. Drain mushrooms, reserving liquid; add mushrooms to meat mixture. Cover, and simmer on low heat for 10 minutes. Uncover, and simmer about 5 more minutes, adding reserved liquid, if necessary, for desired consistency. Serve over hot, buttered noodles.

Note: *Chicken with rice soup is the surprise ingredient — but once the stroganoff is cooked, you can't tell it's there. This dish is very easy, yet elegant enough for company.*

Lisa Ondrey

BEEF TENDERLOIN IN MARCHAND DE VIN

Serves 6-8

**1 (4- or 5-pound) whole
  tenderloin
Olive oil**

**Freshly ground pepper
Mrs. Dash seasoning (original,
  salt-free blend)**

Marchand de Vin Sauce:

**½ clove garlic
¼ cup (½ stick) butter, divided
2 tablespoons flour
1½ cups hot beef broth, divided**

**Salt and pepper to taste
1 cup sliced mushrooms
½ cup dry red wine**

Rub tenderloin with olive oil, and sprinkle liberally with pepper and Mrs. Dash seasoning. Let meat stand for 1 hour before roasting. Put meat on rack in shallow baking/roasting pan; insert meat thermometer. Place in preheated 450° oven, and reduce heat to 350.° Roast to 140° on meat thermometer, or to medium-rare (about 45 minutes, depending on weight of tenderloin). Let meat stand 5-10 minutes. Slice ½-inch thick pieces, and serve with Marchand de Vin sauce ladled over each slice.

Make the sauce while the tenderloin is roasting. Rub a saucepan with ½ clove garlic, then melt 2 tablespoons butter in the pan. Stir in 2 tablespoons flour until blended. Stir in 1 cup hot beef broth (canned or made from bouillon cubes.) Permit the sauce to reach boiling point, stirring constantly. Season with salt and pepper to taste; set aside.

Sauté mushrooms in remaining 2 tablespoons butter. Add remaining ½ cup hot beef broth, and simmer for 10 minutes. Add 1 cup of brown sauce prepared above, and ½ cup red wine. Simmer for 20 minutes, then serve over slices of tenderloin.

Hint: *This is nice to serve for a special dinner occasion. Our family loves to have it on Christmas Eve.*

Judy Robinson

~ **Rubbing it in:** *Rubs are highly concentrated blends of herbs and spices used to flavor meat as it cooks. Create your own or use a commercial blend. Rubs can be applied to the exterior surface of meat just before cooking, but for convenience and more pronounced flavor, apply several hours in advance.*

TWO-SOUP ROAST

Serves 8

1 (3½-4 pound) beef round or
    chuck pot roast
2 tablespoons oil
1 (10¾-ounce) can condensed
    cream of mushroom soup

1 pouch dry onion soup mix
1¼ cups water, divided
6 medium potatoes, quartered
6 carrots
2 tablespoons flour

Heat oil in Dutch oven; add roast, and brown on all sides. Spoon off fat. Stir together mushroom soup, dry onion soup mix and 1 cup water, pour over roast. Reduce heat to low, cover, and simmer for 2 hours or until meat is tender, turning occasionally. Add vegetables, cover, and cook an additional 40 minutes or until vegetables are tender. To make gravy, remove roast and vegetables from pan. In a small bowl, stir together the remaining ¼ cup water and 2 tablespoons flour to make a paste. Cook the drippings from the roast over medium heat, until slightly thickened. Add the flour paste gradually, stirring constantly, until the mixture boils and thickens. Serve alongside roast.

Sandy Carlberg

WORLD'S GREATEST MICROWAVE MEATLOAF

Serves 6

1 (8-ounce) can tomato sauce
¼ cup brown sugar
¼ cup vinegar
1 teaspoon prepared mustard
1 egg, slightly beaten

1 medium onion, minced
¼ cup Italian bread crumbs
2 pounds lean ground beef
1½ teaspoons salt
¼ teaspoon pepper

Combine tomato sauce, brown sugar, vinegar and mustard in small bowl, set aside. Combine egg, onion, bread crumbs, ground beef, salt and pepper in a mixing bowl. Add ½ of tomato mixture and blend thoroughly. Shape into an oval loaf in an oblong baking dish. Make a depression in top of loaf, pour remaining tomato mixture over top of meat. Cook, uncovered, on medium power for 25-30 minutes, or until center is cooked. (Rotate ¼ turn at 10-minute intervals.) Cover meat and let stand about 10 minutes before serving.

Note: *Cooking time will vary according to microwave wattage. Meatloaf can be made ahead, then sliced and frozen in portions for smaller servings.*

Linda St. Lawrence

RED, WHITE AND GREEN CANNELLONI

Serves 6

12 cannelloni shells
2 tablespoons grated Parmesan
  cheese
3 cups tomato sauce
½ cup (1 stick) butter, divided

¼ cup plus 2 tablespoons flour
1 cup milk
1 cup whipping cream
⅛ teaspoon white pepper

Beef-Spinach Filling:

¼ cup diced onion
1 teaspoon minced garlic
2 tablespoons olive oil
1 (10-ounce) package frozen
  chopped spinach, thawed,
  drained

1 pound ground beef
¼ cup plus 1 tablespoon grated
  Parmesan cheese
2 tablespoons whipping cream
2 eggs, slightly beaten
½ teaspoon dried whole oregano

Cook cannelloni shells according to package directions; drain, set aside. Combine 2 tablespoons Parmesan cheese and tomato sauce in small saucepan; cook over medium heat, stirring constantly, until mixture is thoroughly heated. Spread 1 cup of red sauce in a lightly greased 13"x9"x2" baking dish; set aside remaining sauce.

To make filling, sauté onion and garlic in olive oil in a large skillet until tender. Add spinach; cook, stirring often, until spinach is just tender. Remove spinach mixture; set aside. Add ground beef to skillet; cook over medium heat until brown, stirring to crumble; drain. Discard drippings from skillet. Add spinach mixture, ¼ cup plus 1 tablespoon Parmesan cheese, 2 tablespoons whipping cream, eggs, and oregano; mix well. Stuff cannelloni shells with ground beef/spinach mixture. Place filled cannelloni on tomato mixture in baking dish; set aside.

To make white sauce, melt ¼ cup plus 2 tablespoons butter in a heavy saucepan over low heat; add flour, stirring until smooth. Cook 1 minute, stirring constantly. Gradually add milk and 1 cup whipping cream; cook over medium heat, stirring constantly, until mixture is thickened and bubbly. Stir in pepper. Pour over cannelloni; spoon remaining tomato mixture over cream sauce. Dot with 2 tablespoons butter. Bake uncovered at 375° for 20 minutes.

Betty Bendall

CHERI'S LASAGNA

Serves 6-8

1 (16-ounce) package lasagna noodles, cooked
1 (16-ounce) carton ricotta cheese or cottage cheese
1 (8-ounce) package cream cheese

¼ cup (½ stick) margarine, softened
1 egg, beaten
3 tablespoons chopped chives
6 cups (1½ pounds) grated mozzarella cheese
1 cup grated Parmesan cheese

Meat Sauce:

1½ pounds lean ground beef
½ cup olive oil
½ cup chopped onion
1 clove garlic, minced
2 (6-ounce) cans tomato paste
1 (16-ounce) can tomatoes
1 cup water

¼ teaspoon salt
¼ teaspoon pepper
½ teaspoon sugar
1 tablespoon parsley
1 bay leaf
¼ teaspoon oregano

To make meat sauce, brown ground beef in oil. Add onion and garlic, sauté. Add tomato paste, tomatoes, water and seasonings. Cook in a covered pot over low heat for one hour, stirring occasionally.

Cook lasagna noodles according to package directions, set aside. Cream together ricotta cheese, cream cheese, butter, egg and chives. Grease a 13"x9"x2" baking dish, and cover bottom with thin layer of meat sauce. Layer noodles, meat sauce, ricotta cheese mixture and mozzarella cheese. Repeat layers, ending with noodles. Top noodles with Parmesan cheese. Bake at 350° for 45 minutes. Let stand for 10 minutes before serving.

Note: *This recipe freezes well. It makes a great special-occasion dish!*

Cheri McBurnett

~ **Freezer Meat Storage:** *Maximum storage times for properly wrapped, uncooked meat frozen at 0 degrees are: Beef and lamb, 8-12 months; pork, 4-8 months; ground meat, 3-4 months; sausage, 1-3 months.*

MAMA LOZANO'S LASAGNA

Serves 8

1 pound lean ground beef
1 clove garlic, minced
1 tablespoon basil
1½ teaspoons salt
1 (16-ounce) can stewed
   tomatoes
1 cup water
1 (10-ounce) package lasagna
   noodles

2 eggs
3 cups nonfat cottage cheese
½ cup grated Romano cheese
2 tablespoons parsley flakes
1 teaspoon salt
½ teaspoon pepper
1 pound nonfat grated
   mozzarella cheese

Brown meat slowly, drain fat. Stir in garlic, basil, salt and tomatoes. Add 1 cup water; simmer covered 15 minutes, stirring often. Cook noodles in boiling water until tender, drain. Beat eggs, stir in cottage cheese, Romano cheese, parsley, salt and pepper. Layer half the noodles in a 13"x9"x2" baking dish. Spread half the cottage cheese filling on top of noodles, top with half the mozzarella cheese and then half the meat sauce. Repeat layers. Bake at 375° about 30 minutes or until heated through. Let stand 10 minutes before serving.

Note: *Dish can be assembled ahead and refrigerated. If cold, bake for 45 minutes. Use non-cholesterol egg substitute in place of eggs if desired.*

Cheryl Whitten

SPICY MEATBALLS

Serves 4

1½ pounds ground beef
1 cup crushed gingersnaps,
   divided
½ teaspoon salt
½ cup chopped onion

2 eggs
2 or 3 (8-ounce) cans tomato
   sauce
1½ teaspoons onion salt

Mix together meat, ½ cup crushed gingersnaps, salt, onion and eggs. Form into meat balls. Brown lightly in skillet, drain off grease. Mix tomato sauce, salt and ½ cup gingersnaps together to make sauce; pour over meatballs. Simmer for 30 minutes. Serve over rice, if desired.

Janice Keller

BAKED SPAGHETTI

Serves 10-12

2 pounds ground beef
1 cup chopped onion
1 clove garlic, minced
1 (28-ounce) can tomatoes
1 (16-ounce) can tomato sauce
1 (6-ounce) can tomato paste
2 teaspoons sugar
1½ teaspoons oregano

1 teaspoon salt
1 teaspoon basil
1 (8-ounce) package spaghetti,
    cooked and drained
8 cups (2 pounds) shredded
    mozzarella cheese
½ cup grated Parmesan cheese

Cook ground beef with onion and garlic; drain. Stir in tomatoes, tomato sauce, tomato paste, sugar, oregano, salt and basil; simmer, uncovered, for 30 minutes. Stir in cooked, drained spaghetti. Put half the spaghetti mixture in a greased 13"x9"x2" baking dish. Cover with half the mozzarella cheese. Add rest of spaghetti, and top with remaining mozzarella cheese. Sprinkle with Parmesan cheese. Bake at 375° for 30 minutes.

Note: *This is a great party dish to fix ahead of time. With a green salad and French bread, it goes a long way in serving a large group.*

Debbie Gentry

PIZZA CASSEROLE

Serves 6

1½- 2 cups cooked elbow
    macaroni
1 (14-ounce) jar Ragu Pizza
    Quick Sauce
1 (8-ounce) carton cottage
    cheese

1½ cups (6-ounces) shredded
    mozzarella cheese
½ pound ground beef, cooked
    and drained
½ pound mild Italian sausage,
    cooked and drained

Combine all ingredients; place in 2-quart casserole dish. Bake uncovered at 350° for 30-35 minutes. Other pizza "toppings" (sautéed onion and bell pepper, chopped pepperoni, sliced mushrooms or black olives, etc.) may be added. Dish freezes well, but must be thawed before baking.

Cindy Cathcart

CRESCENT ITALIAN CASSEROLE

Serves 4-6

1½ pounds ground beef
¼ cup chopped onion
¼ cup chopped bell pepper
1 (8-ounce) can tomato sauce
½ teaspoon salt
¼ teaspoon pepper
½ teaspoon garlic salt
½ teaspoon Italian seasoning

1 cup sour cream
1 cup (4-ounces) grated Cheddar
  cheese
1 (8-ounce) can crescent
  refrigerator rolls
2 tablespoons butter or
  margarine, melted
⅓ cup Parmesan cheese

Cook ground beef in skillet until brown. Add onion and bell pepper; cook until tender. Add tomato sauce, salt, pepper, garlic salt and Italian seasoning. Mix well, pour into lightly oiled 12"x8"x2" baking dish. Spread sour cream over meat mixture, and sprinkle grated cheese on top. Separate rolls into four rectangles, place over cheese. Brush with melted butter and sprinkle Parmesan cheese on top. Bake at 375° for 20-25 minutes. Cut into squares.

Roberta Hemphill

SPINACH FANDANGO

Serves 8

1 pound ground beef or sausage
1 teaspoon oregano
Salt and pepper to taste
2 (10-ounce) packages frozen
  chopped spinach, thawed,
  drained

1 (10¾-ounce) can condensed
  cream of celery soup
1 (6-ounce) jar of mushrooms,
  drained
¼ teaspoon garlic powder
2 cups (8-ounces) grated
  mozzarella cheese

Brown meat, add oregano, salt and pepper to taste. Drain. Add spinach, soup, mushrooms and garlic powder. Pour into shallow baking dish; cover with grated cheese. Bake at 350° for 15-20 minutes.

Tammi Blevins

MEXICAN LASAGNA

Serves 8

1½ pounds ground beef
1 teaspoon seasoned salt
1 (1¼ ounce) package taco
   seasoning mix
1 cup diced tomatoes (fresh or
   canned)
2 (8-ounce) cans tomato sauce
1 (4-ounce) can diced green
   chilies

1 (8-ounce) carton ricotta
   cheese
2 eggs
9 corn tortillas
2½ cups (10-ounces) grated
   Monterey Jack cheese
Sour cream (optional)

Brown ground beef in skillet until crumbly, drain fat. Add seasoned salt, taco seasoning mix, tomatoes, tomato sauce and chiles. Bring to a boil; reduce heat and simmer, uncovered, 10 minutes. Combine ricotta cheese and eggs. In bottom of 13"x9"x2" baking dish, spread ½ meat mixture. Top with ½ the tortillas and spread with ½ the grated cheese. Repeat once more, ending with grated cheese. Bake at 350° for 20-30 minutes. Let stand 10 minutes before cutting into squares. Serve with sour cream, if desired.

Schelli Martin

TACO PIE

Serves 4-6

1 pound ground beef
2 (8-ounce) cans tomato sauce
1 (1¼-ounce) package taco
   seasoning mix
1 (8-ounce) can crescent
   refrigerator rolls

½ pound Velveeta Mexican
   cheese, cubed
Optional:
1 cup shredded lettuce
½ cup chopped tomato
¼ cup sliced black olives

Brown meat, drain. Stir in tomato sauce and taco mix. Simmer 5 minutes. Press crescent roll dough onto bottom and sides of ungreased 12-inch pizza pan, pressing edges together to seal. Prick bottom and sides with fork. Bake crust at 375° for 10-12 minutes, or until golden brown. Cover crust with meat mixture, top with Velveeta Mexican cheese. Bake at 375° until cheese melts. If desired, top with lettuce, tomatoes and olives, serve with sour cream.

Jenny Pennington

MEXICAN CORNMEAL CASSEROLE

Serves 8

1 pound ground beef, browned
1 cup cornmeal
1 cup milk
1 teaspoon salt
1 teaspoon baking soda
2 eggs, beaten
⅓ cup cooking oil

1 cup (4-ounces) grated Cheddar cheese
1 (16½-ounce) can cream-style corn
1 medium onion, finely chopped
4 fresh jalapeños, chopped, OR 1 (4-ounce) can diced green chiles

In large mixing bowl, combine cornmeal, milk, salt, baking soda, eggs, oil, cheese, cream-style corn, onion, and jalapeños. Mix well, add ground beef that has been browned and drained well. Pour into a greased 13"x9"x2" pan. Bake at 350° for 45 minutes or until golden brown on top. Cut into squares to serve.

Note: *This makes an easy one-dish meal. It microwaves well, and kids love it!*

Becky Gilliland

EASY MEXICAN CASSEROLE

Serves 6-8

1 pound ground beef
1 cup chopped onion
½ can (5-ounces) diced tomatoes with chiles

1 (10¾-ounce) can condensed cream of chicken soup
½ cup milk
9 flour tortillas, torn in pieces
1 cup (4-ounces) grated cheese

Brown meat and onion in skillet. Remove skillet from heat, add diced tomatoes with chiles, soup and milk. Stir until well blended. Layer ½ the meat mixture in a baking dish, top with ½ the torn flour tortillas. Repeat layers. Top with grated cheese. Bake at 350° for 30 minutes.

Missy Funk

BOB'S FRANKS

Serves 4

1 (16-ounce) package franks
1 tablespoon butter
½ cup chopped onion
¾ cup ketchup
3 tablespoons vinegar
4 teaspoons Worcestershire
  sauce

4 teaspoons sugar
1 teaspoon paprika
1 teaspoon mustard
½ teaspoon black pepper
¼ teaspoon hot pepper sauce

Slice franks in half lengthwise. Sauté onion in butter in a large skillet. Mix all other seasonings in skillet, add frankfurters. Simmer covered for 20 minutes.

Barbara Franklin

FRANKFURTER-VEGETABLE CASSEROLE

Serves 6

1 cup chopped carrot
½ cup celery
½ cup chopped onion
1 tablespoon vegetable oil
1 pound frankfurters, sliced

1 (16-ounce) can baked beans
1 (10¾-ounce) can condensed
  bean soup
1 soup can of milk

Cornmeal dumplings:

½ cup cornmeal
½ cup flour
1 tablespoon sugar
1½ teaspoons baking powder

½ teaspoon salt
⅓ cup milk
1 egg, beaten
2 tablespoons vegetable oil

Sauté carrots, celery and onion in 1 tablespoon oil until tender. Add sliced frankfurters, cook for about 2 minutes. Add beans, soup and milk; mix thoroughly. Put bean mixture in lightly oiled 2-quart casserole dish. Stir together cornmeal, flour, sugar, baking powder and salt; set aside. Mix milk, beaten egg and 2 tablespoons oil; add dry ingredients. Put cornmeal dumplings on top of bean mixture; bake at 350° for 40 minutes.

Note: *Kids love this meal!*

Diane Hill

SAUSAGE-STUFFED YAMS

Serves 6

6 medium yams
2 tablespoons butter or
  margarine
2 tablespoons milk
1 egg

1 teaspoon salt
¼ teaspoon dried leaf oregano
4 ounces link sausages, cooked
  and sliced

Wash and dry yams. Place in shallow pan and bake at 350° for 40 minutes or until soft. Cut tops from yams, carefully scoop out centers and mash in large bowl. Add butter, milk, egg, salt and oregano; beat until smooth. Add sausage, mix well. Pile into yam shells and bake at 400° for 15 minutes.

Denice Foose

SAUSAGE-BROCCOLI LOAF

Serves 6

¾ pound bulk sausage
1 loaf frozen bread dough,
  thawed
2 cups (8-ounces) shredded
  mozzarella cheese

1 (10-ounce) package frozen,
  chopped broccoli, thawed and
  well drained

Cook sausage well; drain. On lightly floured surface, roll dough to 15"x8" rectangle. Sprinkle cheese over dough, leaving a 1-inch border around all edges. Top with sausage and broccoli. Bring long sides of dough together; seal. Seal ends. Place loaf seam-side down on a greased baking sheet. Bake at 350° for 30-35 minutes. Let stand 8-10 minutes. Cut into slices to serve.

Peggy Schrott

ZUCCHINI-SAUSAGE CASSEROLE

Serves 3-4

3-4 small zucchini, peeled and
  sliced
¼ pound sausage
½ cup chopped onion
½ cup cracker crumbs

1 egg, beaten
½ cup (2-ounces) shredded
  Cheddar cheese
¼ teaspoon garlic salt
¼ teaspoon thyme

Steam zucchini. Brown sausage and onion, drain. Combine all ingredients; pour into greased baking dish. Bake at 350° until set, about 30-35 minutes.

Ann Ragsdale

SPICY SAUSAGE CASSEROLE

Serves 8

1 pound sausage
2 medium onions, chopped
1 teaspoon salt
1/8 teaspoon pepper
4 tablespoons diced green chiles
10 eggs
2 cups half-and-half cream
1 (2¼-ounce) can sliced black
  olives, drained

1 (8¾-ounce) can whole kernel
  corn, drained
1 (10-ounce) can diced tomatoes
  with chiles
3 cups (12-ounces) shredded
  Monterey Jack cheese
Avocado slices for garnish

Fry sausage in large skillet until brown. Add onion; sauté until tender. Drain fat. Stir in salt, pepper and chiles, remove from heat. In large bowl, mix eggs and cream until blended. Stir in meat, olives, corn, tomatoes and cheese; pour into 13"x9"x2" glass dish. Bake at 375° for 30 minutes, or until knife inserted in center comes out clean. Let stand 10 minutes. Garnish with avocado.

Jane Koontz

HAM GOULASH

Serves 4-6

1/3 cup chopped green pepper
2/3 cup chopped onion
1/4 cup (1/2 stick) margarine
2 cups cooked, cubed ham
2 (16-ounce) cans stewed
  tomatoes, partially drained
1 (4-ounce) can sliced
  mushrooms, drained

1 (10-ounce) package large shell
  macaroni, cooked
2 cups cubed longhorn Cheddar
  cheese
Grated longhorn cheese for
  topping

Sauté green pepper and onion in margarine until tender. In a very large bowl, mix all ingredients except grated cheese. Place in a lightly greased 3-quart casserole dish, top with grated cheese. Bake at 350° until bubbly, about 30-40 minutes.

Note: *This recipe is great to make the day before it is used. Refrigerate or freeze casserole, and bake when needed. Increased baking time if chilled.*

Carol Bohley

WITLOOF (Belgian Endive With Ham)

Serves 4

8 Belgian endives
2 tablespoons margarine
2 tablespoons flour
1 cup milk (or more, as needed)

2 cups (8-ounces) grated
 Gruyère or Gouda cheese
8 slices ham

Wash endives, use tip of sharp knife to remove inner core from bottom of endive. (The core can be bitter, so should be removed.) Place endive in shallow pan with 1 inch water; gently boil for about 5 minutes. Use tongs to remove endive from pan; allow to drain. Reserve fluid from pan. Melt margarine in a heavy pan, add flour until a smooth thick paste forms. Measure endive water up to a cup, and use milk to make 2 cups of liquid. Add to flour mixture, stir well. Add cheese; stir until melted. Remove from heat. Roll each endive in a piece of ham, lay in a baking dish, and pour cheese sauce over all pieces. Bake at 350° for about 20 minutes, or until bubbly. Serve with mashed potatoes or small white potatoes, and fruit.

Note: *This recipe comes from the Netherlands. Every Dutch and Belgian housewife has a variation of this dish for her family.*

Carol Bohley

HAM ROLLS ELEGANTE

Serves 4-6

1 (10-ounce) package frozen
 broccoli spears
8 rectangular slices Swiss cheese
2 (4-ounce) packages 4"x7" ham
 slices (8 slices)

1 (10¾-ounce) can condensed
 cream of mushroom soup
½ cup sour cream
1 teaspoon prepared mustard

Cook broccoli according to package directions, just until crisp- tender; allow to cool. Place slice of cheese on each slice of ham. Divide broccoli; place ⅛ portion on each ham stack. Roll up securely; place in large shallow baking dish, seam-side down. Thoroughly blend soup, sour cream and mustard; pour over ham rolls. Bake, uncovered, 20 minutes or until bubbly. Cream of chicken soup may be substituted for mushroom soup.

Bonnie Novosad

HAM LOAF

Serves 6-8

1½ pounds ground smoked ham	1 cup milk
1½ pounds ground fresh pork	1 green pepper, chopped
2 eggs	1 cup bread crumbs

Sauce:

1 cup brown sugar	¼ cup vinegar
1 cup water	½ teaspoon cloves or mustard

Combine ham, pork, eggs, milk, green pepper and bread crumbs. Shape into large loaf, place in loaf pan. To make sauce, combine sugar, water, vinegar and cloves or mustard. Pour half of sauce over loaf, bake at 350° for 2 hours. Baste loaf with remaining sauce during baking.

Denice Foose

MICROWAVE HAM-BROCCOLI CASSEROLE

Serves 4-6

2 (10-ounce) boxes frozen broccoli spears	1 cup (4-ounces) shredded Cheddar cheese
2 cups cubed cooked ham	1 (10¾-ounce) can condensed cream of mushroom soup
1 (2.8-ounce) can French-fried onion rings, divided	¼ cup milk

Place broccoli in a microwave, cook on high 5 minutes. Drain well, arrange in 13"x9"x2" baking dish, alternating heads and stems. Top with cubed ham, half the onion rings and cheese. Blend soup and milk, pour over casserole. Cover with wax paper, microwave on high for 8-10 minutes, or until broccoli is crisp-tender. (Rotate halfway through cooking time.) Sprinkle with remaining onion rings, microwave uncovered for 5-6 minutes on high, or until thoroughly heated.

Linda St. Lawrence

SWEET 'N SPICY PORK CHOPS

Serves 4

4 pork chops
½ cup apricot-pineapple
preserves

¼ cup soy sauce
¼ cup white wine

Spray large skillet and shallow baking dish with non-stick cooking spray. Brown pork chops in skillet, turning to brown both sides. Remove pork chops from pan, and place side-by-side in the prepared baking dish. Combine preserves, soy sauce and wine; pour over chops. Cover and bake at 350° for 45 minutes, or until tender. Serve with brown rice.

Susan Laver

PORK CHOPS WITH GARDEN VEGETABLES

Serves 4-6

4-6 thick, lean pork chops
1 tablespoon vegetable oil
½ pound fresh green beans, cut
in bite-size pieces
4 red potatoes, cubed

4 medium carrots, sliced
¼ teaspoon dried basil (slightly
less if using fresh basil)
2 envelopes dry onion soup mix
⅔ cups water

In large skillet with tight fitting lid, brown chops on both sides in oil. Drain. Add vegetables and basil. Mix soup and water; pour over chops and vegetables. Bring to boil, cover; simmer 45 minutes or until vegetables are tender.

Jane Ray

PORK CHOP CASSEROLE

Serves 4-6

4-6 pork chops
4 potatoes, sliced thin
1 onion, sliced in rings
1 green pepper, sliced in rings

1 (10¾-ounce) can condensed
cream of mushroom soup
1 soup can of milk
Salt and pepper to taste

Layer thinly sliced potatoes with onion and green pepper rings in a lightly oiled 13"x9"x2" baking dish. Mix soup and milk, pour over potato mixture. Season with salt and pepper to taste. Place raw pork chops on top of potatoes. Cover dish with aluminum foil, bake at 350° for 1 hour.

Sue Allen

JUNE'S PORK TENDERLOIN WITH CHERRY GLAZE

Serves 6

3 (¾-pound) pork tenderloins
1 cup chicken broth
¼ cup soy sauce
¼ cup vegetable oil
¼ cup honey
2 tablespoons sherry

1 tablespoon lemon juice
½ teaspoon cinnamon
1 clove garlic, pressed
1 teaspoon salt
2 tablespoons cornstarch

Cherry Glaze:

1 cup cherry preserves
2 tablespoons light corn syrup
1 tablespoon red wine vinegar

¼ teaspoon cinnamon
¼ teaspoon ground cloves
¼ teaspoon nutmeg

Combine broth, soy sauce, oil, honey, sherry, lemon juice, cinnamon, garlic and salt. Marinate pork in mixture for several hours or overnight, in refrigerator. Preheat oven to 325°. Drain meat; roll in cornstarch. Bake 1½ hours, uncovered, basting frequently with marinade. During last 15 minutes of baking time, brush meat with cherry glaze. To make glaze, melt preserves in small saucepan. Add other ingredients; mix well. Cook over low heat for 5 minutes.

Hint: *For an attractive presentation, serve on a platter lined with purple kale and garnish with cherries.*

Christy McConnell

SWEET AND SOUR SAUCE

✓ *Quick to fix*   *Yields about 1 cup*

½ cup ketchup
¼ cup white vinegar

½ cup peach or apricot
  preserves

Mix all ingredients, simmer in a saucepan for 2 minutes. Do not overcook. Cool to serve.

Lana Booher

PORK MEDALLIONS IN MUSTARD SAUCE

Serves 4

2 (¾-pound) pork tenderloins
3 tablespoons vegetable oil
1 tablespoon coarse-grain
   mustard
½ teaspoon salt

½ teaspoon pepper
¼ cup dry white wine
Fresh basil leaves for garnish
   (optional)

Mustard Sauce:

1¾ cups whipping cream
¼ cup coarse-grain mustard

¼ teaspoon salt
⅛ teaspoon white pepper

Combine oil, 1 tablespoon mustard, ½ teaspoon salt and ½ teaspoon pepper; mix well. Rub mixture over pork. Put tenderloins in a plastic bag; refrigerate 8 hours. Place tenderloins on rack in shallow roasting pan; insert meat thermometer into thickest part of meat. Bake at 375° for 25 minutes, or until thermometer registers 160°. Baste every 10 minutes with wine. To make mustard sauce, heat cream in heavy saucepan until cream cooks down to 1¼ cups (about 15 minutes.) Do not boil. Stir in ¼ cup mustard, ¼ teaspoon salt and white pepper; heat 1 minute. (Yields 1¼ cups sauce.)

Slice tenderloins into ¾-inch thick slices; arrange 4 slices on each dinner plate. Spoon Mustard Sauce around slices on plate. Garnish with fresh basil leaves.

Terrie Lumsden

VENISON GRILLADES

Serves 6

2 pounds venison steak
1½ teaspoons salt
2-3 tablespoons vegetable oil
2-3 tablespoons flour
2 quarts tomatoes
1 onion, chopped

½ green pepper, chopped
3 tablespoons parsley, chopped
3 cloves garlic, minced
½ teaspoon black pepper
½ teaspoon oregano
¼ teaspoon cayenne pepper

Cut venison into ½-inch slices; tenderize. Season with salt; lightly brown in a skillet with oil. Remove meat, add flour. Cook until roux is dark brown. Add all other ingredients. Mix well; bring to a boil. Reduce heat, return meat to skillet, and simmer, covered, 1½ hours or until meat is tender. Add water if needed. Serve on bed of rice.

Delores Smith

CITRUS LAMB ROAST WITH ORANGE GRAVY

Serves 6

1 (3-pound) center-cut leg of lamb roast
⅓ cup sliced green onions
¼ cup snipped parsley
2 tablespoons butter or margarine

1 teaspoon finely shredded orange peel
¼ teaspoon pepper
⅛ teaspoon salt

Orange Gravy:

¼ cup pan drippings
⅔ cup orange juice
1 tablespoon cornstarch

½ teaspoon instant chicken bouillon granules
¼ teaspoon crushed, dried basil
Salt and pepper to taste

Have the butcher bone, roll, and tie the roast. Combine green onions, parsley, butter, orange peel, pepper and salt. Unroll the roast, spread the onion mixture over the meat to within 1-inch of the side. Re-roll and tie the roast securely. Place fat-side up on a rack in a shallow roasting pan. Roast at 325° for 1½ to 1¾ hours, or until meat thermometer registers 150°. Let stand 15 minutes. Remove strings. Slice roast; serve with orange gravy.

To make gravy, skim fat from pan juices (place drippings in refrigerator until fat solidifies to simplify skimming.) Measure ¼ cup drippings and set aside. In a small saucepan, combine orange juice, cornstarch, bouillon granules and basil. Stir in pan drippings, and cook over medium heat until thick and bubbly. Lower heat and cook 2 minutes longer. Season with salt and pepper to taste.

Note: *This recipe gets rave reviews every time I serve it. Because of the seasonings, there is no need to offer mint jelly to weaken the lamb flavor.*

Linda St. Lawrence

MEAT SAFETY REMINDERS

...Defrost meat in the refrigerator, never at room temperature.

...Keep uncooked ground meat and poultry in the refrigerator for a maximum of 2 days.

...Put cooked meat on a clean plate, not the one used to carry it to the grill.

Desserts

CHILDREN'S MUSEUM
1989 - to present

From look-only scavenger hunts to hands-on learning displays, members of the Junior Service League's Children's Museum Committee like to keep youngsters and their parents coming back for more. Members of this service project plan special events at the Brazosport Museum of Natural Science, highlighting the facility's Nature Center, Nature Trail and Children's Museum. A series of popular Discovery Days, begun in 1992, has helped attract many first-time visitors to the museum.

PEACHES IN CHAMPAGNE

❤ *Low-fat*   *Serves 8*

2 pounds fresh peaches, peeled, halved and pitted	1 tablespoon sugar
¼ cup fresh lemon juice	1 split (small) bottle champagne

Cut peach halves into ½-inch long, finger-size slices. Place slices in bowl, add lemon juice and sugar; mix well. Pour champagne over peaches, cover tightly and allow to marinate in refrigerator several hours before serving. Spoon into dessert goblets and serve with biscotti or other delicate cookie.

Note: *This makes a very elegant, light dessert, perfect after a heavy meal and very nice for formal dinners. Each half-cup serving (excluding cookies) contains approximately 74 calories with negligible fat.*

Maureen Schefsky

STRAWBERRIES ROMANOFF

✓ *Quick to fix*   *Serves 8*

2 pints red, ripe strawberries	⅓ cup Grand Marnier or Cointreau
⅓ cup plus 2 tablespoons sugar, divided	1 orange
	¾ cup heavy cream

Remove stems from strawberries. Rinse well and drain, pat dry with paper towel. Place strawberries in a bowl, add ⅓ cup sugar and Grand Marnier. Using a swivel-bladed potato peeler, cut around the orange to produce a very thin spiral of peel. (Do not cut into the white pulp.) Cut peel into wafer-thin shreds. Add to strawberries and fold together gently. (Use the orange in another dish.) Cover bowl and refrigerate until ready to serve. Whip the cream; flavor it with the remaining 2 tablespoons of sugar. Serve the cream with the strawberries.

Denice Foose

~ **To peel a peach:** *Submerge peaches, plums or nectarines in boiling water for about 30 seconds, remove with slotted spoon and dip immediately into cold water. The skins will easily peel off.*

STRAWBERRIES AND CREAM

Serves 4

1 envelope unflavored gelatin
1 cup water
1 cup heavy cream
1 cup sugar

1 cup (½ pint) vanilla yogurt
2 teaspoons vanilla extract
1 pint strawberries

Put water in saucepan, sprinkle gelatin over water. Heat; add cream and sugar. Use spatula to stir over low heat until sugar dissolves. Remove from heat, add yogurt and vanilla; beat until blended. Stir in sliced strawberries. Serve dish by itself; over pound cake or angel food cake; or as the sauce in a trifle recipe.

Jo Ann Brown

CANTALOUPE MOUSSE

Serves 4

1¾ cups cubed cantaloupe
  (about 1 small melon)
2 tablespoons sugar
1 envelope unflavored gelatin
¼ cup water
½ cup whipping cream

1½ cups (9-ounces) semisweet
  chocolate pieces
2 tablespoons shortening
Toasted coconut for garnish
Cantaloupe slices for garnish

Place cubed cantaloupe in a blender or food processor; cover, blend until smooth. In a 1-quart saucepan, stir together sugar and gelatin; stir in water. Let stand 5 minutes; then cook and stir over low heat until gelatin is dissolved. Stir in pureed cantaloupe. Chill to consistency of corn syrup, stirring occasionally. Remove from refrigerator. (Gelatin will continue to set.) In a small bowl, whip cream with electric mixer until soft peaks form. When gelatin is set (consistency of unbeaten egg whites), fold in whipped cream. Pour into four 6-ounce custard cups or molds. Chill about 4 hours, or until firm.

To make sauce, combine chocolate pieces and shortening in a heavy, small saucepan. Stir over low heat until chocolate begins to melt. Immediately remove pan from heat; stir until smooth. To serve, spoon about 3 tablespoons of warm sauce into individual shallow plates or bowls. Unmold each cantaloupe mousse and place atop chocolate sauce. Drizzle 1-2 tablespoons sauce over each mousse. (Reserve extra sauce.) Garnish with toasted coconut and cantaloupe slices.

Terrie Lumsden

RASPBERRY CRÈME BRÛLÉE

❤ *Low-fat* *Serves 4*

2 cups fresh raspberries (about 1 pint)
2 tablespoons sugar
2 teaspoons cornstarch
1 egg, lightly beaten
1 cup skim milk
2 tablespoons low-fat sour cream
1 teaspoon vanilla extract
4 teaspoons brown sugar

Gently rinse raspberries; drain. Divide raspberries evenly among 4 (6-ounce) ovenproof ramekins or custard cups; set aside. Combine sugar and cornstarch in small saucepan; stir well. Add egg; stir well. Gradually add milk, stirring well. Cook over low heat 12 minutes or until thickened, stirring constantly. Remove from heat; let cool 5 minutes. Add sour cream and vanilla; stir well. Spoon mixture evenly over raspberries. Place ramekins on a baking sheet. Sprinkle each with 1 teaspoon brown sugar. Broil 4-5 inches from heat 2 minutes or until sugar melts. Serve warm.

Note: *This dessert has about 122 calories per serving, with 2.6 grams of fat. Other fresh berries such as strawberries, blackberries or blueberries may be used.*

Jody Epps

RASPBERRY TOPPING

❤ *Low-fat,* ✓ *Quick to fix* *Yields 2½ cups*

1 (10-ounce) package frozen raspberries, thawed
½ cup hot water
1 tablespoon lemon juice
⅓ cup sugar
1 tablespoon cornstarch
¼ teaspoon salt
2 tablespoons kirsch or other cherry-flavored liqueur

Drain raspberries, reserving liquid; set aside. Combine reserved raspberry juice, hot water, lemon juice, sugar, cornstarch and salt in medium saucepan. Bring to a boil; reduce heat to medium and stir constantly until mixture begins to thicken. Add raspberries; continue to cook 3 minutes. Remove from heat; stir in kirsch. Serve warm or chilled over cake or ice cream. Sauce may be covered and refrigerated until ready to use.

Cary Rosenbohm

~ **Melting chocolate:** *When melting chocolate by itself, it's best to use a double boiler over barely simmering — never boiling — water.*

EASY FRUIT PIZZA

Serves 6-8

1 (18-ounce) roll slice-and-bake
 cookie dough
1 (8-ounce) package cream
 cheese, softened
4½ ounces whipped topping
Fresh fruit in season, sliced

½ cup sugar
1 tablespoon cornstarch
½ cup orange juice
2 tablespoons lemon juice
½ cup water
Dash of salt

Slice cookie dough into ⅛-inch slices, spread on a pizza pan or cookie sheet; press to seal. Bake at temperature indicated on package until light brown, let cool. Mix together cream cheese and whipped topping; spread on baked cookie crust. Arrange fruit in a single layer atop cream cheese. Mix sugar, cornstarch, orange juice, lemon juice, water and salt. Using a pastry brush, carefully cover each piece of fruit with citrus mixture to prevent fruit from turning brown. Chill for several hours; slice like a pizza to serve.

Hint: *Try thinly sliced apples, strawberries, kiwi, bananas or grapes; diced fresh pineapple, or canned pineapple slices.*

Carol Bohley

RUTH'S BLACKBERRY COBBLER

Serves 4

3 cups fresh blackberries
1 prepared pie crust
1 cup water
1 cup sugar

1½ tablespoons cornstarch
2 tablespoons butter
Cinnamon to taste
Extra sugar for sprinkling

Wash and pick over fresh blackberries. Roll out pie crust about 4 inches larger, and carefully place in 1½-quart casserole. Whisk together water, sugar and cornstarch in saucepan; bring to boil for 1 minute until clear. Add blackberries; pour into crust. Dot with butter; sprinkle in cinnamon and extra sugar to taste. Fold over pie crust. Sprinkle on a little more sugar, and bake at 400° for 30 minutes or until top is golden.

Hint: *Use fresh-picked blackberries for a treat that is out of this world!*

Ruth Bondurant

FAT-FREE FRUIT PIZZA

♥ *Heart healthy,* ✓ *Quick to fix*   *Serves 8*

1 (8-ounce) package Health
   Valley fat-free raspberry
   cookies
2 (8-ounce) packages fat-free
   cream cheese
⅓ cup sugar

1 teaspoon vanilla extract
Fresh fruit in season, or canned
   fruit with no sugar added
1 (10-ounce) jar raspberry
   spreadable fruit
"Lite" Cool Whip (optional)

Spray 13"x9"x2" baking dish with non-stick cooking spray. Crumble cookies into bottom of dish. Moisten fingers and press cookie crumbs together to form a crust. Set aside. Combine cream cheese, sugar and vanilla; spread over crust. Slice attractive fruit (peaches, strawberries, kiwi, seedless grapes, pears, etc.) in single layer to cover entire crust. Remove metal lid from spreadable fruit jar and microwave until spread becomes liquid, about 45 seconds. Stop and stir several times as needed. Pour over crust evenly, and refrigerate. Serve cold. Top with dollop of "Lite" Cool Whip, if desired. (Light version has less than 1 gram fat per tablespoon.)

Note: *This makes a great summer dessert for children and adults alike.*

Alexa Kincannon

MILLIONAIRE PIE

✓ *Quick to fix*   *Serves 6*

1 (8-ounce) tub Cool Whip
1 (14-ounce) can sweetened
   condensed milk
1 (8-ounce) can crushed
   pineapple

3 tablespoons lemon juice
1 cup chopped pecans
Graham cracker pie shell

Mix Cool Whip, milk, pineapple, lemon juice and pecans; pour into pie shell. Refrigerate.

Note: *Add sliced bananas or drained mandarin oranges to filling if desired.*

Denice Foose

~ **Ripening fruit:** *Fruit that is not quite ripe may be kept at room temperature in a loosely closed paper bag or in a ripening bowl. Ripe fruit can be stored a few days in the refrigerator.*

FRUIT TART

Serves 6-8

¾ cup (1 ½ sticks) butter, softened

1 ½ cups flour
½ cup powdered sugar

Filling:

1 (10-ounce) package vanilla chips, melted
1 (8-ounce) package cream cheese, softened
⅓ cup whipping cream

2-3 apples, sliced
2-3 pears, sliced
2-3 kiwis, sliced
Strawberries to taste, sliced
Bananas to taste, sliced

Glaze:

¼ cup sugar
½ cup pineapple juice

1 tablespoon cornstarch
½ teaspoon lemon juice

To make tart, combine softened butter, flour and powdered sugar, mix well. Spread dough on a 12-inch pizza pan; bake at 300° for 20-25 minutes until lightly brown. To make filling, mix chips, cream cheese and whipping cream with a wire whisk. Spread over tart, and top with any variation of sliced fruit. To make glaze, cook ingredients over medium heat in a small saucepan. Stir constantly until thickened. Allow to cool, and spoon over fruit.

Alice Rodgers

SWEET PINEAPPLE BAKE

Serves 8

6 tablespoons flour
1 cup sugar
2 (20-ounce) cans chunk pineapple, drained

2 cups (8-ounces) grated Cheddar cheese
¾ sleeve of Ritz crackers
½ cup (1 stick) butter

Mix flour and sugar. Add pineapple and cheese. Pour into greased casserole dish. Bake at 350° for 30-40 minutes. Sprinkle crushed Ritz crackers on top, and pour the melted butter over crackers.

Sharon Shaver

~ *Lemon does the job:* To prevent discoloration of freshly cut fruit or avocado, dip the exposed edges in citrus juice such as lemon juice.

BUTTERFINGER TREATS

✓ *Quick to fix*   *Serves 12*

1 cup sugar
½ cup light corn syrup
1 cup peanut butter

3 cups corn flakes
1 (12-ounce) package chocolate
chips

Mix sugar and corn syrup in saucepan; boil for 1 minute. Add peanut butter and corn flakes. Press into greased 9"x9" pan, and sprinkle with chocolate chips. Heat under broiler until chips are melted. Spread chips evenly to frost. Cut while warm. Do not store tightly covered, or chocolate will stay soft.

Janice Keller

CINNAMON ICE CREAM

Serves 6

1 pint (2 cups) half-and-half
cream
1 pint (2 cups) heavy cream
1 vanilla bean, sliced in half

6 cinnamon sticks
1 teaspoon lemon peel
12 egg yolks
¾ cup sugar

Steep half-and-half, heavy cream, vanilla bean, cinnamon sticks and lemon peel for 15 minutes. Lightly beat yolks, and add sugar. Add cream mixture; cook over medium heat until thick, stirring constantly. Strain mixture; cool prior to freezing. Freeze according to ice cream machine instructions. Serve with fresh fruit slices on the side, if desired.

Sandra Frazier

CINNAMON CANDY

Serves 20

3¾ cups granulated sugar
1½ cups light corn syrup
1 cup water

1 teaspoon cinnamon oil
Food coloring (red or green)
Powdered sugar for sprinkling

Sprinkle an 18"x22" sheet of aluminum foil with powdered sugar. Mix granulated sugar, corn syrup and water; stir over medium heat until sugar has dissolved. Boil without stirring until syrup reaches 310° or drops in a brittle string in cold water. Remove from heat. Stir in oil and coloring. Pour onto foil. When cool, break into pieces and sprinkle with powdered sugar.

Jackie Brewer

FOOLPROOF MICROWAVE PEANUT BRITTLE

✓ *Quick to fix*   *Serves 6-8*

1 cup granulated sugar
1 - 1½ cups raw peanuts
½ cup white corn syrup
⅛ teaspoon salt (optional)

1 teaspoon butter
1 teaspoon vanilla extract
1 teaspoon baking soda.

Lightly grease a cookie sheet, set aside. In a 1½-quart casserole dish, stir together sugar, peanuts, syrup and salt if desired. Microwave on high 4 minutes. Add butter and vanilla; blend well. Microwave on high 1-2 minutes longer. Peanuts should be lightly browned and syrup very hot. Add baking soda; gently stir until light and foamy. Quickly pour mixture onto prepared cookie sheet, spreading thin. Let cool, then break into small pieces. Store in air-tight container.

Lana Booher/ Lisa Ondrey/ Julia Slaydon

MOSTLY MICROWAVE MILLIONAIRES

Yields 3 dozen candies

1 (14-ounce) package caramels
2 tablespoons margarine
2 tablespoons water
1 teaspoon vanilla extract

3 cups finely chopped pecans
1 (8-ounce) milk chocolate bar
⅓ block paraffin

Lightly grease cookie sheet. Microwave caramels, margarine and water in a 1-quart glass measuring cup on 80% power for 4-5 minutes, or until caramels are melted. Add vanilla and pecans. Mix well and quickly drop by teaspoonful onto prepared cookie sheet. Cool.

Melt chocolate bar and paraffin in the top of a double boiler. Remove from heat, but keep mixture over hot water. Immediately dip candy with a toothpick into chocolate mixture, completely covering candy. Place on waxed paper to cool.

Cindy Williams

~ **Buying pecans:** *When buying unshelled nuts, pick those that feel heavy, indicating more meat inside.*

YUMMY PECAN PRALINES

Yields 4 dozen pralines

3 cups granulated sugar
¾ cup white corn syrup
¾ cup water
3 cups pecan halves

6 tablespoons (¾ stick)
   margarine
1½ tablespoons vanilla extract

Combine sugar, syrup, water and pecans in heavy saucepan. Stir over medium heat until sugar is dissolved and mixture comes to a boil. Cook, stirring occasionally, until mixture reaches the soft ball stage using a candy thermometer. Remove from heat; stir in margarine and vanilla. Beat candy with spoon or wire whisk as it cools until it starts to become creamy and opaque. (Do not wait too long!) Using two tablespoons, drop onto wax paper. Work quickly because pralines will soon become too firm to shape.

Note: *This recipe comes from a cooking class taught by Arlette Hardoin.*

Becky Gilliland

TEXAS PECAN PRALINES

Yields 4 dozen pralines

4 cups brown sugar
½ cup half-and-half cream
1 teaspoon vanilla extract

¼ teaspoon salt
1 tablespoon butter
2 cups pecan halves

Combine sugar, cream, vanilla, salt and butter. Cook over slow heat, stirring constantly. When mixture will form soft ball in cold water, remove from heat and stir in pecans. Beat until mixture begins to thicken slightly. While pourable, drop by tablespoon onto waxed paper.

Dina Dornburg

~ Shelling nuts: Use the microwave to make shelling nuts an easier job. Place 2 cups nuts with 1 cup water in a 1-quart casserole; cook 4-5 minutes. Nut meats slip out easily after cooking.

CALIFORNIA WHITE CHOCOLATE FUDGE

Serves 8-10

1½ cups sugar
¾ cup sour cream
½ cup (1 stick) margarine
12 ounces white chocolate,
    coarsely chopped

1 (7-ounce) jar marshmallow
    creme
¾ cup chopped walnuts or
    pecans
¾ cup chopped dried apricots

In a saucepan, bring sugar, sour cream and margarine to full boil. Continue boiling 7 minutes or until candy thermometer reaches 234°, stirring constantly. Remove from heat; stir in chocolate until melted. Stir in marshmallow creme, nuts and apricots until blended. Pour into greased 9"x9" baking dish. Cool several hours before cutting into squares.

Linda Meche

CHOCOLATE-MARSHMALLOW FUDGE

Serves 10-12

4 cups sugar
1 (14-ounce) can evaporated
    milk
½ cup (1 stick) margarine

1 (7-ounce) jar marshmallow
    creme
3 (6-ounce) packages chocolate
    chips
2 cups chopped pecans

Combine sugar, milk and margarine. Bring to a boil; continue boiling for 9 minutes. Remove from heat; add marshmallow creme, chocolate chips and pecans. Stir and pour into greased 9"x9" pan. Chill. Cut into squares to serve.

Dee Swope

*~ **Microwaving magic:** Microwave chocolate chips uncovered on full power, but use 50% power for chocolate squares melted alone. When it's ready, the chocolate will look shiny and lose its shape when stirred. Avoid overcooking.*

OLD-FASHIONED BREAD PUDDING

Serves 12

4 cups bread crusts
4 cups milk
5 eggs, beaten
1½ cups sugar

1½ cups raisins (or strained
 fruit)
2 teaspoons vanilla extract
½ teaspoon nutmeg

Place bread crusts with milk in bowl. Chop with spoon until well softened. Beat eggs with hand beater until light; add to bread crusts. Add sugar, fruit and vanilla. Pour into buttered 13"x9"x2" glass dish; sprinkle with nutmeg. Bake uncovered at 350° for 50 minutes or until pudding springs back to touch.

Penny Daigle

PATTERSON PUDDING

Serves 10-12

1 (8-ounce) package cream
 cheese
3 cups milk
2 teaspoons vanilla extract
1 (6-ounce) box French vanilla
 instant pudding

1 (12-ounce) tub Cool Whip
1 (14-ounce) can sweetened
 condensed milk
1 box vanilla wafers
4 bananas, sliced (or to taste)

Soften cream cheese. Mix milk, vanilla and instant pudding until thickened, but not too thick to stir. Combine cream cheese and ½ the Cool Whip; mix with condensed milk. Mix pudding and cream cheese mixtures together. Layer vanilla wafers on bottom of serving dish, reserving some cookies for garnish. Layer banana slices on top of cookies, and pour pudding mixture over top. Top with remaining Cool Whip. Decorate with reserved cookies. Chill in refrigerator to set.

Ronnye Patterson

CHOCOLATE ÉCLAIR SURPRISE

Serves 10-12

1 box whole graham crackers
2 (3.9-ounce) boxes French
  vanilla instant pudding

3 cups milk
1 (8-ounce) tub Cool Whip

Frosting:

1 cup sugar
1/8 teaspoon salt
1/3 cup cocoa

1/4 cup milk
1/4 cup (1/2 stick) butter
1 teaspoon vanilla extract

Butter a 13"x9"x2" dish. Line the bottom with whole graham crackers. Mix pudding with milk; beat 2 minutes. Fold in Cool Whip. Pour half of mixture over graham crackers. Add a second layer of graham crackers and pudding mixture. Add a top layer of graham crackers.

To make frosting, combine sugar, salt, cocoa and milk in a saucepan. Bring to a boil, and cook 1 minute. Remove from heat; add butter and vanilla, stir until spreadable. Pour over top layer of graham crackers. Let chill in refrigerator 1 hour before serving.

Tonya Heard

CHOCOLATE FONDUE

✓ *Quick to fix*   *Yields 3 cups*

1 pound semi-sweet chocolate
1/2 cup heavy cream

1/4 cup Jack Daniels whiskey

Melt chocolate, add cream and whiskey. Stir until smooth. Use as a dip with graham crackers, fresh fruit or coffee cake.

Denice Foose

*~ **Crusty variations:** Add variety to graham cracker crusts by mixing in the flavor of your favorite cookie. Try half graham cracker crumbs and half chocolate, vanilla or shortbread crumbs for a change of pace.*

OVERNIGHT LAYERED CHOCOLATE

Serves 6

First layer:

1 cup unsifted flour
½ cup (1 stick) margarine or
    butter

½ cup chopped nuts (or more,
    to taste)

Second layer:

1 (8-ounce) package cream
    cheese

1 cup powdered sugar
4 ounces Cool Whip

Third layer:

1 (3.9-ounce) box chocolate
    fudge instant pudding
1 (3.9-ounce) box vanilla instant
    pudding

2¾ cups cold milk or half-and-
    half cream
Whipped cream (optional)
Chocolate shavings for garnish
    (optional)

First layer: In an 8"x8" greased baking dish, mix and spread flour, butter and nuts. Coat bottom and sides of dish. Bake at 350° for 15 minutes or until golden brown. Cool before spreading next layer.

Second layer: Mix cream cheese, powdered sugar and Cool Whip; spread over first layer.

Third layer: Mix the two puddings with cold milk. Refrigerate to thicken. Pour over second layer; spread evenly. Cover with foil; refrigerate overnight. Top with layer of whipped cream and garnish with shaved chocolate if desired.

Binnie Bauml

~ ***Making chocolate curls:*** *To make chocolate curls, melt 3 squares semisweet chocolate. Pour melted chocolate onto wax paper, and spread to a 3-inch-wide strip. Let stand until cool but not firm. Scrape a vegetable peeler across the chocolate. Store curls in the freezer.*

~ ***...For white curls,*** *melt 4 ounces white chocolate with 1 tablespoon solid vegetable shortening. Pour into small square plastic container; freeze 30 minutes until firm. Remove block from freezer; use vegetable peeler or cheese slicer to make curls.*

LEMON WHIPPERSNAPPERS

Yields 4 dozen cookies

1 (18.25-ounce) box lemon cake
   mix
2 cups Cool Whip

1 egg
1½ cups sifted powdered sugar

Grease cookie sheets or coat with non-stick spray. Combine cake mix, Cool Whip and egg in large bowl; stir until well blended. Drop dough by teaspoonful into powdered sugar; roll to coat. Place ½ inch apart on cookie sheet. Bake at 350° for 10-15 minutes, until light golden brown. Remove from cookie sheet to cool.

Missy Funk

CREAM CHEESE COOKIES

Yields 2-3 dozen cookies

¼ cup (½ stick) margarine,
   softened
1 (8-ounce) package cream
   cheese, softened

1 egg
¼ teaspoon vanilla extract
1 (18.25-ounce) box yellow cake
   mix

Cream butter and cream cheese; blend in egg and vanilla. Add dry cake mix, ⅓ portion at a time. Mix well after each addition. If using mixer, stir last third of cake mix by hand. Cover; chill for 30 minutes. Preheat oven to 325°. Drop dough by teaspoonful onto ungreased cookie sheet; bake 8-10 minutes. Let cool slightly before removing from cookie sheet.

Penny Daigle

SAND TARTS

Yields 2-3 dozen cookies

1 cup (2 sticks) margarine
10 tablespoons plus ¼ cup
   powdered sugar, divided

1 cup finely chopped pecans
¾ tablespoon vanilla extract
2 cups flour

Cream margarine and powdered sugar. Add nuts, vanilla and flour; mix thoroughly. Chill dough. Roll into balls; bake on ungreased cookie sheet at 350° for 20 minutes. Cool; then roll in ¼ cup powdered sugar to coat.

Nancy Chamberlain

EXTRA-CRISP SUGAR COOKIES

Yields 6-8 dozen cookies

1 cup (2 sticks) real butter
2 cups sugar
2 eggs
1 cup vegetable oil
1 teaspoon butter flavor extract

1 teaspoon vanilla extract
½ teaspoon salt
5 cups flour
2 teaspoons baking soda
2 teaspoons cream of tartar

Cream butter and sugar; add eggs, oil, butter flavoring, vanilla and salt. Add flour, soda and tartar; mix until very smooth. Chill several hours. Use ice teaspoon to drop dough onto cookie sheet. Flatten dough with bottom of a drinking glass that has been buttered and dipped into sugar. (Re-dip glass in sugar for each cookie; there is no need to re-butter.) Bake at 350° for 8-10 minutes, until edges are slightly browned. These cookies freeze well.

Jane Ray

SUGAR CHIPS

Yields 12 dozen cookies

1½ cups (¾ pound) margarine or
    shortening
½ teaspoon salt (if using
    shortening)

3 cups sugar
3 eggs
5 cups sifted flour
1 teaspoon vanilla extract

Cream margarine or shortening with sugar. (Add salt if using shortening.) Add eggs, then flour and vanilla; mix well. Chill dough several hours or overnight. Roll out very thin (⅛-inch thick or less) on floured pastry cloth. Cut dough with cookie cutters; place on ungreased cookie sheet. Bake in preheated 400° oven about 4 minutes, only until very light brown.

Hint: Watch first batch closely. Note baking time, and use for remaining batches. Prepare ⅓ the recipe if time is short.

Cindy Cathcart

~ Freeze for later: When you've got time to mix but not bake, mix up a batch of dough and freeze it. Most cookie doughs, especially refrigerator cookies, take well to this treatment.

OLD-FASHIONED TEA CAKES

Yields 5 dozen cookies

1 cup (2 sticks) butter
2 cups sugar
4 eggs
7 cups flour
2 teaspoons baking powder
½ teaspoon baking soda

½ teaspoon salt
1 teaspoon vanilla extract
¼ cup milk, plus 3 tablespoons
   milk, divided
2 cups powdered sugar

Cream butter and sugar. Add eggs, one at a time. Sift together flour, baking powder, soda and salt. Slowly add to butter mixture. Midway through addition, add vanilla and ¼ cup milk. Continue adding flour until all ingredients are well mixed. Roll out dough ¼-inch thick and cut with cookie cutters. Bake at 325° for 8 minutes. Cookies should be very soft — do not let them get brown or crunchy. Make icing by mixing 3 tablespoons milk with 2 cups powdered sugar to form glaze. Frost cookies.

Barbara Lundahl

GINGER CRINKLES

Yields 4 dozen cookies

⅔ cup vegetable oil
1 cup plus ¼ cup granulated
   sugar, divided
1 egg
4 tablespoons molasses

2 cups flour
2 teaspoons baking soda
½ teaspoon salt
1¼ teaspoons cinnamon
2 teaspoons ginger

Preheat oven to 350°. Mix oil and 1 cup sugar thoroughly. Add egg, beat until thick. Stir in molasses; beat well. Sift flour, soda, salt, cinnamon and ginger together; add to sugar mixture. Drop by teaspoon into ¼ cup sugar, and form into ball coated with sugar. Place on ungreased cookie sheet 3 inches apart. Bake for 10-12 minutes for crisp cookies, or 7 minutes for soft cookies. Cool on rack.

Becky Lowery

TEA PARTY COOKIES

Yields 5 dozen cookies

1 cup (2 sticks) butter, softened
1/3 cup whipping cream

2 cups flour
Granulated sugar

Filling:

1/4 cup (1/2 stick) butter, softened
3/4 cup powdered sugar

1 teaspoon vanilla extract
Food coloring

Mix butter, cream and flour thoroughly. Cover and chill. Heat oven to 375°. Roll about 1/3 dough at a time, 1/8-inch thick on flour-covered surface. Keep remaining dough chilled. Use a small biscuit cutter to cut dough into 1/2-inch circles. Transfer rounds to a shallow pan that contains granulated sugar; turn each round so both sides are coated with sugar. Place on ungreased cookie sheet. Prick rounds with fork 3 or 4 times. Bake 7-9 minutes, just until set but not brown. Cool. Prepare filling by creaming butter, powdered sugar and vanilla until smooth and fluffy. Tint with a few drops food coloring. Sandwich two cookies together with filling in middle. Store in air-tight container.

Note: These are delicate little cookies that are baked for every special occasion in our family. They are pretty with pink and green tinted filling for Christmas; pink and blue for baby showers and pretty pastels for Easter, bridal showers or a special tea.

Laura Muskopf

FORGOTTEN COOKIES

Yields 5 dozen cookies

2 egg whites
2/3 cup sugar
Pinch of salt

1 cup chopped pecans
1 cup chocolate chips

Preheat oven to 350°. Beat room temperature egg whites until thick and foamy. Gradually add sugar until peaks form. Stir in salt, pecans and chocolate chips. Drop by spoonfuls on aluminum foil and place in oven. Turn off oven and leave overnight.

Laura Muskopf

MEXICAN WEDDING CAKES

Yields 5 dozen cookies

1 cup pecans
2 cups flour
¼ teaspoon salt
1 cup (2 sticks) butter or
   margarine, softened

¼ cup sugar
2 teaspoons vanilla extract
Powdered sugar

In food processor, finely chop nuts ½ cup at a time. Be careful not to overprocess. Combine nuts, flour and salt in a bowl, set aside. Mix butter, sugar and vanilla in processor bowl until blended. Stop processor as necessary to push mixture down around blades with a rubber spatula. Add flour mixture to processor bowl, and mix only until a smooth dough forms. (If you do not have a food processor, combine ingredients with an electric mixer, and use nuts that are very finely chopped.)

Cover dough, chill for about 30 minutes. Shape by teaspoonful into crescents or small flattened balls, and place on ungreased cookie sheet. Bake at 325° for 20 minutes. While cookies are still warm, place 4-5 cookies at a time in a bag with powdered sugar, and shake gently to coat. Repeat process until all cookies are sugared. Store cookies in air-tight container.

Note: *These cookies melt in your mouth, and never last long at our house!*

Lisa Ondrey

COWBOY COOKIES

Yields 10 -12 dozen cookies

1 cup shortening
1 cup granulated sugar
1 cup brown sugar
2 eggs
1 teaspoon vanilla extract
2 cups flour

½ teaspoon baking powder
½ teaspoon baking soda
½ teaspoon salt
2 cups rolled oats
1 (24-ounce) package chocolate
   tidbits

Mix shortening, granulated sugar and brown sugar. Beat in eggs and vanilla. Add flour, baking powder, soda and salt. Add rolled oats and chocolate. Drop by teaspoonful onto greased sheet; bake at 350° for 10-15 minutes.

Barbara Allen

KATZMAN'S GERMAN CHOCOLATE COOKIES

Yields 6½ dozen cookies

4 cups all-purpose flour
¼ cup unsweetened cocoa
1 teaspoon salt

2 cups powdered sugar
2 cups (4 sticks) butter, softened
4 teaspoons vanilla extract

Filling:

⅔ cup evaporated milk
⅔ cup granulated sugar
2 egg yolks, beaten
⅓ cup (⅔ stick) butter

1 teaspoon vanilla extract
¾ cup chopped pecans
1¼ cups shredded coconut

Topping:

½ cup semisweet chocolate
   morsels
2 tablespoons water

2 tablespoons butter
½ cup sifted powdered sugar

Preheat oven to 350°. Sift together flour, cocoa and salt. In a large mixing bowl, using an electric mixer, cream powdered sugar, butter and vanilla until light. Blend flour mixture into butter mixture. Dough will be stiff. Use hands, if necessary, to knead ingredients together. (If not well mixed, parts of the dough will be too soft and other parts too dry.) Using about 2 tablespoons dough, form dough into balls. Put balls on ungreased baking sheet; make an indentation in center of each ball with your finger. Bake at 350° for 12-14 minutes, or until cookies are slightly browned around the edges. Remove from baking sheet immediately, and cool on wire racks.

To make filling, combine undiluted evaporated milk, granulated sugar, egg yolks, butter and vanilla in a saucepan. Cook, stirring constantly, over medium heat. In about 5-8 minutes, mixture will be slightly thick and gold in color. Mixture will thicken as it cools. Remove from heat; add pecans and coconut. Let cool about 15-20 minutes, then drop a small amount of filling in the indentation of each cookie. Let cool.

For topping, combine chocolate morsels, water and butter in a saucepan. Heat, stirring constantly, until smooth. Add sugar, beat until smooth. Drizzle topping over cookies. Store in air-tight container or freeze.

Christy McConnell

PEANUT BLOSSOMS

Yields 7 dozen cookies

1¾ cups sifted flour
1 teaspoon soda
½ teaspoon salt
½ cup (1 stick) butter or
  margarine
½ cup peanut butter

¾ cup granulated sugar, divided
½ cup brown sugar, firmly
  packed
1 egg
1 teaspoon vanilla extract
84 Hershey chocolate kisses

Sift together flour, soda and salt. Cream together butter and peanut butter. Gradually add ½ cup granulated sugar and brown sugar. Continue creaming. Add egg and vanilla. Add dry ingredients gradually to creamed mixture. Using rounded teaspoons, shape dough into balls. Roll in ¼ cup sugar. Place on ungreased cookie sheet; bake at 375° for 8 minutes. Remove from oven. Press one unwrapped Hershey Kiss on each cookie so it cracks around edges. Return to oven and continue baking 2 -3 minutes.

Binnie Bauml

THUMBPRINT COOKIES

Yields 6-7 dozen cookies

⅔ cup brown sugar
1 cup (2 sticks) butter or
  margarine, softened
1 egg yolk

¼ teaspoon baking powder
¼ teaspoon salt
½ teaspoon vanilla extract
2¼ cups flour

Frosting:

1 cup sugar
⅓ cup milk
1 tablespoon butter

14 large marshmallows
1 cup chocolate chips
½ teaspoon vanilla extract

Mix brown sugar, butter, egg yolk, baking powder, salt, vanilla and flour. Form into small balls; place on cookie sheet. Make indentations in center of each ball with your thumb. Bake at 350° until light brown. Let cool. To make frosting, combine sugar, milk and butter in saucepan. Bring to boil for 1 minute. Remove from stove; add marshmallows, chocolate chips and vanilla. Beat until creamy. Fill cookie indentations with frosting.

Kristi Abild

THE BEST CHOCOLATE CHIP COOKIES

Yields 9 dozen cookies

2 cups (4 sticks) butter
2 cups granulated sugar
4 cups brown sugar
4 eggs
2 teaspoons vanilla extract
5 cups blended oatmeal
4 cups flour
1 teaspoon salt
2 teaspoons baking powder
2 teaspoons baking soda
1 (24-ounce) bag chocolate chips
1 (8-ounce) Hershey chocolate bar, grated
2 cups chopped nuts

Cream butter and both sugars. Add eggs and vanilla. To make blended oatmeal, measure 5 cups oatmeal into a blender, and grind to a flour/cornmeal consistency. Add blended oatmeal, flour, salt, baking powder and baking soda to butter mixture. Add chocolate chips, grated chocolate bar and nuts; mix well. Roll dough into balls; place 2 inches apart on cookie sheet. Bake at 375° for 6-8 minutes. Recipe can be halved.

Cheri McBurnett

TRIPLE CHOCOLATE FROZEN FRAGMENTS

Yields 4 dozen pieces

½ cup (1 stick) butter or margarine, room temperature
½ cup brown sugar
1 egg yolk, beaten
1 cup sifted flour
½ teaspoon vanilla extract
1 (8-ounce) milk chocolate bar
1 (4-ounce) dark chocolate bar
1 (4-ounce) Baker's German chocolate bar
½ cup broken pecan pieces

Preheat oven to 350°. Cream butter and brown sugar. Add egg yolk, flour and vanilla; mix well. Spread on ungreased 9"x13" jelly roll pan; bake at 350° for 15 minutes. Meanwhile, melt all three chocolate bars in top of double boiler. Immediately spread melted chocolate on warm, baked cookie "crust." Sprinkle pecans over chocolate; place in freezer. When completely frozen, break into random-sized pieces by stabbing with a knife. Keep frozen until ready to serve.

Christy McConnell

APPLE-OATS CRISP

Serves 6

4 cups sliced, pared apples
⅔ to ¾ cup brown sugar, packed
½ cup flour
½ cup regular oats

¾ teaspoon ground cinnamon
¾ teaspoon ground nutmeg
⅓ cup (⅔ stick) butter or
margarine, softened

Heat oven to 375°. Grease 8"x8" baking pan. Arrange apple slices in pan. Mix brown sugar, flour, oats, cinnamon, nutmeg and butter with fork; sprinkle over apples. Bake until apples are tender and topping is golden brown, about 30 minutes. Serve with ice cream if desired.

Kristi Abild

CINNAMON APPLE CRISP

Serves 6

6 large apples, peeled and sliced
½ cup orange juice
½ cup granulated sugar
½ teaspoon cinnamon

¾ cup sifted flour
½ cup light brown sugar, packed
¼ teaspoon salt
6 tablespoons (¾ stick) butter

Preheat oven to 350°. Arrange apples in greased 11"x7"x2" baking dish. Pour orange juice over apples. Combine granulated sugar and cinnamon, sprinkle over apples. Combine flour, brown sugar, salt and butter to make a crumbly mixture. Spread over apples. Bake at 350° until apples are tender and crust is lightly brown, about 45 minutes.

Note: *For a nuttier flavor, add ¼ cup oats and 1 additional tablespoon butter to flour mixture.*

Kathy Creel

COUNTRY APPLE DESSERT

Serves 8-12

1 (18.25-ounce) box yellow cake mix with pudding
⅓ cup (⅔ stick) butter or margarine
2 eggs, divided
1 (21-ounce) can apple pie filling

⅓ cup brown sugar, firmly packed
½ cup walnuts, chopped
1 teaspoon ground cinnamon
1 cup sour cream
1 teaspoon vanilla extract

Preheat oven to 350°. Combine cake mix, butter and one egg by hand or using low speed on electric mixer. Place in an ungreased 13"x9"x2" baking dish. Using hands, press mixture to form a bottom crust. Spread apple pie filling evenly over crust. Combine brown sugar, nuts and cinnamon; sprinkle over apples. In a small bowl, blend sour cream, remaining egg and vanilla; spread over sugar mixture. Bake at 350° for 45 minutes or until topping is golden. Serve warm or cold. Refrigerate leftovers.

Roberta Hemphill

CARAMEL-APPLE WALNUT SQUARES

Serves 10-12

1¾ cups unsifted flour
1 cup quick cooking oats
½ cup firmly packed brown sugar
½ teaspoon baking soda
½ teaspoon salt

1 cup (2 sticks) cold margarine or butter
1 cup chopped walnuts
1 (14-ounce) can sweetened condensed milk
20 caramels, unwrapped
1 (21-ounce) can apple pie filling

Preheat oven to 375°. In large bowl, combine flour, oats, brown sugar, baking soda and salt; cut in margarine until crumbly. Reserve 1½ cups of crumb mixture. Press remainder on bottom of 13"x9"x2" baking pan. Bake at 375° for 15 minutes. Add walnuts to reserved crumb mixture. In heavy saucepan, over low heat, melt caramels with sweetened condensed milk, stirring until smooth. Spoon apple filling over prepared crust; top with caramel mixture, then reserved crumb mixture. Bake 20 minutes or until set. Cool. Serve warm with ice cream.

Peggy Schrott

PUMPKIN BARS

Serves 10

2 cups flour
2 teaspoons baking powder
1 teaspoon baking soda
½ teaspoon salt
1 teaspoon cinnamon
2 teaspoons pumpkin pie spice
2 eggs

1½ cups granulated sugar
½ cup brown sugar
1 cup vegetable oil
2 tablespoons amaretto
2 cups fresh pumpkin
½ cup chopped pecans
2 cups mini chocolate chips

Cream Cheese Frosting:

2 to 3 tablespoons half-and-half
  cream
1 (3-ounce) package cream
  cheese
1 teaspoon vanilla extract

Pinch of salt
1 (16-ounce) box powdered
  sugar
Chopped pecans

Combine flour, baking powder, soda, salt, cinnamon and pumpkin pie spice; set aside. Preheat oven to 350 °. Grease and flour 10"x15" jelly roll pan. In large bowl, beat eggs. Add granulated sugar, brown sugar, oil, amaretto and pumpkin; blend until smooth. Add flour mixture; mix thoroughly. Stir in nuts and chocolate chips. Pour into prepared pan; bake at 350° for 30-40 minutes. Let cool. To make frosting, combine half-and-half, cream cheese, vanilla and salt. Add powdered sugar, beat until fluffy. Spread over cooled bars; sprinkle with pecans.

Diane Hill

CHOCOLATE SQUARES

Serves 12

1 (18.75-ounce) box devil's food
  chocolate cake mix
½ cup (1 stick) margarine
3 eggs, divided
1 cup chopped nuts

1 (8-ounce) package cream
  cheese
1 (16-ounce) box powdered
  sugar

Mix cake mix, margarine, 1 egg and nuts. Press into a greased 13"x9"x2" pan to form a layer. Mix cream cheese, sugar and 2 eggs; pour mixture over cake layer. Bake at 350° for 45 minutes. Cut into squares to serve.

Jane Koontz

CARAMEL BROWNIES

Serves 24

1 (18.75-ounce) box German
   chocolate cake mix
¾ cup (1½ sticks) butter, melted
⅔ cup evaporated milk, divided

1 cup chopped nuts
1 (14-ounce) bag caramels
1 (6-ounce) bag chocolate chips

Preheat oven to 350°. Mix cake mix, butter, ⅓ cup evaporated milk and chopped nuts. Bake ½ mixture in greased 13"x9"x2" pan for 6 minutes. Meanwhile, melt caramels and ⅓ cup evaporated milk on stove. After mix bakes, sprinkle chocolate chips on top. Drizzle caramel mixture over chocolate chips. Spoon remaining batter on top. Bake at 350° for 18 minutes.

Jeanne Howard

BLACK BOTTOM CUPCAKES

Serves 12

1½ cups flour
1 cup sugar
¼ cup cocoa
1 teaspoon baking soda

½ teaspoon salt
1 cup water
⅓ cup vegetable oil
1 tablespoon vinegar

Filling:

1 (8-ounce) package cream
   cheese
⅛ teaspoon salt

1 egg
⅓ cup sugar
1 cup chocolate chips

Mix together the dry ingredients; add water, oil and vinegar. Fill cupcake liners ⅓ full with mixture. Mix all ingredients for filling except chips and beat well. Add chips, and mix. Place 1 tablespoon of the filling in the center of the cupcake. Sprinkle with sugar and bake at 350° for 30 minutes.

Nancy Germano

EASY SHORTCAKE

Serves 8-10

2 eggs, separated
³⁄₈ cup hot water (not boiling)
¾ teaspoon lemon juice
1 cup sugar

1 cup flour
1½ teaspoons baking powder
¼ teaspoon salt

Preheat oven to 325°. Combine egg yolks, hot water and lemon juice in a large bowl. With an electric mixer on low speed, stir in sugar, flour, baking powder and salt. Beat egg whites until stiff. Fold egg whites into mixture. Pour into a well-greased 13"x9"x2" pan. Bake at 325° for 40 minutes. Cool and cut into squares.

Note: *This cake is great for coffee breaks!*

Barbara Franklin

SWEDISH CAKE

Serves 20

2 cups sugar
2 cups flour
2 eggs
1 (20-ounce) can crushed
   pineapple, undrained

1 teaspoon baking soda
1 teaspoon vanilla extract
¾ cups chopped pecans

Icing:

1 (8-ounce) package cream
   cheese
½ cup (1 stick) margarine

2 cups powdered sugar
½ cup chopped pecans
1 teaspoon vanilla extract

Mix all cake ingredients by hand. Place in 13"x9"x2" pan and bake at 350° for 35-45 minutes. To make icing, mix all ingredients with hand mixer. Spread over warm cake.

Patti Hoffmann

GEORGIA POUND CAKE

Serves 12

1½ cups (3 sticks) margarine or
   butter
2½ cups sugar
8 eggs

1½ teaspoons cream of tartar
3 cups sifted flour
1½ teaspoons vanilla extract
Chopped nuts (optional)

Cream together margarine and sugar with electric mixer. Beat in eggs and cream of tartar. Add flour and vanilla. Beat on medium speed for 10 minutes. Add nuts to batter if desired. Grease Bundt pan or spray with non-stick spray. Pour batter in prepared pan; bake at 300° for 1 hour and 30 minutes to 1 hour and 45 minutes, taking care not to over-bake. Cool in pan, then turn out on serving platter.

Missy Funk

COCONUT POUND CAKE

Serves 12

1 cup shortening or butter
3 cups sugar
5 eggs
½ teaspoon salt

1 teaspoon baking powder
3 cups flour
1 cup milk
1 package frozen coconut

Whip sugar and shortening together. Add eggs one at a time, mixing well. Mix in the remaining ingredients, alternating dry and liquid. Pour batter into greased Bundt pan; bake at 325° for 90 minutes.

Jackie Brewer

*~ **Tube cake tips:** Always grease and flour tube pans when baking butter cakes. Allow cake to cool in mold for 10 minutes. To remove cake, carefully loosen edges with non-metallic spatula, then invert.*

LEMONADE CAKE

Serves 12

1 (18.75-ounce) box lemon cake
  mix
1 (3.9-ounce) box instant lemon
  pudding

4 eggs
1 cup water
¼ cup vegetable oil

Lemon Glaze:

1 (6-ounce) can frozen
  lemonade concentrate,
  thawed

2 cups powdered sugar plus
  powdered sugar for sprinkling

Mix cake mix, dry pudding, eggs, water and oil; beat for 4 minutes. Pour batter into greased and floured Bundt pan; bake at 350° for 50-55 minutes. Remove from oven, let stand 5 minutes. Mix lemonade concentrate and powdered sugar to make glaze. Prick entire top of cake with toothpick, and pour glaze over cake. Let stand in pan for 15 additional minutes. Remove from pan; sprinkle with powdered sugar, if desired.

Jan Davis

BLUEBERRY CAKE

Serves12-15

1 envelope Dream Whip
1 cup granulated sugar
1 cup powdered sugar
1 (8-ounce) package cream
  cheese, softened

1 (16-ounce) can blueberry pie
  filling
1 large angel food cake

A day in advance, prepare envelope of Dream Whip according to package directions. Mix with granulated sugar, powdered sugar and cream cheese; cover and refrigerate. Refrigerate unopened can of blueberry pie filling, overnight if possible. The next day, slice angel food cake in 3 layers. Place first layer on cake plate and top with whipped mixture and a layer of pie filling. Place second layer of cake on top and repeat process. Place third layer of cake on top and completely frost top and sides of cake. Spoon remaining pie filling on top of cake and drizzle over sides.

B. J. Smith

PLUM FUN CAKE

Serves 12

2 cups sugar
1 cup oil (fill less than full)
3 eggs
2 cups self-rising flour

1 teaspoon cinnamon
1 teaspoon cloves
2 jars junior baby food plums
1 cup chopped nuts

Glaze:

1 cup powdered sugar

Lemon juice

Mix sugar, oil and eggs. Add flour, cinnamon and cloves, then add plums and nuts. Bake in greased and floured Bundt pan at 350° for 1 hour. Mix powdered sugar with enough lemon juice to make glaze. Pour over cooled cake.

Kay Wright

APPLE CAKE

Serves 12

4 cups peeled, sliced Winesap
   apples (5 or 6 apples)
2 cups sugar
1 cup chopped pecans
3 cups flour
½ teaspoon salt

½ teaspoon cinnamon
2 teaspoons baking soda
2 eggs, beaten
1 teaspoon vanilla extract
1 cup vegetable oil

Preheat oven to 350°. Combine, apples, sugar and pecans. Let stand until it makes 1½ cups juice. Combine flour, salt, cinnamon and soda; add to juice mixture. Add eggs, vanilla and oil; mix well by hand. Pour mixture into greased and floured tube pan; bake at 350° for 1 hour and 15 minutes.

Kathy Creel

PUMPKIN PIE CAKE

Serves 20

1 (18.75-ounce) box yellow cake
  mix

½ cup (1 stick) margarine,
  melted
1 egg

Filling:

1 (30-ounce) can pumpkin pie
  filling
2-3 eggs
⅔ cup evaporated milk

½ cup brown sugar
½ cup granulated sugar
1½ teaspoons cinnamon

Topping:

1 cup reserved cake mix
½ cup brown sugar
½ cup chopped nuts

¼ cup (½ stick) margarine,
  softened
Whipped cream

Remove 1 cup dry mix from cake mix; set aside. Mix remaining cake mix with ½ cup melted margarine and 1 egg. Mix well; press into bottom of greased 13"x9"x2" pan.

For filling, combine pumpkin, eggs, evaporated milk, ½ cup brown sugar, granulated sugar and cinnamon in a large bowl. Beat well; pour over crust.

For topping, combine reserved cake mix with ½ cup brown sugar, chopped nuts and ¼ cup soft margarine to make a crumb mixture. Sprinkle over filling layer. Bake at 350° for 50-60 minutes. Serve with whipped cream. Keep refrigerated.

Sherrie Ezell

*~ **Picnic savvy:** Frosted cakes don't often survive their transportation to picnics. For a prettier cake, wrap the cake layers and carry them to the picnic in cake pans. Mix up the frosting, seal in a plastic bag and carry along to frost after you arrive.*

EASY SPICE CAKE

Serves 16

1 (18.75-ounce) box white "Lite Recipe" cake mix
¾ teaspoon cinnamon
¼ teaspoon ground cloves

½ teaspoon nutmeg
½ teaspoon allspice
½ teaspoon vanilla extract
¼ cup brown sugar

Smooth Caramel Icing:

½ cup (1 stick) margarine or butter
1 cup light brown sugar

¼ cup milk
1 teaspoon vanilla extract
2-4 cups powdered sugar

Follow package directions for preparing cake mix. Add additional spices and brown sugar; bake as directed on package. Cool cake completely.

To make frosting, melt butter in saucepan and stir in brown sugar. Add milk; continue stirring until mixture boils well. Cool to lukewarm. Add vanilla and 2 cups sugar while beating with electric mixer on low speed. Beat on high speed until mixture is of spreading consistency. Adjust consistency with additional sugar if needed. Spread on cake at once.

Cindy Cathcart

CHOCOLATE CHIP APPLESAUCE CAKE

Serves 20

1 (24-ounce) jar applesauce
½ cup (1 stick) margarine, melted
1 teaspoon vanilla extract
2 cups flour
1 cup sugar
2 teaspoons baking soda

1 teaspoon cinnamon
1 teaspoon ground cloves
½ teaspoon salt
1 egg, beaten
1 (6-ounce) package chocolate chips

Mix applesauce, melted margarine and vanilla; combine with flour, sugar, baking soda, cinnamon, cloves and salt. Mix well. Add beaten egg, mix well. Stir in chocolate chips. Bake in greased and floured 13"x9"x2" pan at 350° for 25-35 minutes.

Note: *This fast, easy recipe produces a moist spice cake.*

Debbie Gentry

RUM CAKE

Serves 12

½ cup chopped pecans
1 (3.9-ounce) package vanilla
   instant pudding
1 (18.75-ounce) box yellow
   butter cake mix

½ cup light rum
½ cup water
½ cup vegetable oil
4 eggs

Glaze:

1 cup sugar
½ cup (1 stick) butter

¼ cup water
¼ cup rum

Grease and flour Bundt pan. Crumble nuts in bottom of pan. In large bowl, pour pudding and cake mix. Add ½ cup rum, ½ cup water, oil and eggs; mix 2 minutes. Pour into cake pan; bake at 325° for 50-60 minutes.

To make glaze, mix sugar, butter, ¼ cup water and ¼ cup rum in pan; boil 2-3 minutes. Drizzle hot glaze over cake.

Donna Schwertner

SAD CAKE

Serves 12

2 cups Bisquick baking mix
1 (16-ounce) box brown sugar
4 eggs
2 teaspoons vanilla extract,
   divided
1 cup chopped pecans

1 (3-ounce) package cream
   cheese, softened
2 cups powdered sugar
1 tablespoon milk (more if
   needed)

Combine Bisquick, brown sugar, eggs, 1 teaspoon vanilla and pecans; mix well. Bake in greased and floured 13"x9"x2" pan at 350° for 30-35 minutes. Cake will rise, then fall in the middle. To make icing, mix together softened cream cheese, powdered sugar and 1 tablespoon milk. Add more milk if needed for proper spreading consistency. Frost while cake is still warm.

Alice Rodgers

CHOCOLATE RUM CAKE

Serves 6-8

3 (9-inch) yellow or sponge cake
   layers
1 cup (2 sticks) butter, softened
8 ounces semisweet chocolate

½ cup rum
1 (16-ounce) box powdered
   sugar

Rum Syrup:
½ cup water
½ cup granulated sugar

½ cup rum

To make rum syrup, combine water and granulated sugar in a small saucepan. Bring to a boil over moderate heat; cook 1 minute without stirring. Remove from heat, let cool slightly, and stir in ½ cup rum. (Makes 1 cup.)

Use mix or favorite recipe for cake layers. Split each layer into 2 thinner layers. Prick layers with tines of a fork, and sprinkle with rum syrup to moisten. In top of a double boiler, melt together ½ cup butter and semisweet chocolate; stir until smooth. Remove from heat and add ½ cup rum. Beat in remaining ½ cup softened butter alternately with powdered sugar. Frost the top of each cake layer, and stack layers to make 6-layer cake. Spread remaining frosting over top and sides of cake. Refrigerate for one hour, or freeze.

Note: *Rum Syrup is excellent on fruits as well as cake.*

Serena Andrews

MILK CHOCOLATE CHIP CAKE

Serves 12

1 (18.25-ounce) box yellow
   butter cake mix
1 (3.9-ounce) box instant
   chocolate pudding
1 (8-ounce) carton sour cream

4 eggs
1 cup vegetable oil
1 (6-ounce) package milk
   chocolate chips

Mix all ingredients thoroughly. Bake in greased and floured Bundt pan at 350° for 1 hour.

Cary Rosenbohm

LAVERNE'S CHOCOLATE CAKE

Serves 20

½ cup (1 stick) margarine
½ cup vegetable oil
4 tablespoons cocoa
1 cup water
½ cup milk
2 teaspoons vinegar

2 cups flour
2 cups sugar
2 eggs
1 teaspoon baking soda
1 teaspoon vanilla extract

Icing:

½ cup (1 stick) margarine
4 tablespoons cocoa
6 tablespoons milk
1 (16-ounce) box powdered
  sugar

1 teaspoon vanilla extract
1 cup coconut
1 cup chopped pecans

In a saucepan, combine margarine, oil, cocoa and water. Make sour milk by combining ½ cup milk with 2 teaspoons vinegar; add sour milk to pan. Bring mixture to a boil. Combine flour and sugar in large mixing bowl, pour in the boiling chocolate mixture. Add eggs, soda and vanilla; mix. Bake in a 13"x9"x2" pan at 375° for 20 -25 minutes.

While the cake is cooking, combine ½ cup margarine, cocoa and milk in a saucepan; bring to a boil over low heat. Remove from heat; add powdered sugar, vanilla, coconut and pecans. Pour over hot cake. Cut in squares to serve.

Note: *This is a wonderful rich cake that goes well with ice cream for a great dessert. It can be kept for several days because it stays so moist.*

Carol Ann Adam

CHOCOLATE CAKE, HUNGARIAN STYLE

Serves 6

5 large eggs, separated
¼ teaspoon salt
1 cup sifted powdered sugar
¼ cup sifted unsweetened cocoa
1 teaspoon vanilla extract

1 cup heavy cream, whipped and
   sweetened
Sliced toasted almonds
   (optional)

Chocolate glaze:

½ cup sugar
1½ tablespoons cornstarch
1 ounce square unsweetened
   chocolate

Dash salt
½ cup water
1½ tablespoons margarine
½ teaspoon vanilla extract

Separate eggs and beat whites until stiff, but not dry. Add salt. Beat in 1 cup sifted powdered sugar, one tablespoon at a time. Fold in cocoa. Beat yolks until thick and lemon colored. Fold into cocoa mixture. Add vanilla. Spread in 15"x10" pan lined with waxed paper and sprayed with non-stick cooking spray. Bake at 350° about 20 minutes. Turn out on towel that has been sprinkled with powdered sugar. Gently peel off wax paper and let cake cool. Cut cool cake crosswise in quarters. Put layers together with sweetened whipped cream.

To make glaze, combine sugar, cornstarch, chocolate, salt and water in a small saucepan. Cook over medium heat, stirring constantly, until chocolate is melted and glaze thickens. Remove from heat; add margarine and vanilla. While hot, spread on top layer of cake. Decorate with almonds if desired. Chill and slice.

Marilyn Matthews

RED DEVIL'S FOOD CAKE

Serves 20

½ cup shortening
1½ cups granulated sugar
2 large eggs
3 tablespoons cocoa
1 teaspoon red food coloring

2 tablespoons brewed coffee
2 cups flour
1 teaspoon baking soda
1 teaspoon salt
1 cup buttermilk

Icing:

½ cup (1 stick) margarine
1 (16-ounce) box powdered
 sugar

3 tablespoons cocoa
2 tablespoons brewed coffee
Milk

Cream granulated sugar and shortening. Add eggs one at a time. Make a paste of the cocoa, food coloring and coffee; add to sugar mixture. Mix together flour, baking soda and salt. Add to sugar mixture alternately with buttermilk, ending with buttermilk. Pour batter into greased and floured 13"x9"x2" pan, bake at 350° for 25-30 minutes. Check often — do not overcook. Let cool before icing.

To make icing, melt butter. Mix together sugar, cocoa and coffee; stir into melted butter. Slowly add just enough milk to make frosting spreadable.

Note: *This is a delicious, moist cake with wonderful fudge frosting!*

Dee Eddins

GERMAN CHOCOLATE DELUXE CAKE

Serves 15

1 (18.75-ounce) box chocolate
 cake mix
1 can German chocolate ready-
 made frosting
4 eggs

½ cup vegetable oil
1 cup water
1 (12-ounce) package mini
 chocolate chips
Powdered sugar for sprinkling

Preheat oven to 350°. Combine cake mix, frosting, eggs, oil and water in bowl; beat with mixer for 4 minutes. Add chocolate chips; stir well. Pour batter into greased, floured Bundt pan; bake at 350° for 1 hour, 15 minutes. Cool 10 minutes; remove from pan. Sprinkle with powdered sugar when cooled.

Sharon Schwing

CHOCOLATE SHEATH CAKE

Serves 16

2 cups sugar
2 cups flour
½ cup (1 stick) margarine
½ cup vegetable oil
4 tablespoons cocoa
1 cup water

½ cup buttermilk
2 eggs, slightly beaten
1 teaspoon baking soda
1 teaspoon cinnamon
1 teaspoon vanilla extract

Icing:

½ cup (1 stick) margarine
4 tablespoons cocoa
6 tablespoons milk
1 teaspoon vanilla extract

1 (16-ounce) box powdered
  sugar
1 cup chopped pecans

To make cake, sift sugar and flour together in a bowl. In saucepan, bring margarine, oil, cocoa and water to a rapid boil; pour over flour mixture. Stir well. Add buttermilk, eggs, soda, cinnamon and vanilla; mix well. Pour into greased 16"x11"x3" pan. Bake at 400° for 20 minutes. To make icing, melt margarine in saucepan. Add cocoa and milk, bring to a boil. Remove from heat. Stir in vanilla, powdered sugar and pecans; beat well. Spread on cake while still hot.

Linda Jordan

CHOCOLATE DECADENCE CAKE

Serves 12

1 (18.25-ounce) box German
  chocolate cake mix
1 (12-ounce) bottle Smucker's
  caramel ice cream topping

1 (12-ounce) carton Cool Whip
  topping, thawed
3 (1.4-ounce) frozen Skors candy
  bars

Prepare cake and bake in a 13"x9"x2" pan according to package directions. While cake is warm, use a fork to poke holes along entire top at half-inch intervals. Slowly pour room-temperature caramel topping over entire top. Let cake cool, then refrigerate several hours or overnight. Frost with Cool Whip. Place frozen candy bars in plastic bag; beat to break into crumbs. Sprinkle over surface of cake. Store cake in refrigerator.

Susan Plowman

MOCHA CHEESECAKE

Serves 10-12

2 cups graham cracker crumbs
½ cup (1 stick) butter, melted
2 tablespoons sugar

Whipped cream
Chocolate curls

Filling:

8 ounces semi-sweet chocolate
1 (8-ounce) carton sour cream,
  divided
3 (8-ounce) packages cream
  cheese, softened

1 cup sugar
2 eggs
½ cup strong brewed coffee,
  cold
1 teaspoon vanilla extract

Combine graham cracker crumbs with melted butter and 2 tablespoons sugar. Press into bottom of 10" springform pan. To make filling, melt chocolate; remove from heat, stir in 2 tablespoons of sour cream. Cool. Beat cream cheese until fluffy. Add 1 cup sugar, then add eggs one at a time. Add chocolate, remaining sour cream, coffee and vanilla. Mix well. Pour into crust. Bake at 350° for 45 minutes. Chill 8 hours. Garnish with whipped cream and chocolate curls just before serving.

Hint: *Place a shallow pie pan of water in the bottom of the oven while baking to help prevent cracks in the cheesecake.*

Laura Muskopf

QUICK CHEESECAKE

Serves 10-12

1 (8-ounce) package cream
  cheese
1 cup sweetened condensed milk
⅓ cup lemon juice

1 teaspoon vanilla extract
1 graham cracker pie shell
1 (16-ounce) can cherry pie
  filling

Mix softened cream cheese, milk, lemon juice and vanilla; pour into graham cracker pie shell. Chill at least 2 hours. Top with cherry pie filling. Blueberry or strawberry filling can be substituted.

Doris Aldrich

AMARETTO CHEESECAKE

Serves 12

Crust:

1½ cups graham cracker crumbs
2 tablespoons sugar
1 teaspoon ground cinnamon

¼ cup (½ stick) margarine plus 2 tablespoons margarine, melted

Filling:

3 (8-ounce) packages cream cheese, softened
1 cup sugar

4 eggs
⅓ cup amaretto

Topping:

1 (8-ounce) carton sour cream
1 tablespoon plus 1 teaspoon sugar
1 tablespoon amaretto

1 (1.2-ounce) chocolate candy bar, grated
¼ cup toasted sliced almonds

To make crust, combine cracker crumbs, 2 tablespoons sugar, cinnamon and margarine; mix well. Firmly press mixture into bottom and half-inch up sides of a 9-inch springform pan.

To make filling, beat cream cheese with electric mixer until light and fluffy. Gradually add 1 cup sugar, mixing well. Add eggs, one at a time, beating well after each addition. Stir in ⅓ cup amaretto. Pour filling into prepared crust. Bake at 375° for 45-50 minutes or until set.

To make topping, combine sour cream, 1 tablespoon plus 1 teaspoon sugar and 1 tablespoon amaretto; stir well. Spoon over baked cheesecake filling. Refrigerate 24-48 hours. (Cheesecake is best when thoroughly chilled and flavors have time to ripen.) Garnish with grated chocolate and almonds.

Donna Schwertner

~ *Closing the cracks: If your cheesecake cracks, it's probably because you whipped the ingredients too thoroughly. Avoid beating too much air into the mixture.*

CHOCOLATE CHIP CHEESECAKE

Serves 8-10

1½ cups finely crushed Oreo
  sandwich cookies
¼ cup (½ stick) butter or
  margarine, melted
3 (8-ounce) packages cream
  cheese, softened

1 (14-ounce) can sweetened
  condensed milk
3 eggs
2 teaspoons vanilla extract
1 cup mini chocolate chips
1 teaspoon flour

Preheat oven to 300°. Combine cookie crumbs and melted butter; pat firmly onto bottom of 9-inch springform pan. In large mixer bowl, beat cream cheese until fluffy. Add condensed milk; beat until smooth. Add eggs and vanilla, mix well. In small bowl, toss together ½ the chips with flour to coat; stir into cheese mixture. Pour into prepared pan, and sprinkle remaining chocolate chips over top. Bake 1 hour, or until cake springs back when lightly touched. After cake cools to room temperature, place in refrigerator until chilled. Remove side of pan. Store in refrigerator.

Nancy Standlee

CHOCOLATE CREAM CHEESE PIE

Serves 6-8

12 ounces cream cheese,
  softened
1¼ cups sugar
3 eggs
Pinch of salt

½ teaspoon vanilla extract
2 blocks (8-ounces) unsweetened
  chocolate, melted
1 (8-inch or 9-inch) graham
  cracker crust

Topping:

1 cup sour cream
⅓ cup sugar

½ teaspoon vanilla extract

Using food processor or mixer, beat cream cheese until smooth. Add sugar gradually. Beat in eggs one at a time. Add salt and vanilla; stir in melted chocolate. Pour into graham cracker crust; bake at 375° for 20 minutes. Cool 1 hour. Combine topping ingredients, pour over pie and return to 375° oven for 10 minutes. Cool and refrigerate until firm.

Roberta Hemphill

MOM'S PEACH PIE

Serves 6-8

4 cups fresh sliced peaches
1 cup sugar plus ⅓ cup sugar, divided
2 tablespoons flour plus ⅓ cup flour, divided
1 egg, beaten

1 teaspoon vanilla extract
1 cup (8-ounces) sour cream
1 (10-inch) unbaked pie crust
¼ cup butter
1 teaspoon cinnamon

Combine peaches, 1 cup sugar, 2 tablespoons flour, egg, vanilla and sour cream; pour into pie crust. Combine ⅓ cup sugar, ⅓ cup flour, butter and cinnamon; sprinkle on top of pie filling. Bake at 400° for 15 minutes. Reduce heat to 300° and bake 40 minutes longer.

Marcie Allen

NO MESS PIE CRUST

✓ *Quick to fix*   *Yields 2 pie crusts*

2 cups flour
½ teaspoon salt
⅓ cup (⅔ stick) margarine or butter

⅓ cup vegetable shortening
Ice water (about ⅓ cup)

Mix salt into flour. Cut butter and shortening into flour with pastry cutter, or by crossing two knives against each other, until bits of shortening are pea-size. Moisten dough with ice water by stirring with a fork. Pat into two balls, wrap in wax paper and chill thoroughly.

Spray insides of two 2-gallon (13"x15") zipper-top plastic bags completely with no-stick cooking spray. Place one ball of dough inside each bag. Use rolling pin on outside of each bag to flatten dough into a circle that reaches to the edges of the bag. Cut the bag along the seams and lay the pie crust in a 9-inch pie pan. Place a favorite filling in the shell and bake according to pie's directions.

Note: *This dough handles easily, and bakes very well.*

Patti Hoffmann

KINNEY'S BUTTERMILK PIE

Serves 8

1½ cups sugar
4 tablespoons flour
½ cup (1 stick) margarine, melted
3 eggs, slightly beaten

1 cup buttermilk
1 teaspoon vanilla extract
1 unbaked pie shell
Nutmeg

Preheat oven to 400°. Mix sugar, flour and melted margarine. Mix in slightly beaten eggs, buttermilk and vanilla. Pour filling into unbaked pie shell. Sprinkle with nutmeg. Bake at 400° for 10 minutes. Reduce heat to 375°, and cook for 35 minutes more, or until knife inserted in filling comes out clean.

Note: *Triple recipe for two 10-inch pies. Pie may be frozen after it is baked.*

Eva Kinney

NANNY'S LEMON CHESS PIE

Serves 6-8

4 eggs
2¼ cups sugar
¾ cup (1½ sticks) butter, melted
Dash of salt

1½ teaspoons lemon extract
1½ tablespoons vinegar
1 (9-inch) unbaked pastry shell

Beat eggs in large mixing bowl. Add sugar, melted butter and salt. Stir in lemon extract and vinegar. Pour into pastry shell and bake at 350° for approximately 1 hour.

Note: *This is my grandmother's recipe, and deserves a homemade pastry shell. It is very rich and is best served warm.*

Karen Moran

GRANDMA'S SWEET POTATO PIE

Serves 6-8

1 large or 2 small sweet potatoes
1½ cups sugar
¼ cup (½ stick) margarine
3 eggs

1 teaspoon cinnamon
¼ teaspoon allspice
½ cup milk
1 (9-inch) pie shell

Boil sweet potatoes in water until tender; drain and mash. (You should have 2-3 cups of pulp.) Add sugar, margarine, eggs, cinnamon and allspice. Beat together until smooth. Add milk, and mix. Pour into pie shell; bake at 350° for 40 minutes.

Note: *My grandmother in Alaska always made this pie at Thanksgiving, but never recorded it in recipe form. It took many long-distance telephone conversations to get the measurements just right!*

Jody Epps

MRS. PARKS' PECAN PIE

Serves 6-8

3 eggs
⅔ cup sugar
1 cup dark or light corn syrup
⅓ cup (⅔ stick) butter or
    margarine, melted

Dash of salt
1 cup pecan halves
1 (9-inch) unbaked pie shell

Preheat oven to 350°. Beat 3 eggs with sugar. Add corn syrup, melted butter and salt, mix by hand. Stir in pecans. Pour into pie shell; bake for 50 minutes or until knife inserted into middle comes out clean. Cover edges of pie crust with foil if necessary to keep from burning.

Kathy Creel

CHOCOLATE LOVER'S PIE

Serves 6-8

2 eggs
½ cup flour
½ cup granulated sugar
½ cup brown sugar
1 cup (2 sticks) margarine,
    melted at room temperature

1 (6-ounce) package chocolate
    chips
1 cup chopped nuts
1 (9-inch) unbaked pie shell
1 (8-ounce) tub Cool Whip

Using mixer, beat eggs in large mixing bowl. Beat in flour, granulated sugar and brown sugar. Blend in melted margarine. Stir in chocolate chips and nuts; pour into pie shell. Bake at 350° for 1 hour. Serve warm with whipped topping.

Lisa Solis

GERMAN CHOCOLATE PIE

Serves 6-8

1 cup (2 sticks) margarine
1 block (4-ounces) unsweetened
    German chocolate
3 cups sugar

6 eggs
6 heaping tablespoons flour
2 teaspoons vanilla extract
2 cups pecan halves

Melt margarine with German chocolate. To melted mixture, add sugar, eggs and flour. Mix well; then add vanilla and pecans. Bake in 10-inch pie pan at 325° for 45 minutes. (Pie will make its own crust.)

Julia Slaydon

~ Pie on a pedestal: Add a touch of flair to formal dinners or holiday get-togethers by bringing your elegant dessert pie to the table on a cake pedestal. Cut and serve as your admiring guests look on.

CHERYL'S CHOCOLATE PIE

Serves 6

½ cup (1 stick) butter, melted
1 cup sugar
2 eggs
½ cup sifted flour
1 square (1-ounce) bitter
   chocolate, melted

¾ cup chocolate chips
½ cup pecans
1 teaspoon vanilla extract
1 (8-ounce) tub chocolate Cool
   Whip

Preheat oven to 325°. Beat butter and sugar together, add eggs and beat thoroughly. Add flour, blend well. Add chocolate, chocolate chips, pecans and vanilla. Pour into greased 9-inch glass pie pan, bake 25 minutes. When pie has cooled, top with chocolate whipped topping and refrigerate.

Note: *This pie is New Orleans-style, and very rich!*

Cheryl Whitten

GRANDMA'S FUDGE PIE

Serves 6-8

4 tablespoons cocoa
4 tablespoons flour
1 cup sugar
2 eggs, beaten

1 teaspoon vanilla extract
¼ cup (½ stick) margarine,
   melted
1 unbaked pie shell

Mix together cocoa, flour, sugar, eggs, vanilla and margarine. Bake in pie shell at 375° for 25 minutes. Serve with whipped topping or vanilla ice cream. Use 8 tart shells and bake a few minutes less, if desired.

Note: *This pie is a tradition in our home on Thanksgiving. It is a very quick and easy pie.*

Susan Laver

AUNT KATE'S CHOCOLATE PIES

Yields 2 pies

Pie crusts:

2 cups flour
¾ cup shortening

1 teaspoon salt
5-6 tablespoons cold water

Pie Filling:

3 cups sugar
1 cup flour
¾ cup cocoa
Pinch of salt
5 tablespoons cornstarch

3 cups milk
7 eggs, separated
¼ cup (½ stick) margarine
1 teaspoon vanilla extract

Meringue:

7 egg whites
⅓ cup sugar
½ teaspoon vanilla extract

¼ teaspoon cream of tartar
(optional)

To make crusts, cut together flour, shortening and salt. Add water gradually while kneading. Divide dough in half; roll each portion out on floured surface. Place rolled dough in two 9-inch pie plates. Prick with a fork and weight for baking. Bake at 350° for 10 minutes or until golden brown.

For filling, mix sugar, flour, cocoa, salt and cornstarch; set aside. Separate eggs, and reserve whites for meringue. Beat yolks. Combine dry ingredients with milk, and cook in top portion of a double boiler over medium high heat until mixture begins to boil. Add a small amount of heated mixture to beaten egg yolks, and stir. Add egg mixture to double boiler, and cook until filling thickens to pudding consistency. Add margarine and vanilla, stir well until margarine is melted. Remove from heat, cool slightly and pour into two baked 9-inch pie shells.

To make meringue, beat egg whites until peaks form. Continue beating while gradually adding sugar. When stiff peaks appear and meringue appears "glossy," add vanilla and cream of tartar. Spread over chocolate mixture, making certain all edges are sealed. Bake at 350° for 10 minutes or until meringue is golden brown. Do not overcook.

Ann Ragsdale

PEANUT BUTTER PIE

Serves 6

4 ounces cream cheese, softened
1 cup powdered sugar
⅓ to ½ cup peanut butter
½ cup milk

1 (8-ounce) carton Cool Whip
Baked or crumb pie shell
Hot fudge sauce

Beat cream cheese and powdered sugar together until mixture is smooth. Add peanut butter and milk; beat until smooth. Fold in Cool Whip. Spoon into baked or crumb pie shell; freeze. Top with hot fudge sauce drizzled over pie or individual slices.

Note: *This recipe comes from the Sweet Onion Restaurant in Midland, Michigan.*

Barbara Monical

FROZEN PEANUT BUTTER PIE

Serves 8-10

1 (3-ounce) package cream cheese, softened
1 (14-ounce) can sweetened condensed milk
½ cup creamy peanut butter
¼ cup small chocolate chips (optional)
¼ cup coarsely chopped peanuts

1 cup whipping cream, stiffly whipped (not whipped topping)
1 ready-to-use graham cracker, vanilla wafer or chocolate cookie crust
Chocolate chips and peanuts for garnish (optional)

In large mixing bowl, beat cream cheese until fluffy. Beat in condensed milk and peanut butter. Stir in chocolate chips and peanuts. Gently fold in whipped cream. Pour into crust. Freeze for 4 hours, or until firm. Remove from freezer 10 minutes before serving. Garnish with additional chocolate chips and peanuts if desired. Return any leftover pie to freezer.

Note: *This pie tastes great on hot summer days!*

Deani Farrar

TOFFEE ICE CREAM PIE

Serves 8

18 vanilla wafers, crushed
2 tablespoons margarine
 plus ¼ cup (½ stick)
 margarine, divided
2 pints vanilla ice cream,
 softened

1¼ cups crushed Heath bar,
 divided
1½ cups sugar
1 cup evaporated milk
¼ cup light corn syrup

Combine wafers and 2 tablespoons melted margarine in food processor; process to make fine crumbs. Press into 9-inch pie pan or square pan. Spread ½ of the ice cream on crust; sprinkle with ½ of crushed candy bar. Add rest of ice cream and freeze. To make sauce, combine sugar, evaporated milk, ¼ cup margarine and corn syrup; boil on low for 1 minute. Add rest of candy; cool. To serve, cut pie into wedges or squares. Heat sauce and pour over individual slices.

Katy Engen

ICE CREAM PIE SUPREME

Serves 8

1 cup graham cracker crumbs
½ cup chopped pecans
¼ cup (½ stick) butter, melted

1 pint coffee ice cream, softened
1 pint vanilla ice cream,
 softened

Brown Sugar Sauce:

3 tablespoons butter
1 cup firmly packed brown sugar
½ cup half-and-half cream

1 cup chopped pecans
1 teaspoon vanilla extract

Combine cracker crumbs, pecans and ¼ cup melted butter; stir well. Press mixture firmly into buttered 9-inch pie plate. Bake at 350° for 8-10 minutes, cool. Spoon coffee ice cream into cooled crust, spreading evenly; freeze until almost firm. Spread vanilla ice cream over coffee ice cream, and freeze until firm. To make Brown Sugar Sauce, melt 3 tablespoons butter in heavy saucepan over low heat; add brown sugar. Cook 5-6 minutes, stirring constantly. Remove from heat, and gradually stir in cream. Return pan to heat, cook mixture for 1 minute. Remove from heat, stir in pecans and vanilla. Spoon sauce over pie slices when serving.

Karen Parrett

Specialties
of the House

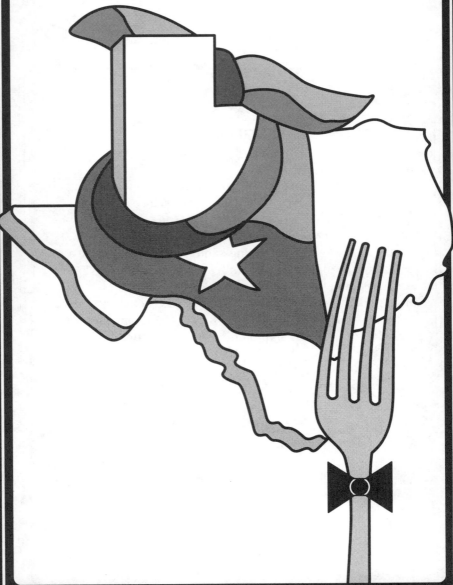

SCHOLARSHIPS
1986 - to present

Helping the youth of our community achieve their educational goals is the motivation for the Junior Service League Scholarship Fund. The scholarships were established in 1986 to honor the memory of Manon Ray Murray, a JSL member from 1972 - 1985. Every spring, deserving seniors from Brazosport and Brazoswood high schools are awarded scholarships to the college or university of their choice. In the program's first year, two students received scholarships of $500 each. In 1990, the award amount was raised to $750, and six students received scholarships. In 1993, six promising students were each awarded $1,000.

SAUCE NEW ORLEANS

Yields about 3 cups

½ cup (1 stick) butter
¼ cup chopped onions
1 tablespoon finely chopped
   garlic
2 cups heavy cream

½ teaspoon cayenne pepper
½ teaspoon salt
½ teaspoon white pepper
½ cup dry vermouth
   (or brandy)

Melt butter in saucepan. Add chopped onions and garlic; sauté over low heat until onions are soft. Slowly stir in the cream; raise heat to medium. Add cayenne pepper, salt and white pepper, stirring often to make sure cream does not burn. Reduce the sauce on the stove until it becomes very thick. Remove sauce from heat and slowly add in vermouth. Serve over baked fish, other seafood, or vegetables.

Note: *This rich cream sauce is used as the basis for Snapper New Orleans, Shrimp Fettuccine and Crab Florentine.*

Red Snapper Inn
Surfside, Texas

MOTHER TERESA'S EGGPLANT PARMESAN

Serves 6-8

1 large, firm eggplant (about
   ½ pound) or 2 medium
3 tablespoons olive oil
½ cup bread crumbs, divided
1 (16-ounce) jar Mother
   Teresa's Pasta Sauce
¼ cup water

3 tablespoons grated
   Parmesan cheese
1 cup (4-ounces) shredded
   mozzarella cheese, divided
Fresh ground black pepper
Salt to taste

Peel eggplant and slice thin. Brush sliced eggplant with olive oil on both sides. Place on baking sheets in broiler for a few minutes until golden brown. (Turn slices as necessary.) Remove from oven when golden brown, and dip in bread crumbs. Heat pasta sauce, and add ¼ cup water to sauce.

Spread a portion of the sauce on the bottom of an 8"x10" baking dish. Arrange some of the sliced eggplant on top of sauce. Sprinkle with some of the Parmesan cheese, mozzarella and pasta sauce. Add fresh ground pepper and salt if desired. Continue layering until all ingredients are used, reserving 2 tablespoons of mozzarella.

Bake at 400° for 18-20 minutes. Sprinkle remaining bread crumbs plus the reserved mozzarella on top a few minutes before taking out of the oven. Garnish with fresh chopped basil and parsley. Serve with risotto, if desired.

Mother Teresa's Cuisine
Clute, Texas

SHRIMP FAJITAS

Serves 4-6

Pico de Gallo:

1 green onion, chopped
¼ cup cilantro, chopped
1 fresh jalapeño chile,
 stemmed and chopped

1½ cups (2-3 medium)
 tomatoes, diced
1 teaspoon seasoning salt
 (or to taste)
1 tablespoon Italian dressing

Shrimp Fajitas:

2 garlic cloves, chopped fine
½ cup (1 stick) unsalted
 butter
1½ pounds fresh jumbo
 shrimp (16-20 count),
 peeled

¼ cup dry white wine
2 cups pico de gallo
½ tablespoon seasoning salt
 (or to taste)

To make pico de gallo: Combine onion, cilantro and jalapeño in a glass bowl. Add tomatoes; mix together thoroughly. Adjust salt to taste, and add Italian dressing to smooth out flavor. Set aside.

To make shrimp fajitas: In a large skillet, sauté garlic with butter until light brown. Watch carefully and don't let it burn. After 3-4 minutes, add shrimp and sauté until pink. Add white wine and let simmer for 3-4 minutes, then add pico de gallo and seasoning salt to taste. Use a slotted spoon to transfer to plate. Serve with Mexican rice, guacamole, refried beans and plenty of tortillas!

Note: *This has been a favorite recipe at Cafe Laredo since it first appeared on the menu in 1985.*

Leonard Botello III, Owner
Cafe Laredo
Lake Jackson, Texas

DEUTSCHE RINDSROULADEN (Beef Rolls)

Serves 4

4 thin slices of beef
Prepared mustard
Salt and pepper to taste
2 ounces (55 grams) fat
bacon, diced
2 ounces onions, chopped

2 ounces fat
2 cups (570 ccm) water
1-2 teaspoons Oetker Gustin
(cornstarch powder)
1 tablespoon cold water

Ask the butcher to hand-cut your slices of beef. Beat beef slices lightly, brush with mustard and sprinkle with salt and pepper. Mix together the diced bacon and chopped onions; spread mixture onto the beef. Starting at the narrow end, roll up the slices of meat and secure them with a skewer or with thread.

Heat the fat, and brown the beef rolls well. Add about 1 cup (285 ccm) boiling water very carefully, cover, and braise gently until done (about 2-2½ hours). Make up any water lost during cooking, and thicken the gravy with Gustin blended with 1 tablespoon cold water. Season to taste. Serve with Haricot beans, cauliflower, salsify or macaroni, if desired.

Note: *The sauce also may be seasoned with paprika, tomato puree, lemon juice or sour cream.*

Bernie and Marlies Buschbom, Owners
Wursthaus German Deli and Restaurant
Lake Jackson, Texas

STUFFED BEEF TENDERLOIN

Serves 6-8

¼ cup (½ stick) butter
1 medium onion, chopped
½ cup diced celery
1 (4-ounce) can sliced
  mushrooms, drained
2 cups soft bread crumbs

Salt to taste
⅛ teaspoon black pepper
½ teaspoon basil leaves
⅛ teaspoon parsley flakes
3 pounds beef tenderloin
4 slices bacon

Melt butter in a small skillet over low heat. Sauté onion, celery and mushrooms until onion is transparent. Place bread crumbs in a 1-quart bowl. Mix in salt, pepper, basil and parsley flakes. Pour in onion-butter mixture; lightly mix until well blended.

Make a lengthwise cut ¾ of the way through the tenderloin. Lightly place stuffing in the pockets formed by the cut. Close the pockets with wooden toothpicks. Place bacon strips on top diagonally covering the cut. Place in a 3-quart baking dish; bake uncovered at 350° for 1 hour.

Kuality Katering
Lake Jackson, Texas

~ **Brew without boiling:** *Using boiling water to steep tea can release oils and acids that make tea bitter. Try these alternatives for iced tea:*

~ **...For sun tea,** *place 4 teabags in a quart jar or 7 bags in a gallon jar. Fill with cold water, cover jar and place in a sunny spot for 4-6 hours. Remove tea bags, pour into ice-filled glasses.*

~ **...For overnight tea,** *place 4 teabags in a quart of cold water or 7 bags for a gallon jar. Cover and let stand at room temperature over-night. Remove tea bags in the morning, refrigerate tea. To serve, pour into ice-filled glasses.*

ENGLISH STEAMED PLUM PUDDING

Serves 112

1 cup (2 sticks) margarine or
   butter
2 cups granulated sugar
1 cup brown sugar, packed
1 cup ground suet
6 eggs, slightly beaten
2 teaspoons baking soda
2 cups buttermilk
1 cup dark corn syrup
1 cup sorghum molasses
3 teaspoons cinnamon
2 teaspoons nutmeg
1¼ teaspoons cloves
2 teaspoons brandy flavoring
2 teaspoons vanilla extract
2 good-size apples, peeled
   and chopped
1 cup currants
1 cup raisins
2 cups chopped, sugared
   date pieces
2½ cups fine bread crumbs
   (not toasted)
5 cups sifted flour

Cream margarine and sugars until light and fluffy. Add ground suet; blend. Add beaten eggs; blend. Combine soda and buttermilk; add to mixture. Add syrups and flavorings. Combine apple, currants, raisins and dates with crumbs. Add crumb mixture alternately with flour to first mixture. Use three (2-pound) coffee cans and one (1-pound) coffee can. Grease cans heavily all the way up. Line bottom with wax paper and grease again. Fill cans about ⅔ full or 4 inches up from bottom of 2-pound coffee can. (If can has 3 indented rings, filling line will be half-way between 2nd and 3rd ring up.) Seal tops with foil and plastic lid from can.

Fill a canner or large vessel with enough boiling water to rise at least 2 inches on cans. Cover vessel with lid; keep water boiling at that level for 3-3½ hours. (Take out the 1-pound can after 2-2½ hours.) Lift cans from boiling water and place on a rack to cool slightly. After puddings have cooled for about an hour, or can be handled easily, run knife gently around inside of can and turn out gently on a convenient surface to cool. When entirely cool, wrap in heavy foil, folding edges together and tucked under to preserve moisture. The large puddings will be used for the guests, the smaller one for the servers, singers and instrumentalists. Serve with lemon sauce.

Madrigal Feast
Brazosport Center for the Arts and Sciences

CHOCOLATE POUND CAKE

Serves 12

1 cup (2 sticks) butter	3 cups flour
½ cup shortening	½ teaspoon salt
3 cups sugar	1 teaspoon baking powder
½ cup cocoa	1⅛ cups milk
4 eggs	1 teaspoon vanilla extract

Combine butter, shortening, sugar, cocoa and eggs; mix well. Sift flour, salt and baking powder together; add to butter mixture alternately with milk and vanilla. Grease and flour a large tube pan; pour batter into pan. Bake at 350° for about 1 hour and 15 minutes. Do not overbake.

Mary Reed, Caterer
Lake Jackson, Texas

~ **Glamorous garnishes:** *Dress up iced tea or fruit drinks with garnishes. Try sprigs of fresh mint, melon balls, strawberries on a skewer, clove-studded orange slices , pineapple sticks, maraschino cherries or thin strips of peel cut from oranges, lemons or limes.*

~ **Entertaining ideas:** *Give ice cubes a touch of class by adding tasty tidbits to each section in the ice cube tray before adding water. Try a maraschino cherry, sprig of mint, a slice of lemon, lime or orange, a piece of pineapple or other fruit.*

~ **Frosty-edged drinks:** *For a sweet touch, dip the rim of drinking glasses in citrus juice, then into granulated sugar.*

~ **Keeping its punch:** *Keep iced tea or punches cold without diluting flavor by freezing some of the beverage into ice cubes or floating rings. Use ice cube trays or a 5½-cup ring mold, freeze until firm.*

~ **Picnic pleaser:** *Beverages sealed in plastic bags, frozen and transported in coolers arrive at the picnic grounds frosty cold for drinking. Try water, iced tea, lemonade or fruit juices.*

SHRIMP BOIL AND FISH FRY

Serves 4,500

3,200 pounds shrimp (heads off)
2,200 pounds cod fish fillets
1,000 pounds new potatoes
5,000 (3-inch) ears of corn

400 pounds pinto beans
14 (shiny and new!) large garbage cans of cole slaw
15 gallons red sauce

Invite several thousand of your closest friends; cook it all up and have a great time!

Rotary Shrimp Boil,
Rotary Club of Brazosport

BACKYARD BARBECUE, TEXAS-STYLE

Serves 2,000

23 beef briskets

800 pounds sausage

Coleslaw:

250 pounds cabbage
66 pounds yellow onion
22 pounds green bell pepper

65 pounds sugar
11 gallons vinegar
6 gallons vegetable oil

Mix well, and feed the multitudes!

Methodist Men's Barbecue,
First United Methodist Church of Lake Jackson

BROWNIE TOAST

✓ *Quick to make* *Serves 4*

4 slices bread
¼ cup brown sugar

4 teaspoons shredded coconut
Margarine or butter

In a small bowl, mix brown sugar and coconut. Place bread on cookie sheet, and toast on one side under broiler. Remove from oven, turn bread over, and spread untoasted side with margarine. Top each slice with about 1 tablespoon of the brown sugar/coconut mixture. Return to broiler, and toast until bubbly and brown.

Missy Funk

FLUTTER-BY BUNS

Serves 8

1 (9.5-ounce) can refrigerated
quick cinnamon rolls with
icing

8 maraschino cherries with
stems

Preheat oven to 400°. Separate dough into 8 rolls. Remove stems from cherries; reserve stems. Cut each cherry into 6 wedge-shaped pieces. To assemble a butterfly, cut one roll in half. Place halves, topping-side up with rounded edges touching, on ungreased cookie sheet. Make three ½-inch slits in center of each roll half; insert cherry pieces to decorate. Cut 1 cherry stem in half; insert pieces into biscuit halves to look like butterfly antennae. Repeat to assemble all butterflies, using remaining rolls and cherries.

Bake at 400° for 13-17 minutes, or until golden brown. Remove from pan, allow to cool slightly. Spoon contents of icing container into small pastry bag fitted with plain writing tip; decorate rolls. (Or use a small plastic sandwich bag. Seal opening; cut ⅛-inch from one bottom corner and squeeze icing through opening to decorate.) Serve warm.

Barbara Lundahl

APPLE TEETH

✓ *Quick to make*   *Serves 8*

2 large red apples, sliced   **1 (8-ounce) bag of mini**
8 teaspoons peanut butter   **marshmallows**

Slice each apple into 8 wedges. Spread each slice on one side with ½ teaspoon peanut butter. Take 8 wedges, and line mini marshmallows on top of the peanut butter. Sandwich remaining apple wedges on top, with the peanut butter side down. The treats will look like red lips with teeth.

Barbara Lundahl

BACON & EGGS

✓ *Quick to make*   *Yields 50 treats*

1 (8-ounce) package pretzel   **½ cup yellow plain M & M**
sticks   **candies**
4 ounces white chocolate,
melted

Arrange pretzel sticks in groups of four with sides touching. Drop 1 teaspoon melted white chocolate on top of each pretzel grouping, centering the chocolate over the middle two pretzels. Place 1 yellow candy in the center of the white chocolate. Let stand for 10 minutes or until set. The treats will look like eggs on bacon.

Christy McConnell

STOPLIGHT STOPPERS

✓ *Quick to make*   *Yields 12 treats*

12 rectangle-shaped crackers or   **12 each red, yellow and green**
wafers   **round candy pieces**
6 teaspoons creamy peanut
butter

Spread ½ teaspoon peanut butter on each cracker. Arrange 3 colors of candy pieces on each to look like a traffic light.

Barbara Lundahl

DINOSAUR FOOD

✓ *Quick to make*   *Serves 20*

¼ cup dirt (cocoa)
½ cup swamp water (milk with green food coloring)
2 cups crushed bones (sugar)

½ cup fat (butter)
2 cups grass (uncooked oatmeal)
½ cup squashed bugs (peanut butter)

In a dinosaur skull (bowl), mix dirt, swamp water, crushed bones and fat. Heat to a boil, and boil for 3 minutes. Add grass and squashed bugs. Stir with a big bone (spoon), then drop on dinosaur skin (waxed paper) by the boneful (spoonful). Let cool.

Jeanne Howard

OCEAN OCTOPUS SOUP

Serves 8

2 (12½-ounce) cans chicken broth
2 soup cans water

1 (12-ounce) bag spinach noodles
8 weiners

Boil soup and water in large pot; add spinach noodles and cook until tender according to package directions. Cut weiners in half and make 8 vertical slits from bottom, leaving about ½-inch intact at top of weiner. Put the weiners in the boiling soup. Its "legs" will curl up, to resemble an octopus swimming in a green sea.

Barbara Lundahl

~ Advice For Eating Spinach: "*Divide into little piles, re-arrange again into new piles. After five or six maneuvers, sit back and say you are full...*"

Delia Ephron

KANGAROO KRUNCH

✓ *Quick to make* *Yields 8 cups*

**8 cups popped popcorn
(unsalted)**

**¼ cup (½ stick) butter
¼ cup peanut butter**

Heat peanut butter and butter together; pour over popped corn. Let children take turns stirring the mixture to coat it well. Allow the snack to cool. Let children try forming the letter "K" or other letters with their popcorn before they eat it.

Note: *Substitute ¼ cup brown sugar for the peanut butter, if desired. Prepare as directed above, and sprinkle with cinnamon.*

Barbara Lundahl

NO-BAKE CHOCOLATE DROP COOKIES

✓ *Quick to make* *Yields 3 dozen cookies*

**¼ cup cocoa
2 cups sugar
½ cup milk
½ cup (1 stick) margarine**

**½ cup peanut butter
1 teaspoon vanilla extract
3 cups quick oats**

Combine cocoa, sugar, milk and margarine in a saucepan, heat to a boil. Continue boiling on medium heat for 3½ to 4 minutes. Add peanut butter, vanilla and quick oats. Drop by teaspoonful onto waxed paper.

Susie Hanchey

NO-BAKE CORNFLAKE COOKIES

✓ *Quick to make* *Yields 4-5 dozen cookies*

**1 cup sugar
1 cup light corn syrup**

**¾ cup peanut butter
6 cups corn flakes**

Combine sugar and syrup in saucepan; bring to boil for 1 minute. Remove from heat and stir in peanut butter. Add cornflakes, stir until well coated. Spread on wax paper until cool. Cut into squares to serve.

Kristi Abild

DODGEBALL PUDDING

✓ *Quick to make*   *Serves 6*

1 (6-ounce) box instant pudding   **2 (gallon-size) zipper-top, heavy-**
**   (any flavor)**   **   duty plastic bags**
3 cups cold milk

Pour cold milk into 1 plastic bag; add instant pudding. Seal bag's zipper-top carefully. Place first bag inside a second plastic bag; seal well. Let children form a circle and play catch with the bag, tossing it back and forth. (It will hold up to rough handling, or missed catches.) Pudding will be ready to eat after 5 minutes of vigorous dodgeball. Use a long-handled spoon to scoop pudding into paper cups or serving dishes. Double or triple recipe for larger groups, and get several "dodgeballs" flying at once.

Cynthia Lancaster

FROSTY FRUIT POPS

Yields 12 popsicles

44 pieces Starburst fruit chew   **1¾ cups applesauce**
**   candies (about half a 1-pound**   **12 (5-ounce) paper cups**
**   bag)**   **12 popsicle sticks**
2½ cups water, divided

Unwrap candies, combine in heavy saucepan with ¼ cup water. Cook over low heat, stirring frequently, until candies are melted and well blended. Add remaining water and applesauce; mix well. Pour about ⅓ cup mixture into each paper cup; and freeze until partially set, about 1 hour. Insert 1 popsicle stick into the center of each partially frozen pop; freeze until firm. To serve, peel paper cups from frozen pops.

Nancy Standlee

~ **On Children and Eating:** *"In general, my children refused to eat anything that hadn't danced on TV..."*

Erma Bombeck

STRAWBERRY PIZZA

Serves 8-10

Ready-made pie crust
1 (8-ounce) package cream
cheese, softened
1 pint strawberries, sliced

1 (12-ounce) carton Cool Whip,
thawed
1 package strawberry glaze

Press pie crust into a round pizza pan and cook according to directions on package. Cool. Spread cream cheese over pie crust. Layer sliced strawberries on cream cheese, reserving some for garnish. Spread glaze over strawberries. Top with Cool Whip and decorate with reserved strawberries. Slice with a pizza cutter into pizza-size wedges to serve.

Schelli Martin

MOTHER'S GOOFY WHITE FUDGE

Serves 6

3 tablespoons real butter,
divided
2 china-teacups of sugar
1¾ china-teacups of milk

Pinch of salt
1 teaspoon vanilla extract
1 cup chopped pecans

Butter a plate with 1 tablespoon butter. Use a real china cup to measure 2 teacups of sugar and 1¾ teacups of milk. Combine in pan with a pinch of salt. Bring to a boil; do not stir. When mixture is brown on the bottom, add remaining butter and vanilla.

Remove from heat and beat like mad for at least 5 minutes, until mixture thickens and loses its gloss. Add pecans, and pour mixture onto plate until set.

Note: *My mother made this recipe by mistake, and it has become a family favorite. Be sure to use a real china teacup for measuring.*

Ruth Bondurant

PEPPERMINT CRUNCH

✓ *Quick to make* *Yields 1 pound*

2 blocks (16-ounces) white chocolate

4 ounces red and green mint chips

Microwave white chocolate in glass bowl until melted. Stir in mint chips. Pour mixture onto a waxed paper-lined baking sheet. Place in freezer for 5 minutes. Break into bite-size pieces.

Hint: *Fill decorative containers, and use for child-made gifts that children can give to teachers and other special people.*

Christy McConnell

SWEET TREAT JELLY

Fills 10 baby-food jars

2 cups water
1 box plus 2 tablespoons powdered pectin

3½ cups plus 4 tablespoons sugar, divided
1 (6-ounce) can frozen juice concentrate (any flavor)

Pour 2 cups water into a bowl; slowly add powdered pectin, stirring well. Let mixture stand for 45 minutes. Stir frequently. Open the can of fruit juice concentrate, and pour it into a second bowl. Add 1¾ cups sugar. Stir well, but don't expect all of the sugar to dissolve. When the pectin mixture is ready, add remaining sugar. Stir until sugar dissolves. Add the juice mixture to the pectin mixture. Stir well until all of the sugar dissolves. Pour jelly into 10 baby-food jars (or decorative containers.) It will be solid in minutes.

Barbara Lundahl

These playdough recipes are for playing, not for eating!

HOMEMADE PLAYDOUGH

Yields 1½ cups

1 cup water	**½ cup salt**
Food coloring	**1 tablespoon cream of tartar**
1 cup flour	**1 tablespoon cooking oil**

Add food coloring of choice to 1 cup water. Combine colored water, flour, salt, cream of tartar and oil in a saucepan; stir and cook over low-medium heat until rubbery. Remove from heat, allow to cool slightly. When cool enough to handle, knead dough to desired texture. Cool and store in a plastic bag in the refrigerator.

Note: *Add a scent such as peppermint to the playdough if desired.*

Peggy McKnight / Helen Baker

Microwave Playdough: *Combine 1 cup flour, 1 cup salt, 1 cup water, 2 tablespoons vegetable oil, 2 teaspoons cream of tartar and food coloring of choice. Place in microwave for 5 minutes at 50% power. Stir often. Continue cooking until mixture reaches proper consistency. (Yields 1½ cups.)*

Helen Baker

FINGERPAINT

Yields 4 cups paint

⅔ cup dry starch	**1 cup Ivory soap flakes**
1 cup cold water	**Food coloring**
3 cups boiling water	**3 drops oil of cloves (optional)**

Dissolve starch in cold water, smooth out lumps. Bring 3 cups water to a boil in pan; add dissolved starch to boiling water and boil for 1 minute. Stir constantly and be careful not to let mixture boil over. Remove pan from heat, add soap flakes, food coloring and oil of cloves if desired as a preservative. Let cool; and paint.

Nancy Standlee

FOOD WEIGHTS AND MEASURES

WEIGHT/ MEASURE:	EQUIVALENT:
Dash	Less than ⅛ teaspoon
1½ teaspoons	½ tablespoon
3 teaspoons	1 tablespoon
2 tablespoons	⅛ cup (1 fluid ounce)
4 tablespoons	¼ cup (2 fluid ounces)
5⅓ tablespoons	⅓ cup
8 tablespoons	½ cup (4 fluid ounces)
10⅔ tablespoons	⅔ cup
12 tablespoons	¾ cup (6 fluid ounces)
16 tablespoons	1 cup (8 fluid ounces)
⅜ cup	¼ cup plus 2 tablespoons
⅝ cup	½ cup plus 2 tablespoons
⅞ cup	¾ cup plus 2 tablespoons
1 tablespoon	½ fluid ounce
1 cup	½ pint (8 fluid ounces)
2 cups	1 pint (16 fluid ounces)
4 cups	1 quart (32 fluid ounces)
2 pints	1 quart
2 quarts	½ gallon
4 quarts (liquid)	1 gallon
8 quarts (dry)	1 peck
4 pecks	1 bushel
16 ounces (dry)	1 pound
1 gram	.035 ounces
1 kilogram	2.21 pounds
1 ounce	28.35 grams
1 teaspoon	4.9 milliliters
1 tablespoon	14.8 milliliters
1 cup	236.6 milliliters
1 liter	1.06 quarts or 1,000 milliliters

EMERGENCY SUBSTITUTIONS

INGREDIENT:	AMOUNT:	SUBSTITUTION:
Baking powder	1 teaspoon	¼ teaspoon baking soda plus ½ teaspoon cream of tartar
Buttermilk	1 cup	1 cup plain yogurt OR 1 tablespoon vinegar plus milk to equal 1 cup OR 1 tablespoon lemon juice plus milk to equal 1 cup
Cake flour	1 cup	1 cup minus 2 tablespoons sifted all-purpose flour
Chocolate, unsweetened	1 ounce (1 square)	3 tablespoons unsweetened cocoa plus 1 tablespoon butter or margarine
Cornstarch	1 tablespoon	2 tablespoons all-purpose flour
Corn syrup	2 cups	1 cup granulated sugar
Cream, light	1 cup	1½ tablespoons butter plus whole milk to equal 1 cup
Cream, whipping	1 cup	⅓ cup butter plus whole milk to equal 1 cup
Egg yolk	2 yolks	1 whole egg (not for piecrust or sauces)
Egg, whole	1 egg	2 egg yolks (for baking: 2 egg yolks plus 1 tablespoon water)
Herbs, fresh	1 tablespoon	1 teaspoon dried herbs
Honey	1 cup	1¼ cups granulated sugar
Lemon juice	1 tablespoon	1 tablespoon distilled white vinegar
Milk, skim	1 cup	⅓ cup nonfat dry milk plus ¾ cup water
Milk, whole	1 cup	½ cup evaporated milk plus ½ cup water
Molasses	1 cup	¾ cup granulated sugar
Mushrooms, fresh	1 pound	12 ounces canned mushrooms, drained
Mustard, dry	1 teaspoon	1 tablespoon prepared mustard
Sour cream	1 cup	3 tablespoons butter plus buttermilk or yogurt to equal 1 cup
Sugar, brown	1 cup	1 cup granulated sugar
Sugar, granulated	1 cup	1¾ cups powdered sugar (not for baking)
Tomato juice	3 cups	1½ cups tomato sauce plus 1½ cups water OR 1 (6-ounce) can tomato paste plus 3 cans water, dash salt and pepper
Tomato sauce	1 cup	3-ounces tomato paste plus ½ cup water
Yogurt	1 cup	1 cup buttermilk

INDEX

~ *Snacks: How much serves how many:*

Potato chips: *1 (16-ounce) package = 16 servings*

Corn or tortilla chips: *1 (16-ounce) package = 16 servings*

Cheese curls: *1 (12-ounce) package = 24 servings*

Pretzels: *1 (12-ounce) package = 12 servings*

Sour cream dip: *1 (8-ounce) container = 8 servings*

Mixed nuts: *1 (56-ounce) container = 56 servings*

Junior Service League of Brazosport
P.O. Box 163
Lake Jackson, TX 77566

Please send _____copies   @ $16.95 each _____
   Postage and handling   @ $3.00 each _____
   Texas residents add sales tax   @ $1.31 each _____
                                 TOTAL _____

Name _____
Address _____
City _____State _____Zip _____

Make checks payable to Junior Service League of Brazosport

- -

Junior Service League of Brazosport
P.O. Box 163
Lake Jackson, TX 77566

Please send _____copies   @ $16.95 each _____
   Postage and handling   @ $3.00 each _____
   Texas residents add sales tax   @ $1.31 each _____
                                 TOTAL _____

Name _____
Address _____
City _____State _____Zip _____

Make checks payable to Junior Service League of Brazosport

- -

Junior Service League of Brazosport
P.O. Box 163
Lake Jackson, TX 77566

Please send _____copies   @ $16.95 each _____
   Postage and handling   @ $3.00 each _____
   Texas residents add sales tax   @ $1.31 each _____
                                 TOTAL _____

Name _____
Address _____
City _____State _____Zip _____

Make checks payable to Junior Service League of Brazosport

Reorder Additional Copies

Names and addresses of bookstores, gift shops, etc. in your area would be appreciated.

_____

_____

_____

_____

_____

_____

— —

Names and addresses of bookstores, gift shops, etc. in your area would be appreciated.

_____

_____

_____

_____

_____

_____

— —

Names and addresses of bookstores, gift shops, etc. in your area would be appreciated.

_____

_____

_____

_____

_____

— —